Literary Contexts

Shakespeare

Literary Contexts recognises that literature is always rooted in its social milieu and that we need to study literary cultures in all their complexity and connections. It offers the thrill of locating a text within its context and seeing a context reflected in a literary/cultural text.

Each of the books in the series offers students of English and other literatures concise, informative insights into the history of ideas embodied in literary texts, authors and movements. Organised around themes and ideas with extensive examples from literary and cultural texts, the books enable students to understand how the "literary" takes shape in an intellectual milieu and discover manifestations of abstract ideas in literary texts. Written by scholar-teachers who have taught and researched literature for several years, each volume in the series is a stand-alone reference book for students and teachers alike.

Series editor

Pramod K. Nayar teaches at the Department of English, University of Hyderabad. His most recent books include *The Transnational in English Literature: Shakespeare to the Modern* (2015), *Citizenship and Identity in the Age of Surveillance* (2015), *The Postcolonial Studies Dictionary* (2015) and *Postcolonial Studies: An Anthology* (2015). His forthcoming work includes a book on the Indian graphic novel.

Also in the series

American Literature
Modern English Literature, 1890–1960
Postcolonial Literatures
Victorian Literature
Postmodern Literatures
Eighteenth-century English Literature

Literary Contexts

Shakespeare

Anna Kurian

Series Editor
Pramod K. Nayar

Orient BlackSwan

All images used in this book are by courtesy of Wikimedia Commons.

ORIENT BLACKSWAN PRIVATE LIMITED

Registered Office
3-6-752 Himayatnagar, Hyderabad 500 029, Telangana, India
Email: centraloffice@orientblackswan.com

Other Offices
Bengaluru, Bhopal, Chennai, Ernakulam, Guwahati, Hyderabad, Jaipur, Kolkata, Lucknow, Mumbai, New Delhi, Noida, Patna, Vijayawada

First published 2016

ISBN 978 81 250 6012 3

Typeset in Adobe Caslon Pro 11.5/14 *by*
OSDATA, Hyderabad

Printed and bound at
Graphica Printers, Hyderabad

Published by
Orient Blackswan Private Limited
3-6-752 Himayatnagar, Hyderabad 500 029
Email: hyderabad@orientblackswan.com

For my parents, and my children

Contents

Series Editor's Preface *ix*

A Note on the Shakespeare Quotations *xi*

Introduction 1

Section 1 Socio-cultural Backgrounds

1. Monarchy and Authority 17
2. Gender, Family and Society 46
3. Expanding Worlds and New Peoples 70

Section 2 Shakespeare and/in the Theatre

4. Drama, the Theatre and Stagecraft 97
5. Shakespeare and His Contemporaries 115
6. The Forms of Shakespearean Drama 140

Section 3 Shakespeare Ever After

7. Shakespeare Adaptations 177
8. Shakespeare and Criticism 204

Recommended Reading *232*

Index *242*

Series Editor's Preface

The idea that the literature of every age is rooted in its social milieu is a truism. Mapping the contours of this milieu often requires, for the student, to read through several specialised texts. Titles in *Literary Contexts*, by bringing together the key contexts – both general and specialised – into one volume, offer the student of English and other literatures short, prescient and informative studies that provide the history of ideas embodied in literary texts, authors and movements.

Intellectual history or the history of ideas has always been intertwined with the cultural practices and shifts within them in every age. Therefore titles in the series track the intellectual history of every age through social and historical contexts, whether these were contexts of imperial voyages, "Westward expansion", the Reformation of the Church, great scientific discoveries or nationalist movements. Considerable attention is paid to the contexts of class, literacy, gender relations, the state and its functions in every age.

The series' titles demonstrate how certain dominant ideas in any age operated. To this end, every title in the series draws upon and cites numerous examples from literary texts. This enables the student to get a sense of the literary themes' origins in the intellectual milieu, and discover manifestations of abstract ideas, such as "exceptionalism", "hybrid and displaced identity" or "division of powers of Church and State", in literary texts.

The authors do not seek to establish a direct correspondence between the literary text and the dominant idea of the age, but they offer the student a sense of the dense exchanges between the idea and the literary text. Each title maps ideas across cultural texts – popular forms, high culture, and scientific and philosophical texts – so that it demonstrates how ideas are mobile and cut across genres and domains. The titles in the series also document the conflicts and tensions in every age so that the student is made aware of the complicated nature of both, the history of ideas and the literary expressions of the same, and is alerted to the messy nature of cultural history of any age, in any nation.

Written by scholar-teachers who have taught and researched literature for several years, *Literary Contexts* is student-friendly, being both jargon-free and incisive. The "Recommended Reading" section in each title lists the key secondary reading essential to a fuller understanding of the age, and should further the student's reading towards more specific topics in literary history.

Pramod K. Nayar

A Note on the Shakespeare Quotations

All quotations from Shakespeare's plays, used in this book, are taken from *The Norton Shakespeare*, second edition. (Greenblatt, Stephen, gen. ed. *The Norton Shakespeare: Based on the Oxford Edition*. 2nd ed. Ed. Walter Cohen, Jean E. Howard and Katharine Eisaman Maus. New York: W. W. Norton, 2008. Print.) The quotations from *King Lear* are from *The Tragedy of King Lear: A Conflated Text*, in *The Norton Shakespeare*.

Introduction

Consider if you will the plays of Shakespeare,[1] their characters, themes, situations: characters such as an ass-headed lover for a fairy queen; a sharp-tongued scold who has a sweet-as-honey sister; a duke who wants to marry a nun-to-be; young and old, rich and poor, witty and slow-witted, the honoured and honourable as well as the despised and dishonoured: you find them all, and more, in Shakespeare's plays. His themes display a variety that is difficult to list in a page or two: we can speak of love and hatred, desire and indifference, of appearance and reality, of truth and deception, all in just one play, whether *King Lear* or *Hamlet,* and we would still have touched only the tip of the iceberg. Underlying these overarching themes are the small details, which together evoke another, allied set of themes and ideas that help us to see further into the heart of the play. And then there are the situations: a box of tennis balls being delivered to a young, newly crowned monarch; a bear chasing a man across the stage; eyes being gouged out on stage; a dinner party where the main course is the chief guest's two sons baked into a pie; a melancholic courtier weeping over the killing of deer in a forest; a steward who hopes to marry his mistress, wearing yellow stockings and smiling incessantly, hoping thus to woo her: each play shows us the routine and the everyday and then juxtaposes it with some startling situation, some bizarre happening which we take in our stride, even as we smile at how incongruous it is, or are shocked by it.

The famous, now clichéd, lines about Cleopatra, "Age cannot wither her, nor custom stale / Her infinite variety (*Antony and Cleopatra* II.ii.240–41), are as descriptive of Shakespeare's oeuvre as they are of one of his most famous heroines. His work is infinitely various and that variety extends across not just characters, themes and situations but also the schools of critical thought which can be applied to it, the uses to which it can be put and the many forms in which it exists today: from print through theatre performance and films to comic books, hypertexts and any, and nearly all, forms of popular culture.

And yet the person who comes to a Shakespeare play as part of his or her undergraduate or high school education is often prejudiced before reading even a word of his work: the fact that you have always already known of Shakespeare as "the greatest English dramatist" makes him a legend but also someone who lived long ago, wrote of events from long ago and worst of all, wrote in a style and a language that seems to have little or nothing to do with English as we know it today. The dread of boredom, something all young people are constantly fighting, is very real when asked to read a Shakespeare play: there is also, of course, the problem that these are not one-act plays; there are five long acts, some with as many as seven or twelve scenes, and all of them written, o horror, in poetry. Approaching Shakespeare is sometimes akin to entering into a chamber of horrors! So what does one do when faced with this monumental author and a play that narrates either the life and death of a Roman emperor (*Julius Caesar*), or a murderer who wants the crown (*Macbeth*), or a play that is described as a comedy but where nothing funny actually happens, and people go around falling in love and eventually getting married (*As You Like It* or *Much Ado About Nothing*)? If you are lucky, you have a good teacher and you understand the play and enjoy it; if not, you suffer through it and never really understand what all the fuss is about. Why should Shakespeare be treated as almost a God in the world of literature, and his work as something extraordinary, when, for many, it could be difficult, boring or ordinary?

While some of us never overcome our aversion to Shakespeare, we can still learn to read his plays, we can still achieve a degree of understanding which will then enable us to speak with some knowledge and insight regarding some of his many plays. (Oh yes, yet another of the complaints that students have: why did he write so many plays? Sigh!) And we can learn to see what might have been the reasons that his work is considered significant across languages and cultures even today.

Given that Shakespeare lived and wrote his plays in the sixteenth and seventeenth centuries, in an England very different from England today, why is it that people still read Shakespeare, perform his plays, watch movies based on his plays, read fiction based upon the plots of his plays and so on? The list of how his plays are adapted, transformed, and yet remain his plays in re-mediated and re-genred versions, is extensive, never-ending. So what makes Shakespeare's plays so attractive? Why is it that whether in Arabia or Surinam, Germany, Brazil or China, Shakespeare's plays are still seen as relevant? Is it because when we read these plays we are looking not so much at the particulars of where and how they are located (Scotland, ancient Rome, Venice, Denmark, Illyria, set in medieval times or the fourteenth and fifteenth centuries or in unspecified times), as at the people who populate them: people whom we recognise as akin to ourselves, as recognisably real and human, as we are ourselves? It is this that gives them their relevance, their powers of attraction, that when we read or watch a young man mourning the death of his father and the hasty remarriage of his mother, we see something we recognise. When we look at a young woman mourning the supposed death of her brother but then determining to live her life as she can best do so, we recognise traits we have seen around us, as we do when we watch another young woman swear to mourn for seven years for a dead brother and then forget all about it when she discovers love! We might pity the young man, admire the first woman and laugh at the second, but in each of these reactions to death we also recognise the human element which makes these differences possible and yet makes them all, also, recognisably human. And it is this fact, of an irreducible humanity, a "universal" humanity, that also makes Shakespeare a recognisable name across the world.[2] The themes and the humans whose lives those themes are played out in, are to us "real", "human" and "relatable". The fact that the plays are also filled with specificities regarding location, social mores, stereotypes, facts, dates and times might give us pause; but that is not to deny the universal but to add another dimension to it.

From the Universal to the Particular

No play of Shakespeare's leaves its location unspecified. We know where we are within a few minutes of beginning to read a Shakespeare play: whether that is Venice, Verona, Ephesus, an England in the middle ages, Sicily or Bohemia. But wherever we might find ourselves at the beginning of the play we also know as we read that we are in a world that in many features resembles Shakespeare's England. So time and space within the play might be framing devices but these are almost facades as Shakespeare imagines his plots, characters and themes into a world that is called into being along the lines of the one he was most familiar with: his own. While we might be told that the world of the play is that of ancient Britain, the Roman empire of the triumvirs, or the England of the Wars of the Roses, or any of the locations and times that are to be seen in Shakespeare's worlds, we also see a world that is built along the lines of England during the times of Elizabeth I and James I (and VI). Kingship obtains and displays its authority in ways that are remarkably similar to those employed by the monarchs he was familiar with; gender roles, the prejudices, the antipathies, the stereotypes regarding national, racial, gender or ethnic identities, the views about the larger world outside England, or about the classical world: all these can be seen as modelled upon views prevalent in Early Modern England. Further, when we examine the world of the theatre, the world within which he lived, acted, wrote and performed, Shakespeare appears again, a product of the times. His familiarity with other playwrights; his role as a shareholder, actor and playwright in one of the two major playing companies; his uses of the genres and language of the times: all of these then locate him, again, very specifically as a part of Renaissance England. An England that was beginning to frame itself as a nation, a people who were beginning to enter into a humanist framework of imagining themselves, a language that was slowly gaining strength and a personality of its own: these were the significant integral features of Shakespeare's time. So what did Shakespeare have to do with the new humanism? Or with the making of English into the language it is today?

A Humanist World in the Making

"Humanism" as a term encompasses several aspects, several shades of meaning: there is the everyday definition of humanism which indicates that it is a system of thought which privileges the human rather than the divine; there is the one which connects it to Renaissance Europe and a movement that moved away from medievalist attitudes towards learning and instead focused on empiricism and the classical models of knowledge; there is the now derogatory attitude towards the word which makes of it something almost evil, as it casts the white male and his systems of knowledge and determinations of selfhood as the only possible ones.[3] What are the connections between Shakespeare and humanism?

It remains necessary to remember that "Humanism" as we know it today and study it, in the Humanities, was not codified as such in the Renaissance: the elements were there but, as Davies puts it, "The term 'humanism' denoted nothing in the fifteenth and sixteenth centuries, in Italy or anywhere else, for the reason that no such term existed" (94). Similarly, the humanists of the era did not know themselves as such: these are the labels applied to a period and a set of individuals who were beginning to break away from the forms of knowledge which had held sway till then; they were able to repudiate the all-encompassing authority of the Church and they believed that it was possible for man (and it *is* a gendered humanism that the age put forth) to learn and master the world of knowledge without giving in to the obfuscations of the past. The so-called humanists of the time include Erasmus, Michelangelo, Thomas More, Lorenzo Valla, Petrarch, Castiglione, Rabelais and Montaigne among many more, though they may not have applied the label to themselves.

The Renaissance on the European continent was characterised by a looking back to the classical age, of the Romans and the Greeks, an idealising of the life then, as also of the authors and their works; by movement and collaboration, as many of those who called themselves the *umanisti* knew one another, learned from one another, conveying, as Davies[4] puts it in his book *Humanism*, "ideas, languages and (most importantly) books to schools, universities, private collections and solitary scholars across the European continent and its islands" (74). In addition, the scholars and thinkers of the time benefited from the invention and popularisation of the printing press and the increase in the sheer number of print shops across Europe made it possible for classical literature to spread and also for the new thinkers and scholars to reach a wider audience. The book becomes an important artefact during this period: made possible by the printing press and the spread of education, books are integral to the rise and spread of humanism. Even as they stand in several plays as a potent symbol of the new knowledges and the new cultures of mankind, they are also literal manifestations of the possibilities of a knowledge that could be available to anyone who could read. Books, as emblematic of the new knowledges which were not restricted to monasteries and churchmen, are significant stage props across the plays of the period, most visible in Marlowe's *Doctor Faustus* but also powerfully present in Shakespeare's *Titus Andronicus*, *Hamlet*, *The Tempest*, etc. Indeed *Titus Andronicus* shows an awareness of the classical models of knowledge and learning with its plotlines, incidents and tags drawn from Latin and Greek texts and cultural icons, even as Shakespeare overtops the classical within the time and events of his play. The importance of education within the new humanism, and the aura it had, is seen in the repeated references to reading, writing, letters, etc. as well, in practically all of Shakespeare's plays.

One more characteristic of the humanism of the period is also significant where Shakespeare is concerned: the humanists of the time, even as they harked back to Latin and Greek as the languages most worthy of study, also worked at their own languages, to create in the vernacular a vehicle for the new learning and to make in it a literary idiom which would approximate to Latin and Greek. Thus the modern languages were seen as plastic and malleable. Many of the continental and English humanists deplored the easy familiarity of their own languages and worked at creating a new form of their language which would be learned enough to carry the weight of their learning. This was also because the studies of the humanists were not seen as solitary pursuits to be carried out in private: they were to be shared, spoken out, debated with others and thus, tested to see if they would hold. While books and print can be seen as making of this sharing a more private enterprise, the making of books in the vernaculars illustrates the desire to disseminate the new knowledges as widely as possible. In the process the modern languages of Europe developed a literary style and changed dramatically. Where does Shakespeare stand in this making and remaking of language?

SHAKESPEARE'S LANGUAGE

Bernard Levin famously said,

> If you cannot understand my argument, and declare "It's Greek to me", you are quoting Shakespeare; if you claim to be more sinned against than sinning, you are quoting Shakespeare; if you recall your salad days, you are quoting Shakespeare; if you act more in sorrow than in anger, if your wish is father to the thought, if your lost property has vanished into thin air, you are quoting Shakespeare. . . .

The examples continue for a good many more lines and it provides an excellent instance of the influence Shakespeare has had on the English language. So when readers grumble about how impossible-to-read Shakespeare's works are, how tough the language is and how impossible to understand it all is, they are unaware that several of the phrases and words they, and we, use in our everyday conversation are drawn from Shakespeare's works.

If the previous paragraph demonstrates the extent to which Shakespeare has contributed to English as we know it today, what was the English language like when he first began writing? The Renaissance saw a turn to the classical languages and their literatures but it also saw the growth and spread of the vernaculars of Europe. English, similarly, was being utilised for the writing of poetry, drama and prose treatises. One advantage that English possessed in this period was that it had not been strictly codified: still plastic and flexible, the English language was in a transitional phase and the development of the language was aided by the development of the printing press, the spread of basic education, the Reformation with its emphasis on reading the scriptures in the vernacular and the number of individuals who were writing in English during this period. With the arrival of the printing press and the possibility of possessing texts to read (whether scriptural, erudite or popular), the emphasis on education and the gradual increase in the number of schools, and the Reformation's insistence that people should be able to read the Bible for themselves, English as a language began to grow and develop, incorporating into itself new words and constructions drawn from the classical languages but also altered from existing terms and vocabulary, as also invented.

Shakespeare is part of this movement, often at the forefront, inventing new words and phrases ("assassination", "dwindle", "neither rhyme nor reason", "at one fell swoop", etc.), changing the form of words in unexpected ways (thus he uses "ghost" as a verb), generating new and entertaining insults ("thou base football player") and so on. That his language is seen as difficult is because the English today is quite different from the English of the sixteenth and seventeenth centuries: there is the usage of "you" and "thou" (and the associated "thee") but more confusing are words that have now changed in meaning, their earlier meanings forgotten to a large extent: for example, "fond" which today usually means "affectionate", but which meant "foolish" in his times; "presently" which we use today to mean "in a while" but which meant "immediately" in Shakespeare's times. There are also words that have faded from the language as we know it: thus "bisson" and "mammer" are no longer used, and readers would not know that they mean "blind" and "to hesitate" respectively. There is also the fact that Shakespeare uses images, rhetorical devices and figures of speech that are no longer familiar to the average reader. One way out of this impasse is to read Shakespeare aloud: much that appears incomprehensible when seen as words on a page becomes clear and comprehensible when read, when listened to. The fact that Shakespeare wrote in dramatic verse rather than prose is also significant. The verse is not verse on account of rhyme, though Shakespeare often used rhymed couplets at the end of scenes: the nature of the poetry is in the use of the iambic pentameter.[5] The rhythm created by the use of the iambic pentameter is said to be most akin to the rhythm of English speech by native speakers and Shakespeare exploited the nuances and the sounds of this to the utmost. But, and this is again significant, Shakespeare did not use only poetry in his plays: most of his plays contain some prose as well and some of the prose passages are as poetic as the poetry to be found therein. Nor is the use of the iambic pentameter unvaried: he changed the stresses as he felt the need and depending upon the context, varied both the stress patterns and the number of feet in the dramatic verse within the plays.

SHAKESPEARE'S CANON

Shakespeare is known primarily as a playwright and while this book provides a set of backgrounds against which many of Shakespeare's plays can be read fruitfully, he did not write only plays. There is a large body of non-dramatic verse as well, in addition to the thirty-six or thirty-eight plays that he wrote. The usual consensus of critical opinion is that even if Shakespeare had not written any of his plays he would still have been a well-known literary figure, his reputation resting upon his poetry: a sonnet sequence of 154 sonnets and his longer narrative verse, *Venus and Adonis* and *The Rape of Lucrece*. While some disputes continue as to the authorship of *The Passionate Pilgrim* and *The Phoenix and the Turtle*, they are also usually ascribed to Shakespeare, and find a place in *The Norton Shakespeare*, along with *The Lover's Complaint* that was published with the sonnets in 1609.[6] The sonnets are usually divided into two neat sections:

the "young Man" sonnets (1–126) and the "Dark Lady" sonnets (127–152), with the last two forming a coda to the collection. Written in the English sonnet form of three quatrains and a concluding couplet, they present dramatic situations, questions that the poet raises and then attempts to answer, and a range of moods and tones, from evaluations of what true love is (sonnet 116) to the mocking of conventional ideas of beauty and grace (sonnet 130).[7] Shakespeare's poetry is also useful to understand questions of literary production in his time, as also the issue of noble patronage for poets.

Shakespeare's plays, which are our area of study in this book, are usually accounted to be thirty-six in number, if we go by the contents of the First Folio of 1623. Today, in addition to those, *Pericles, Prince of Tyre* and *The Two Noble Kinsmen* are included as being Shakespearean plays. We also know today that he might have collaborated on other plays as well, with other playwrights of the time.[8] There are also plays such *Cardenio* and *Love's Labour's Won* which are now considered Shakespeare's lost plays. Given that Shakespeare's works were not published by him in his lifetime and that there is no definite dating mechanism by which we can ascertain which play was written and performed in which year, there is no certitude about the chronology of Shakespeare's career trajectory, which is further complicated because some of the plays were published many years after their first performance. Given these complications, we do not offer you a chronology of Shakespeare's plays:[9] the editions used in the classroom usually offer a date for the play's first performance and first publication, and it is wise to go along with that.

****

And so, to the contexts . . .

What is the point of reading this book? How will it aid you to read and understand a Shakespeare play? When we first read a

Shakespeare play, we usually see it from our own, contemporary and presentist viewpoint, a viewpoint shaped by conditions of life and literature and culture that exist *now*. But we also read with considerable ignorance regarding the social and political structures of Shakespeare's time, with little knowledge of how drama and the theatre functioned during his time. In the presence of these gaps, it is easy to understand Shakespeare's works in a skewed manner, imposing our presentist frames on texts that were produced in very different times. What this book tries to do is explain certain backgrounds to Shakespeare's plays, backgrounds and contexts that are found reflected, examined, interrogated and sometimes subverted, in many of his plays, especially those that form a part of courses at college and university levels. Students often puzzle over how Hamlet's uncle becomes king when Hamlet himself is in the line of direct succession: this book gives you a brief overview of the factors which influenced kingship and succession, and which we see playing out in *Hamlet*. To use another example, many students find it difficult to understand why plays such as *Twelfth Night* are called comedies: by examining the features of the comedy as it was understood in Shakespeare's time and by reading about the genres in which Shakespeare wrote, it is possible for a student to gain some answers to her questions regarding the comedic nature of Shakespeare's plays. Thus the book provides doorways through which one can look into the Shakespearean world while also showing how Shakespeare's works have been a part of that and other worlds since their first performance and publication.

Works Cited

Bate, Jonathan. "Shakespeare's Universal Appeal Examined." *DNA India*. 24 April 2012. Web. 22 October 2014. <http://www.dnaindia.com/lifestyle/column-shakespeares-universal-appeal-examined-1679877>.

Davies, Tony. *Humanism.* The New Critical Idiom. London: Routledge, 1997. Print.

Levin, Bernard. "On Quoting Shakespeare." Web. 22 October 2014. <http://inside.mines.edu/~jamcneil/levinquote.html>.

O'Toole, Emer. "Shakespeare, Universal? No, It's Cultural Imperialism." *The Guardian.* 21 May 2012. Web. 22 October 2014. <http://www.theguardian.com/commentisfree/2012/may/21/shakespeare-universal-cultural-imperialism>.

Notes

1. The focus of this book is Shakespeare as dramatist: we will look at the backgrounds and contexts to the study of Shakespeare's plays, *not* his poetry.
2. At this point it is necessary to remember that while Shakespeare's plays were initially taught as part of the syllabus in English colonies, as part of a civilisational mission and to assert cultural superiority, today Shakespeare has been appropriated and used by the former colonies. It is also useful to remember that Shakespeare also continues to be taught and performed in nations and lands that were not part of the British Empire. For two opposing perspectives on the question of Shakespeare's "universality", read the columns by O'Toole and Bate.
3. In recent years humanism has lost its privileged position and to now call someone a "liberal humanist" is to accuse them of being participant in, and colluding with, structures of oppression and exclusion which made it possible to exclude and oppress races other than white, genders other than male, religions other than Christianity, species other than the human. Humanism is seen as responsible, in some measure, for the colonies and empires of the European nations, for the extinction of several animal and other species, and for the devaluing of the black, the Native American, the Indian, the Chinese, the Muslim, etc. By defining the human in terms that were predicated upon white Christian masculinity, all other peoples were immediately less than human; and the wiping out of entire peoples and cultures is, in some measure, a fallout of the humanist project.

4. This discussion of humanism is in large part drawn from Davies's extremely accessible and lucid primer.
5. The iambic pentameter refers to lines of ten syllables, where the first syllable is unstressed, the second stressed and the pattern repeated so that a line consists of five units, each containing two syllables. Each unit is called an iamb, and the form called the iambic pentameter because the iamb was repeated five (penta) times.
6. For a brief but illuminating overview of Shakespeare's career as a poet, see the biography of Shakespeare as poet at <http://www.poetryfoundation.org/bio/william-shakespeare#poet>
7. An excellent website for Shakespeare's sonnets is <http://www.shakespeares-sonnets.com/index.php>
8. These include *The Reign of King Edward the Third* and *Sir Thomas More*.
9. Chronologies for his life and work can be found at <http://search.eb.com/shakespeare/browse?browseId=248456 and http://internetshakespeare.uvic.ca/Library/SLT/reference/chronology/index.html>

Socio-cultural Backgrounds

One

Monarchy and Authority

William Shakespeare's life and work extended across the reign of two English monarchs: Elizabeth I (1558–1603)[1] and James VI and I ([1603–25] he was James VI of Scotland from 1567 before moving to England as James I). Kingship, governance and the roles that rulers play are recurrent themes in Shakespeare's plays from the early Henry VI plays, through the major tragedies to the last plays such as *The Tempest*. To better understand plays such as *Richard II*, *Macbeth* or *King Lear* we need to know how the monarchy was shaped in Shakespeare's time and functioned in his lifetime. But before we can venture upon gaining an in-depth knowledge of the ways in which the monarchy was constructed, operated and was constantly being reinvented in this period, we will need to know actual factual details. To gain an understanding of Shakespeare's times and his uses of the monarchy we need to go back to the reign of Henry VIII, Elizabeth I's father and King of England from 1509 through 1547, because the tumultuous reign of Henry VIII laid the foundation for the reign of his three children, as well as moved England away from the medieval ages firmly into the Early Modern.

This chapter begins with a brief historical account of the English monarchs beginning with Henry VIII and ending with James VI and I. It goes on to look at concepts associated with kingship and kingly authority, ideas which include how authority was derived and sustained by the kings and queens of England during this period and how these then become a background to Shakespeare's plays.

A BRIEF HISTORY

Henry VIII

The Tudors, the dynasty to which Elizabeth I belonged, came to the throne of England in 1485, with the reign of Henry VII (1485–1509). But it was the rule of Henry VIII (1509–47), his son, that consolidated the Tudor reign and also constituted the beginnings of many of the distinguishing features of England as it was in Shakespeare's time. Henry VIII is known today primarily for his many wives but when he became king, at the age of eighteen, he was popular, known and loved by his people for his love of hunting, dancing, athletic activity and religion. He was also content to let his Lord Chancellor, Cardinal Thomas Wolsey, handle the daily working of the kingdom. Having inherited a stable realm and a healthy treasury, the initial years of Henry VIII's reign were positive: he was granted the title 'Defender of the Faith' by the Pope in 1521 for writing a book in which he defended the Catholic Church against the accusations of the German reformer, Martin Luther. Henry's military campaigns were more problematic as they involved considerable expense and did not yield any lasting benefits to England. However, Henry also built up the navy. The prowess of England on the seas is a legacy from Henry VIII's time: his reign began with England possessing a navy of five ships and ended with the number having increased to fifty-three.

However, the lasting significance of Henry VIII's reign can be attributed to two intertwined threads: the succession to the throne and the English Reformation. For a king who defended the Catholic Church to have dissolved all ties with that Church required a powerful impetus: Henry found that impetus in his worry that he would have no male heir to inherit his kingdom. His marriage to Catherine of Aragon had given him a daughter, Mary, but no sons, and as the queen grew older Henry grew ever more desperate: he himself was only the second monarch of the Tudor dynasty, and a daughter inheriting the throne would be a risk for the sovereignty of England and one which could well endanger the kingdom by her marriage. This desire for a male heir led Henry to seek the annulment of his marriage to Catherine. Given that Catholicism did not permit divorce and the fact that Henry had married his brother's widow (in itself questionable under the Biblical law), it was at the highest level that the annulment was sought: from the Pope. The refusal, when it came, was influenced by non-religious reasons primarily: the Pope was in the power of the Holy Roman Emperor and King of Spain, Charles V, who was nephew to Catherine of Aragon. Familial pressures worked in tandem with the fear of an emergent strong England to thwart Henry's desires. By this time Henry had already fixed upon Anne Boleyn as his next queen even in the face of the Pope's refusal. Cardinal Wolsey was unable to change the Pope's views and fell into disfavour with Henry VIII, leading to his arrest and death. His successor, Thomas Cromwell, effected a series of Acts, with the help of the Parliament, which led eventually to England's break with Rome. These Acts initially stopped revenues from ecclesiastical properties in England going to Rome but eventually ended in the excommunication of Henry VIII by the Pope, to which England responded by making the English monarch the head of the Church of England (1534). While these events were in progress, the Archbishop of Canterbury, now no longer answerable to the Pope, declared Henry's marriage to Catherine of Aragon invalid, making it possible for him to marry Anne Boleyn in January 1533. Henry's desire for a son remained unfulfilled as Elizabeth was born, followed by miscarriages, and as Henry was tired of Anne Boleyn, she was arrested on charges of treason and executed in 1536. The new queen was Jane Seymour; and though she died soon after childbirth, the child, the longed-for son, survived, and Henry finally had his male heir: Edward, born in 1537. Henry's next three marriages did not yield any more children, so the succession was now in place: Edward, though the youngest of Henry's three surviving children, by the rule of male primogeniture (the rule that makes it possible for the first-born son to inherit his father's titles, property, etc.), would inherit on the death of his father.

The English Reformation[2] was more a consequence of Henry's marital career than the result of a felt disquiet, revulsion and anger against the iniquities and corruption of the Catholic Church. This top-down imposition would impact the reorganisation of the Church in England in significant ways, leading to England switching from Protestantism to Catholicism and back again depending upon the personal affiliation of the English monarch to Catholicism or Protestantism. However, Henry's avarice furthered more actions as he dissolved the monasteries (1534–40), breaking up lands which belonged to the Church, attaching some, selling others and taking over the valuable possessions of the many Church properties. These were actions that swelled the king's treasuries but also disrupted social order and tore apart the hitherto smooth social fabric.

The final years of Henry VIII's reign were spent in fruitless wars against France, his treasury rapidly emptying; and he finally died in January 1547.

Edward VI

Edward VI (1547–53) was a nine-year-old sickly child on his accession in 1547, though well-read and brought up with the knowledge of his role as the king of England. Though Edward was king in name the kingdom was ruled by a Lord Protector, Edward Seymour, Duke of Somerset. Somerset and the Archbishop of Canterbury, Thomas Cranmer, worked at making

England a Protestant nation: an English prayer book, the *Book of Common Prayer*, was introduced in 1549 across England and marriage was permitted for the clergy. However, there were also rebellions within the country and France threatened war as well. Somerset lost his control over the king (1551) and his life as well (1552) and was replaced by John Dudley, Duke of Northumberland. The reforms to the English Church continued but in an atmosphere of increasing worry as it became apparent that Edward was ailing and in the event of his death Mary, eldest daughter of Henry VIII, and Catherine of Aragon, a staunch Catholic, would ascend the throne. Northumberland attempted to prevent this by altering the line of succession and getting Edward VI to recognise Lady Jane Grey, a great-niece of Henry VIII, as his successor. On Edward's death in 1553, Northumberland did succeed in having Lady Jane Grey enthroned but her reign lasted a mere nine days as Mary rode into London with her followers and deposed, imprisoned and later executed Lady Jane Grey.

Mary I

Becoming queen when she was thirty-seven, Mary (1553–58) saw her coronation as an opportunity to right the wrongs suffered by her mother and the Catholic Church during the reigns of her father and brother. She worked quickly to have Acts of Parliament passed by which Catholicism was reinstated and her mother's marriage to Henry VIII (which had been declared invalid, thus making her a "bastard") was declared valid and legal. Determined to make England a Catholic nation once more, she married Prince Philip of Spain (king of Spain from 1556), hoping for an heir who would then prevent the crown from passing to Elizabeth, in case of her own death.

Mary, known in history as "Bloody Mary", gained the title from her fanatical measures to put down Protestantism: arrest, imprisonment, followed by execution, often by burning at the stake, was the fate of those who refused to recant, including the Archbishop of Canterbury, Thomas Cranmer, who was burnt at the stake in 1556.[3] The numbers included bishops and prelates, commoners and nobles: the earlier imposition of Protestantism by the Crown was seen to have struck roots and grown. Mary's marriage to the Catholic Philip of Spain also incurred the displeasure of the kingdom. As discontentment with Mary's policies spread, England was forced into a war with France in the course of which England lost its last possession in France, Calais, in January 1558. Rendered unhappy by her childlessness, deserted by her husband, unloved by her people, Mary died in November 1558; and with her death, the last hope of a Catholic England ended.

Elizabeth I

Popularly accounted among the greatest of English monarchs, the reign of Elizabeth I is regarded as a "Golden Age" in the history of England. Her rule is marked in the initial years by a painstaking effort to make and constitute England as a Protestant nation. Undoing Mary's efforts, Elizabeth asked for outward conformity, set a middle course, steering England away from the extreme position adopted by Mary and thus brought into existence the Church of England, in the process saving England from divisive religious wars.

With ability, intelligence and a fierce determination, Elizabeth was also fortunate in having a set of loyal ministers who helped her to run her realm efficiently. These included William Cecil, Lord Burghley, her Secretary of State, and Francis Walsingham, in charge of intelligence. The naval prowess first set in place by Henry VIII came into its own during her realm, as English sailors set out on voyages of exploration and discovery: Sir Francis Drake circumnavigated the globe (1580); Sir Walter Raleigh led expeditions to the Americas; the English navy decisively beat the Spanish Armada (1588). Threats to the queen were disposed of with alacrity and efficiency, the most famous being the threat posed by Mary, Queen of Scots, which ended with her imprisonment and eventual execution.

Through the reign of Elizabeth, especially in the early years, there were innumerable suitors for her hand in marriage. With remarkable acumen, she kept everyone guessing as to what her course of action would be. She had favourites among her courtiers (Lord Robert Dudley, Sir Walter Raleigh and Robert Devereux, Earl of Essex, to name just three) but she avoided marriage as marrying an Englishman could lead to factional fighting in the realm and marrying one of the foreign princes might endanger the independence of England. While entertaining embassies and suitors, Elizabeth made it possible for the arts to thrive: she encouraged composers at her court, her courtiers included poets such as Philip Sidney (1554–86), she frequently ordered plays to be performed at court, and miniature painting flourished (as in the work of Nicholas Hilliard [c.1547–1619] and others) during this period. While conscious of being a "weak and feeble woman", she spoke of herself as "a king, and a king of England too" (in her speech to the English troops at Tilbury, in 1588). She projected herself as a monarch devoted to her country and her subjects and often spoke of the "love" she bore her subjects, which was recompensed by the love they bore her, which was, she claimed "the Glory of my crown". The idea of the "Virgin Queen" was one which Elizabeth's subjects had invested in as we see in Shakespeare's *A Midsummer Night's Dream* wherein he speaks of

> A certain aim he (Cupid) took
> At a fair vestal throned by the west,
> And loosed his love-shaft smartly from his bow,
> As it should pierce a hundred thousand hearts.
> But I might see young Cupid's fiery shaft
> Quench'd in the chaste beams of the wat'ry moon,

And the imperial vot'ress passed on,
In maiden meditation, fancy-free. (II.i.157–64)

To further this idea she would often move through her kingdom in ceremonial processions, called "progresses", rarely riding in her carriage, preferring instead to ride on horseback, seeing and being seen by her subjects. Her last speech to the Parliament, in 1601, called the "Golden Speech", endorsed this attitude and helped her, as always, to project herself as the loving and loved queen of a grateful people: "And, though God hath raised me high, yet this I count the glory of my Crown, that I have reigned with your loves" ("The Farewell Speech").

Elizabeth I died in March 1603, thus ending the Tudor line, leaving no heir in the direct line of succession; but though James VI was not formally named as her successor, she did indicate her preference for him to succeed her to the throne of England.

James I of England

The Stuart James had already been king of Scotland for thirty-six years when he was invited to become king of England (1603–25), thus uniting the two countries of Scotland and England under one Crown for the first time. The many fears of the people of England regarding the succession and the lack of an heir were belied as England welcomed James VI of Scotland as James I of England. The welcome accorded James I by the English is seen tangentially in Shakespeare's *Macbeth* where he offers James I the compliment of creating Banquo as a righteous and loyal Thane, knowing that James I claimed Banquo in his ancestral line.

James I with his interests in theology and the theories of kingship wrote several treatises: on witches and witchcraft, on the Divine Right of Kings, on tobacco, etc. But today he is best remembered for authorising and facilitating the King James translation of the Bible (1611), which remained the most popular and widely read translation of the Bible for the next two hundred-odd years. He was also a fairly tolerant monarch in terms of religion: until the Gunpowder Plot of 1605[4] he had only ordered all Catholic priests to leave England, but that event then necessitated the imposition of strict punitive action on Catholics. James I was a patron of the theatre: Shakespeare's company, previously the Lord Chamberlain's Men, was now the King's Men, their patron James I himself. The queen (Anne of Denmark) and the courtiers often took part in masques and interludes acted in the court and Inigo Jones's (1573–1652) work for the theatre, designing costumes, introducing moveable scenery and the proscenium arch, was done during this period.

The relations between James I and the English Parliament were often difficult as James I believed firmly in the Divine Right theory of kingship and resented the power of Parliament to adjudicate upon his powers. Indeed, his address to Parliament in 1609 dealt at length with the idea of kings being equal to God:

> Kings are justly called Gods, for that they exercise a manner or resemblance of divine power upon earth.... I conclude then this point touching the power of kings, with this axiom of divinity, that as to dispute what God may do, is blasphemy . . . so is it sedition in subjects, to dispute what a king may do in the height of his power: But just kings will ever be willing to declare what they will do, if they will not incur the curse of God.

The abrasive relationship between James I and his Parliament was further rendered acrimonious as his expensive tastes and habits meant that he was constantly petitioning Parliament for more funds. The frictions between the monarch and Parliament, and also the fact that James I did not win the affections of his people the way Elizabeth I had done, meant that James I's kingship had a shaky foundation, which though it held up during James I's reign, eventually lead to the execution of his son, Charles I, who succeeded him on his death in 1625.

KINGLY AUTHORITY

> We princes, I tell you, are set on stages, in the sight and view of all the world duly observed.
>
> (Elizabeth I, "In Answer to a Petition from Both Houses of Parliament")

As the above quotation indicates, Queen Elizabeth I recognised the fact that kingship was a performance, a role that was played by the monarch, and where the audience was "all the world". In this section, we will examine the processes by which the authority of kings was derived, instated and endorsed, and also the ways in which the monarchs of Shakespeare's age demonstrated authority. Kings, while they might have become kings due to genealogy and lineage, were also kings because there was an implicit belief in the idea that kingship was divinely ordained, an idea that was articulated as the "Divine Right theory of kingship". But while kings owed their kingship to God and bloodlines, there were other factors as well which made it possible: the power of the people and their affections was one such factor. While it is commonplace to argue for one or the other, the truth remains that all three of these factors had to work together for a king to be accepted and revered in Early Modern England.

Deriving Authority

Divine Right Theory of Kingship

> Not all the water in the rough rude sea
> Can wash the balm from an anointed king;
> The breath of worldly men cannot depose
> The deputy elected by the Lord. (*Richard II* III.ii.50–53)

The Divine Right theory of kingship held that a king was appointed by God in His infinite wisdom and as such there was no earthly authority that could be exerted over a king, nor any authority that could depose him. It also followed from this that as the king had been granted his kingship by God, only God could judge him: this paved the way for the absolute power of the king as (1) he was subject to no earthly power and (2) it was sacrilegious to go against such a king, even if he were to be tyrannical. The only redress that was possible was if God were to intercede and prevent injustice: human powers could not attempt to have control over kings. Thus even if an unjust and despotic king was to be on the throne, the only option for the people was to suffer quietly, for to rise against the king was to incur the wrath of God himself. Resisting such a king meant not just suffering the punishments meted out by the king but also retribution in the afterlife! In addition, a king who believed in this theory also considered all power to be settled on him by God: as such the people had no power over him and he was not accountable to them or to Parliament. It is of course ironical that the clearest articulation of the Divine Right theory of kingship in Shakespeare's plays appears in *Richard II*, wherein he is deposed and forced to abdicate and Henry Bolingbroke takes over the throne as Henry IV.

While this theory had its origins in the medieval belief that earthly power was vested in the king, while spiritual power was vested in the Church, the Christian world view believed that in his body the king was a representative of God here on earth. King James I tried to further popularise and endorse this form of kingship as is evidenced from his speeches to Parliament right from the time of his accession (see the speech of James I quoted above). Even prior to becoming king of England, while he was king of Scotland, James I had written two texts—*The True Law of Free Monarchies* (1598) and *Basilikon Doron* (1599)—in both of which he spoke about absolute monarchy, the divinely ordained position of the king, and the role of parliaments and subjects. The latter of these was written to instruct and advise his son and heir about kingship. As James I put it in the "Sonnet Prefixed to His Majesty's Instructions to His Dearest Son, Henry the Prince", the Argument of *Basilikon Doron*, "God gives not Kings the style of Gods in vain / For on his throne his Sceptre do they sway. . . ." As indicated, kings were next only to God in power, holding their kingdoms under his aegis and being almost God-like in their power and "style".

This belief in divinely ordained monarchy was a feature of the reigns of both Elizabeth I (see the extract from the "Farewell Speech", quoted above) and James I, but more so in the reign of James I. We see it also in Shakespeare's works, especially in *Richard II*, where the Bishop of Carlisle speaks of him:

And shall the figure of God's majesty,
His captain, steward, deputy elect,
Anointed, crowned, planted many years,
Be judged by subject and inferior breath,
And he himself not present? (IV.i.116–20)

The belief that no harm could touch the King, anointed as he was by God finds expression in *Hamlet*, where ironically enough, it is Claudius, who has himself killed a king, who speaks about the divinity that surrounds a king when Laertes comes to assault him:

Let him go, Gertrude; do not fear our person.
There's such divinity doth hedge a king,
That treason can but peep to what it would,
Acts little of his will. (IV.v.119–22)

Thus, even as the Divine Right theory of kingship circulated in society, it was also contested and questioned; literature demonstrated its gaps and fissures and it cannot be claimed that it was the sole basis on which kingship rested. Other factors and features played equally important roles.

The King's Two Bodies

A medieval theory, the idea that the king was possessed of two bodies, was in circulation during Tudor times. The monarch was held to be composed of two bodies: one his natural body, prone to decay and disease and eventually death, and two, "his Body politic is a Body that cannot be seen or handled, consisting of Policy and Government, and constituted for the Direction of the People, and the Management of the public weal, and this Body is utterly void of Infancy, and old Age, and other natural Defects and Imbecilities, which the Body natural is subject to. . . ." (Kantorowicz). Thus while the king would, and did, die, and could even be assassinated, the body politic was immortal, something that could not be killed "for it represented the mystical dignity and justice of the body politic" (Philpott). The Body Politic was held to contain the Body Natural and this gave an additional layer of authority to the monarch: *the indestructible nature of the monarchy was endorsed by this theory* and it was invoked at critical junctures to further validate the authority and position of the king. Thus when one Body Natural died, the Body Politic passed on to the next Body Natural and thus immortality was conferred upon the kingship.

This theorising regarding the two bodies of the king circulated in legal and political circles during Shakespearean times. We see traces of it in *Hamlet* where Hamlet Senior speaks of having died with his sins heavy upon him, in his Body Natural, with his body marred and damaged, but where the Body Politic is seen as having passed on smoothly to Claudius:

> And a most instant tetter barked about,
> Most lazar-like, with vile and loathsome crust,
> All my smooth body.
> Thus was I, sleeping, by a brother's hand
> Of life, of crown, of queen, at once dispatched:
> Cut off even in the blossoms of my sin,

Unhouseled, disappointed, unaneled,
No reck'ning made, but sent to my account
With all my imperfections on my head: (I.v.71–79)

The theory of the king's two bodies can be a crucial tool for reading and interpreting *King Lear* as well. If the king is possessed of two bodies, of which one is indestructible and the other mortal, it then becomes imperative to ask that when King Lear partitions the kingdom he does so in which body. The partition of the kingdom in I.i is done as a father *and* as a king and as such Lear appears to not know the difference between the two bodies of the king. If the Body Politic consists of the kingdom, the subjects and himself, how can the king partition that body? *King Lear* is further complicated because the Body Politic which is whole and one is herein partitioned and segmented, the parts set at odds with one another and the whole ruined: *King Lear*, in effect, offers a salutary lesson against the mixing up of the two bodies of the king and not taking cognisance of them as they were seen during this period: as separate and having an integrity, each of its own.

Genealogy, Lineage and Tradition

I may not be a lion but I am a lion's cub and have a lion's heart.

(Attributed to Elizabeth I)

Given the questionable basis of the Divine Right Theory (which in effect claimed that kingship was constituted by God and therefore a king was unassailable), what could be seen as an adequate reason for elevating someone to the throne? One of the more practical and demonstrable bases for kingship was the bloodline: kings could not be chosen from amongst commoners, kingship rested on genealogy and lineage. The aspirant to the throne had to be related by blood to a previous king or kings (as seen in the epigraph to this section attributed to Elizabeth

I where she invokes her lineage and claims legitimacy from it). Thus even if the crown was not passed directly from parent to child there had to be a blood connection between a person and previous kings, before that person's claims to the throne could even be considered. The history of Elizabethan and Jacobean kingship demonstrates this, over and over again. The many rebellions against an enthroned monarch were always in the name of a claimant whose bloodline gave him/her the legitimacy of aspiring to the throne. Thus during the reign of Elizabeth I the fear and suspicion of Mary, Queen of Scots, was due to the fact of her having a legitimate claim to the throne of England: she was a great-granddaughter of Henry VII and as such had nearly as strong a claim to the English throne as did Elizabeth I. It was also on the basis of this bloodline that the Stuart James I, son to Mary, Queen of Scots, was invited to become king after the death of Elizabeth I. A similar case of lineage lending authority to the claims of a person to the throne was seen in the brief nine days reign of Lady Jane Grey. She too was a great-granddaughter of Henry VII and her family placed her on the throne, hoping to keep England in Protestant hands after the death of Edward VI. Thus family bloodlines, a person's genealogy and near-impeccable lineage (at least in terms of descent), was one of the primary requirements to gaining the throne.

We see this awareness of bloodlines and royalty in *Richard II* from the very first act as Henry Bolingbroke's "high blood's royalty" is referenced by Thomas Mowbray (I.i.58), as one of the reasons he cannot fight against him. That royalty, ingrained in the blood, so to speak, is what makes it possible for Bolingbroke to challenge Richard II later on. (He calls himself "A prince, by fortune of my birth" [III.i.36].) In *Hamlet*, similarly, it is the fact of Claudius being brother to Hamlet Senior that makes him a candidate for the throne and helps him to become king. In several of Shakespeare's plays we can see this emphasis on lineage and bloodlines play out as brothers seek to take over crowns and thrones and kingdoms (from *Titus Andronicus*, where Bassianus and Saturninus vie for the crown, to *The Tempest*, where Prospero is supplanted by his brother as Duke of Milan): a dramatic representation of what was often plotted and planned in the lives of the monarchs of England.

Noble and Popular Support

> Yet this I count the glory of my Crown, that I have reigned with your loves.
>
> (Elizabeth I, "The Farewell Speech")

While the candidates to the throne might have been many, there was still one more factor which went into determining who would eventually rule: gaining access to the throne was also a matter of popular support, as evidenced by the rise to power of Mary I. Even though Lady Jane Grey had been enthroned, Mary, by mobilising mass support, was able to march to London and take back the crown.

The support of the nobility and the masses, while not absolutely essential, was nonetheless an important factor in questions of kingship. During late Tudor times, Elizabeth I time and again evidenced her hold over the people's hearts and thus was able to rule with comparatively little opposition. Her ability to be loving to, and loved by, the ordinary people stood her in good stead through her reign. Indeed so marked was this appeal that many of the nobles, both English and foreign, at her court, commented on it. Thus according to John Harington, her godson and courtier, she converted her reign "through the perpetual love-tricks that passed between her and her people, into a kind of romance" (qtd. in McDonald 313). This romancing of each other had begun during Elizabeth's progress and entry into London prior to her coronation in January 1559, when the people demonstrated a "wonderfull earnest love of most obedient subiectes towarde theyr soveraigne" and she in return held up a "merie countenaunce to such as stode farre of, and most tender and gentle language to those that stode nigh to her grace" ("The passage of our most drad Soveraigne Lady Quene Elyzabeth through the citie of London to Westminster the daye before her coronacion").

The necessity of the support of the people and their love is visible in *Hamlet* where Claudius is afraid to touch Hamlet because of the "great love the general gender bear him" (IV. vii.18), and in *Macbeth* where we are told by the lords how Macbeth finds himself isolated at the end: "Those he commands move only in command, / Nothing in love. . ." (V.ii.19–20). Malcolm states, "Both more and less have given him the revolt" (V.iv.12), and Macbeth himself knows that "the thanes fly from me" (V.iii.51) and every scene in Act V underlines the plight of a king who is deserted by his people, both the nobility and the commoners.

But it comes out most clearly in *Richard II* where we read of an entry into London by the two cousins, Richard II the king and Henry Bolingbroke, who having forced Richard to abdicate is now the heir to the throne:

> Whilst all tongues cried 'God save thee,
> Bolingbroke!'
> You would have thought the very windows spake,
> So many greedy looks of young and old
> Through casements darted their desiring eyes
> Upon his visage, and that all the walls
> With painted imagery had said at once
> 'Jesu preserve thee! Welcome, Bolingbroke!'
> Whilst he, from the one side to the other turning,
> Bare-headed, lower than his proud steed's neck,
> Bespake them thus: 'I thank you, countrymen,' (V.ii.31–41)

This is in stark contrast to how the same crowds greet Richard:

men's eyes
Did scowl on gentle Richard; no man cried 'God save him!'
No joyful tongue gave him his welcome home;
But dust was thrown upon his sacred head, (V.ii.27–30)

While the love of the common people was an important factor in getting and retaining the kingship, it also depended upon being able to command the loyalties of the nobility. This is showcased in *Hamlet* where we are told by Claudius that his accession to his brother's throne and his marriage to his brother's widow have the sanction and accord of the nobles, for which he thanks them:

nor have we herein barred
Your better wisdoms, which have freely gone
With this affair along. For all, our thanks. (I.ii.14–16)

The role of the nobility in supplanting a ruler with another, and its changeable nature, is seen in *The Tempest*, where Prospero tells Miranda how he came to be driven out from his dukedom of Milan, by his brother who

Being once perfected how to grant suits,
How to deny them, who t'advance and who
To trash for over-topping, new created
The creatures that were mine, I say or changed 'em,
Or else new formed 'em; having both the key
Of officer and office, set all hearts i' th' state
To what tune pleased his ear; (I.ii.79–85)

Prospero, like Hamlet, owes his life to the love his people bear him, the reason they were not destroyed as he tells Miranda is: "Dear, they durst not, / So dear the love my people bore me;" (I.ii.140–41).

While Shakespeare's plays show the tensions between various factors that authorise and consolidate monarchy, the real life of the court in post-Shakespearean England also demonstrated this, as James I became unpopular with his people and Parliament, his son Charles I more so, eventually leading to the Civil War, the execution of the latter and the establishing of the Commonwealth.

Demonstrating Authority

> . . . the shining glory of princely authority
>
> (Elizabeth I, "The Farewell Speech")

The reigns of Elizabeth I and James I were built upon ideas of kingship which have been outlined above, but they also gained and consolidated their power and reach by the demonstration of kingly authority via various means. The people were subjected to repeated and enhanced manifestations of the monarch's authority and power which then helped to consolidate it. The dominion of the king was also ineradicably endorsed and added to, by naturalising it and by setting it in a frame which granted it earthly and divine sanction.

Ideas of Order

Early Modern concepts of order were all-pervasive: they extended from the cosmos to every level of earthly life, even to plants and animals.[5] Thus beginning with the heavenly bodies a certain order was imposed by which they existed in a hierarchy which was seen as the key to a harmonious life and society. Among the heavenly bodies the Sun was pre-eminent, God was the highest among the angels and all created works, the king was foremost in the state, the husband and father in the family, the head over all the other members of the body, fire among the elements, the lion among the beasts, and so on. This hierarchic order enabled a naturalising (making it appear that Nature itself had framed it this way) of an ordered society and also of the monarchy. (Its repercussions for familial order we shall consider later.) The king was naturally, and by divine diktat, the head of the state and the nation and as such his power was not to be flouted. Indeed, to try to disrupt this harmonious arrangement was to invite disorder and agitation at all levels. Shakespeare's referencing of this in *Troilus and Cressida* makes it abundantly clear that

> The heavens themselves, the planets and this centre
> Observe degree, priority and place,
> Insisture, course, proportion, season, form,
> Office and custom, in all line of order.
> ....
>
> O when degree is shaked,
> Which is the ladder to all high designs,
> The enterprise is sick! How could communities,
> Degrees in schools, and brotherhoods in cities,
> Peaceful commerce from dividable shores,
> The primogenity and due of birth,
> Prerogative of age, crowns, sceptres, laurels,
> But by degree, stand in authentic place?
> Take but degree away, untune that string,
> And, hark, what discord follows! (I.iii.85–88, 101–10)

This ordering of, and order in, society is often remarked upon by Shakespeare's characters who connect disorder and the shaking of the structures of society to events that have troubled the order of the stars and the natural world. Thus in *Macbeth*, after the killing of Duncan, the Old Man mentions yet another overturning of the natural order of things:

> On Tuesday last,
> A falcon, tow'ring in her pride of place,
> Was by a mousing owl hawked at and kill'd. (II.iv.11–13)

The naturalising of kingship was also further endorsed by religion and the Church which preached the necessity of obedience and loyalty to the king. This became particularly so after England's break with the Catholic Church during the reign of Henry VIII. The Protestant church employed the Sunday sermon as a vital method for promoting values that were seen as acceptable to the Church and the monarchy. Given the fact that the English Reformation was, in its initial stages, a fall out of the King's personal desires and agenda, the Church was intimately connected to the throne; and Elizabeth I, as Supreme Head of the Church, as had her predecessors and would her successors, used this to consolidate her position as monarch of England. The use of the homily in Elizabethan times is of particular interest as the homilies were read from the pulpit to promote particular values, values which were most often such that supported and endorsed particular ideological positions that were crucial to the monarchy. Thus *An Homily against Disobedience and Willful Rebellion* was issued in 1570 as an answer to one of the many rebellions in support of Mary, Queen of Scots.[6] The Church endorsing kingship is a recurrent

The 'ermine portrait' of Elizabeth I   Portrait of James I

feature in several of Shakespeare's English history plays wherein prelates frequently feature as significant characters.

Thus kingship was seen as endorsed by both Nature and God, both powerful validating mechanisms in Shakespeare's England.

Spectacular Authority

To *be* a king was not enough; it was necessary to be *seen* to be a king and no one was more aware of this than the kings and queens of Early Modern England. Even as Nature and God were endorsing mechanisms for kingly authority, the most visible way of demonstrating kingship was by virtue of an appeal to the eye: the spectacle of kingship was proof of kingship. This spectacular presentation of kingship was accomplished via the dress of the monarch, the court and courtly activities, including the royal progresses, and finally the most powerful, visible demonstration of kingship: punitive action and its consequences upon human bodies.

The presence of the monarch signified the court: wherever he or she was present, the court was held to have assembled. Though the kings of England had several palaces (Whitehall, Hampton, Windsor, Greenwich, Westminster, Richmond, etc.), they also stayed at the castles and manor houses of their principal or favourite courtiers: thus wherever the king and his retinue (of courtiers and servants) stayed was the court. The court was during Early Modern times a place of much pomp, ceremony and grandeur, a space wherein the practices were characterised by "ceremonious affection" towards the monarch, as Shakespeare puts it in *King Lear* (I.iv.50).

The grandeur of the court was contributed to by magnificent interiors, distinguished by wooden panelling with extensive decorative carving, ornate, elaborate tapestries and often enough displays of gold and silver plates. Paintings, particularly of the monarch, had also begun to be included in the décor of the royal castles. But the most magnificence was contributed by the courtiers and the monarch him/herself: in their dress and jewellery, they were ostentatious, flamboyant and glitteringly dazzling. This can be noted in the portraits of Henry VIII, Elizabeth I and James I, each of whom is usually dressed magnificently, with a wealth of fine apparel and gorgeous jewels.[7]

The king in his palace, surrounded by his court, presented a spectacle of pomp and finery that constituted his kingly quality even as it demonstrated it. This awareness that it was necessary to "appear" a king is seen in several of Shakespeare's plays as well which focus on the spectacle of the court in their initial scenes: *King Lear* (I.i); *Hamlet* (I.ii); the Senate scene in *Othello* (I.iii); I.i of *Twelfth Night* and *A Midsummer Night's Dream*; and all the scenes at the court of the ruling monarch in the English history plays. *King Lear*, indeed, can be read as a meditation on the nature of kingship and what is necessary to *appear* a king: does Lear remain a king once stripped of the crown, the throne and his courtiers?

While having an ostentatious court was a necessity for the king, Elizabethan England was also careful to observe degree, order and hierarchy in matters of dress. The Sumptuary Laws of England (1562 and 1574) delineated with exactitude what was permitted as outerwear for each rank and each income group. Details included permitted colours (for example, the colour purple), the type of embroidery and material (gold, silver or pearl embroidery and velvet, silk, damask, etc.), the amount of material to be used (in hose, for example), the length of rapiers, etc.[8] As Shakespeare put it in *Hamlet*:

> Costly thy habit as thy purse can buy,
> But not expressed in fancy; rich not gaudy;
> For the apparel oft proclaims the man, . . . (I.iii.70–72)

Thus kingship and nobility was signified not just by birth but also by the clothes that one wore. This was more so in the court where a certain grandeur and flamboyance was the norm rather than the exception. This was particularly so in the case of the monarch who had to display more magnificence than any of her courtiers: this was an expensive proposition but done as a matter of course. An "inventory" of Elizabeth I's wardrobe in 1600 "included almost 300 gowns and several hundred other costumes, in addition to state apparel" ("Elizabethan Fashions"). Kingship was also signified, interestingly, by such customs as the one that decreed that the monarch's head was to be higher than any other's. We see this in operation in the 2008 BBC production of *King Lear*, where in I.i everyone hastens to kneel every time Lear raises his hand. The king's court effected and helped in the circulation of an image of kingship which then further built and endorsed his authority.

The visibility of the monarch as she moved around the country during the summer months in what has come to be called the "royal progress" also helped in circulating the kingly image. The royal progresses were again an opportunity to visibly make manifest kingship via extravagance and ostentation: the homes of courtiers where she lodged overnight or where she chose to stay, sometimes for weeks on end, were furnished with showiness and flamboyance. But more so was the entertainment which was planned for the monarch: no expense was spared and gifts were lavished upon her with no thought to expense. This hospitality often bankrupted the host but was nonetheless one more device by which the monarch made herself visible and impressed her kingship upon her subjects.

One more device, and arguably the most powerful, by which kingliness was made visible was that by which kings effected punitive action, creating of it a spectacle so complete that all who witnessed it carried away with them the awareness and understanding of the absolute power of the monarch. During Shakespeare's times, there were courts at several levels to try different kinds of crimes, but high treason was tried and judged by the monarch herself and her privy council: the punishment meted out was death and after, the head of the condemned man would be exhibited on a pike on London Bridge or in other places of high visibility. Macbeth as he fights with Macduff in the final scene of the play is reminded that he will be the

> show and gaze o' th' time:
> We'll have thee, as our rarer monsters are,
> Painted upon a pole, and underwrit,
> 'Here may you see the tyrant.' (*Macbeth* V.viii.24–27)

Executions and other punishments under the law were often in the nature of a warning even as they were also exemplary punishment for crimes committed. And as all crimes were punished in the name of the monarch, it was the power of the king which was enacted/written upon the body of the perpetrator. Extreme examples included that of "drawing, hanging and quartering", pressing which involved being "pressed to death by huge weights laid upon a board, that lies over their breast, and a sharp stone under their backs" ("Refusing to Enter a Plea"), and this for a refusal to plead guilty, which people did so that their goods could be saved for their families as otherwise these would become crown property. The spectacle of public punishment was thus a device by which kingly authority and its limits (or lack thereof) were inscribed in the minds of the viewers and subjects. More than any other place "London was a nonstop theater of punishments," Greenblatt states, and here it was possible to watch "*the state* brand, cut and kill those it deemed offenders" (emphasis added). This activity of the state (read the king) was one more way of demonstrating absolute power, via the "penal spectacle" (178–79).

* * * *

> To be a King, and weare a Crown, is a thing more glorious to them that see it, then it is pleasant to them that beare it
>
> (Elizabeth I, "The Farewell Speech")

While it is necessary to remember how kingship was constituted and how it played out on the stage of the world in Early Modern times, it is also essential to remember that what we are doing is gazing at the past with our present-day concerns and ideology in place.[9] It is coloured, in addition, with a painstaking knowledge of Shakespeare's plays which appear to question, subvert, endorse and toy with the dominant modes of belief of his times. As we read Shakespeare's plays, kingship becomes an ever-more fraught enterprise, one which conferred authority and power but came with its attendant perils and anxieties. Thus in closing it might be instructive to consider one more quotation in conjunction with the one that is the epigram to this section, from the "Golden Speech" of Elizabeth I. The other is from *Richard II*, the Shakespeare text which has featured more than any other in this discussion of kingship.

> for within the hollow crown
> That rounds the mortal temples of a king
> Keeps Death his court; and there the antic sits,
> Scoffing his state and grinning at his pomp,
> Allowing him a breath, a little scene,
> To monarchize, be feared and kill with looks,
> Infusing him with self and vain conceit,
> As if this flesh which walls about our life,
> Were brass impregnable; and humour'd thus,
> Comes at the last, and with a little pin
> Bores through his castle wall; and farewell, king! (*Richard II* III. ii.156–66)

The ways in which these two quotations speak to each other are illustrative of the limitations of kingship. While Elizabeth I demonstrates an awareness of the fact that kingship is not all pleasure, Shakespeare reminds his readers of the evanescent nature of all life, even that of kings: in the final analysis, "Your worm is your only emperor for diet", as Hamlet reminds Claudius (IV.iii.21–22).

Works Cited

Dollimore, Jonathan. *Radical Tragedy: Religion, Ideology and Power in the Drama of Shakespeare and His Contemporaries*. 1984. New York: Palgrave Macmillan, 2010. Print.

Elizabeth I. "Against the Spanish Armada." 1588. *Modern History Sourcebook*. Paul Halsall. Fordham University. 1997. Web. 12 August 2013.

——. "In Answer to a Petition from Both Houses of Parliament." 12 November 1586. Cited in *The Oxford Shakespeare: Richard II*. By William Shakespeare. Ed. Anthony B. Dawson and Paul Yachnin. New York: Oxford UP, 2011. 259. Print.

——. "The Farewell Speech," 1601. *Modern History Sourcebook*. Paul Halsall. Fordham University. 1998. Web. 12 August 2013.

"Elizabethan Fashions." *Internet Shakespeare Editions*. University of Victoria. n.d. Web. 17 August 2013. http://internetshakespeare.uvic.ca/Library/SLT/stage/costumes/fashion.html

Fischlin, Daniel. "Political Allegory, Absolutist Ideology, and the *Rainbow Portrait* of Queen Elizabeth I." *Renaissance Quarterly* 50.1 (Spring 1997): 175–206. JSTOR. Web. 7 August 2014.

Greenblatt, Stephen. *Will in the World*. New York: W. W. Norton, 2004. Print.

James I. Extract from a speech to Parliament, 21 March 1609. Historic Royal Speeches and Writing. *The Official Website of the British Monarchy*. n.d. Web. 6 August 2014.

——. "Sonnet Prefixed to His Majesty's Instructions to His Dearest Son, Henry the Prince." *The Book of Elizabethan Verse*. Ed. William Stanley Braithwaite. Boston: Herbert B. Turner and Co., 1907; *Bartleby.com*, 2013. Web. 14 August 2013.

Kantorowicz, Ernst. Excerpts from *The King's Two Bodies: A Study in Medieval Political Theology*. Princeton, NJ: Princeton UP, 1957. Library of Social Science.com. Web. 17 August 2014.

McDonald, Russ. *The Bedford Companion to Shakespeare: An Introduction with Documents*. (Second Edition) Boston, MA: Bedford/St Martin's, 2001.

Philpott, Dan. "Sovereignty." *The Stanford Encyclopedia of Philosophy* (Summer 2014 Edition). Ed. Edward N. Zalta. Web. 17 August 2014. <http://plato.stanford.edu/archives/sum2014/entries/sovereignty/>.

"Refusing to Enter a Plea: Pressed to Death. Let the Punishment Fit the Crime." *Internet Shakespeare Editions*. University of Victoria. n.d. Web. 17 August 2013. <http://internetshakespeare.uvic.ca/Library/SLT/history/crime%20and%20the%20law/stocks+1.html#refusing>.

The passage of our most drad Soveraigne Lady Quene Elyzabeth through the citie of London to Westminster the daye before her coronacion. Richard Mulcaster. 1558. "Description of Elizabeth I's Royal Progression through London to Westminster the day before her coronation." *Emotions*. Australian Research Council Centre of Excellence for the History of Emotions. Web. 6 August 2014.

Notes

1. The dates are of the monarch's reign, not his or her life.
2. The Reformation refers to the reform movements begun in Europe by individuals such as Martin Luther and John Calvin. These movements were agitations that protested against the corruption that the Catholic Church had fallen prey to and were meant to reform and improve the Church. The English Reformation, on the other hand, was not aimed at theological improvement, nor at weeding out corruption in the Church: it was primarily the result of Henry VIII's marital entanglements and his desire for an heir.
3. Read a first person account of his execution at <http://englishhistory.net/tudor/pcranmer.html>

4. The Gunpowder Plot refers to an attempt by a small group of Catholics to blow up James I at the opening of Parliament on 5 November 1605.
5. See Arthur O. Lovejoy's *The Great Chain of Being* and E. M. W. Tillyard's *The Elizabethan World Picture* for a fuller understanding of this phenomenon.
6. The homilies were sermons to be read aloud in churches and as such were a useful mode of indoctrination. Read the "Homily against Disobedience and Wilful Rebellion" at <http://www.library.utoronto.ca/utel/ret/homilies/bk2hom21.html>
7. For studies of the representation of the queen in her portraits see Daniel Fischlin on the *Rainbow Portrait* of Queen Elizabeth I.
8. Read about who could wear what at <http://www.elizabethan.org/sumptuary/index.html>
9. Readings of kingship, social and religious order in Shakespeare's plays, as also those of other Renaissance dramatists such as Marlowe and Middleton, can be found in Dollimore's *Radical Tragedy*.

Two

Gender, Family and Society

What beast was't, then,
That made you break this enterprise to me?
When you durst do it, then you were a man;
And to be more than what you were, you would
Be so much more the man. Nor time nor place
Did then adhere, and yet you would make both.
They have made themselves, and that their fitness now
Does unmake you. *I have given suck, and know*
How tender 'tis to love the babe that milks me.
I would, while it was smiling in my face,
Have plucked my nipple from his boneless gums,
And dashed the brains out, had I so sworn
As you Have done to this. (*Macbeth* I.vii.47–59; emphasis added)

Lady Macbeth's (in)famous speech to Macbeth when he refuses to go ahead with their plan of murdering Duncan, the king, calls attention to questions of gendered identity. Even as she questions his masculinity she appears to reject the standards and stereotypes of femininity which define her as a woman. And these ideas regarding masculinity and femininity are visible in much of Shakespeare's work,[1] causing the thoughtful reader to reflect upon what it meant to be a man or woman in Shakespeare's time. This chapter builds upon the basic premise that gender roles and gender identities are constructed and these constructions are then disseminated, validated, contested and subverted by material practices. Masculinity is as much a product of social construction as femininity is and therefore we shall, in the first section, look at the ways in which gender identities and roles are structured and framed by the discourses of law, religion, physiology, medicine, etc. The second section will then examine and demonstrate how these constructions manifest, shaping relationships and roles within the family sphere and in society at large.

Constructions of Gender

When Shakespeare put the words "Frailty, thy name is woman" into Hamlet's mouth in I.ii.146 of the play he was saying something that was accepted as the norm in his time and in his world: women were frail, not just in terms of their morals (as Hamlet says here) but frail vis-à-vis their physical, emotional and intellectual attributes![2] Women in Early Modern England were perceived as inferior to men, and this perception was facilitated by the discourses of religion, biology and law. On the other hand, these very discourses worked to further endorse and validate Hamlet's contention regarding man (and it is not the inclusive noun here but very specifically the masculine):

> What a piece of work is a man! How noble in reason,
> how infinite in faculty, in form and moving how
> express and admirable, in action how like an angel,
> in apprehension how like a god! the beauty of the
> world, the paragon of animals! (II.ii.293–97)

Aristotle's writings—looked up to, and in wide circulation, during the Early Modern period—offered one of the foundation stones upon which the gendering of men and women was based. "The fact is, the nature of man is the most rounded off and complete, and consequently in man the qualities or capacities above referred to are found in their perfection," wrote Aristotle in *Historia Animalium*; and he went on to show the emotional differences between the two genders. These were views that were specifically about men and women but were seen as further authenticated by a study of the animal world as well, based upon the observation of various animal species. The deficiencies of the woman were wide-ranging: she was

> more compassionate than man, more easily moved to tears, at the same time is more jealous, more querulous, more apt to scold and to strike. She is, furthermore, more prone to despondency and less hopeful than the man, more void of shame or self-respect, more false of speech, more deceptive, and of more retentive memory. She is also more wakeful, more shrinking, more difficult to rouse to action, and requires a smaller quantity of nutriment.
>
> As was previously stated, the male is more courageous than the female, and more sympathetic in the way of standing by to help. (Aristotle)

These virtues on the man's part and vices on the woman's were further seen as proved by observing similar patterns of behaviour in several animal species.

If women's characters were seen as imperfect in comparison to that of men, their bodies were also seen as lesser than that of men. While Aristotle spoke of women as "deformed" or "mutilated" men, the theories of humours and elements, which enjoyed widespread credence during this period, further disempowered women. From Hippocrates onwards the ancient world had believed in the theory that in the human body four body fluids occurred and their balance determined the nature and character of the individual. These fluids were choler, phlegm, and black and yellow bile; and each was in turn associated with a personality trait. A perfect balance of all four would mean that the individual in question was perfectly balanced and healthy. When the theory of humours was juxtaposed with that of the four elements (fire, air, water and earth) it gave rise to an understanding of gender which was widely accepted during this period. Thus fire and air were associated with masculinity, while earth and water were seen as typically feminine. Another of the theories which explained gendered roles and traits was that the woman was controlled by the moon whereas the man was controlled by the sun. In *Antony and Cleopatra* when Cleopatra is about to commit suicide she eschews her femininity by first repudiating the moon's control over her:

> My resolution's placed, and I have nothing
> Of woman in me: now from head to foot
> I am marble-constant; now the fleeting moon
> No planet is of mine. (V.ii.234–37)

And as she proceeds to array herself for her death she claims: I am fire and air; my other elements / I give to baser life (V.ii.280–81). Put together these theories gave a (so-called) scientific explanation for the inferiority of women in terms of science and physiology.

If physiology and science helped in engendering a positive set of traits for the male while consequently positing the female as lesser and wanting in nobility, this discourse was further validated and endorsed by religion which performed a similar function, whether in the older Catholic version, the Anglican or the Puritan guise. Building upon select passages from the Bible, religious commentary made it clear that women were lower than men in the Godly scheme of life and as such were inferior to, and were to be submissive to, men. This was evidenced on the basis of passages such as the Book of Genesis, Chapter 2, wherein the creation of Adam and Eve is narrated, wherein Adam is created first and Eve is later formed from his rib by God, for the express purpose of being a "helper suitable for him". The creation of Eve taking place after the creation of Adam and expressly to be a helper for him was thought to be evidence of Eve's distance from God in comparison to Adam. Further, the story of the fall from the Garden of Eden and the role of the woman in that "Fall" was seen as indicative of the frailty of woman, easily led astray by the wiles of Satan and also capable of causing man's downfall. These early narratives were then buttressed by select portions from the Pauline epistles wherein women were asked to be subject to their husbands (Ephesians 5: 22–23), were asked to cover their heads while praying (I Corinthians 11: 4–16), were asked not to have authority over men and to remain silent (I Timothy 2: 11–15). These passages built upon the two primary narratives from the Creation story for the necessity of women's silence and meekness. Used repeatedly by Bible commentators, writers of advice manuals, social commentators and others, these Biblical precepts, actually used in very specific contexts in the Bible, were taken as God's pronouncements on the subject of women's roles within the family, the Church and society at large.

These passages ordained that women were to be largely silent and docile, that they were to have no public roles in the Church and its doings, that they were to learn in submission to their husbands and that they were to demonstrate obedience and compliance to masculine authority in all the spheres of their life. Added to the theories of the humours and elements, which were seen as formative of women's bodies, these worked together to create an ideology which situated women as the weaker frailer gender, one which was easily led astray, which was prone to physical and mental frailty. Thus when Hamlet says, "Frailty, thy name is woman", he was voicing an opinion that was widely held in the Early Modern period, seen also in "An Homily of the State of Matrimony" where it was said, ". . . the woman is the more frail part". Juxtaposed against this was the ideology that posited man as next to the angels in the hierarchical models that circulated in the period. He was seen as possessing faculties and characteristics that were in "the image of God" and as such was superior to the animals and to women who were created second.[3]

Further augmenting this ideological bias were circumstances that restricted the activities and movements of women: the distribution of labour in evolving societies meant that women occupied home spaces while men went out; the lack of contraception meant that women spent a considerable period of their fertile years pregnant and caring for small children within the spaces of the home. These were also interpreted as consequences of the frailty of women, as painful childbirth and labour was indicated in the Bible as a consequence of woman's culpability for the Fall. Additional ammunition in this ideological war against women was provided by societal structures and edifices which disempowered them further. Thus women could not own property legally; they were not permitted to own and run businesses and they were denied formal education (though some of them were schooled privately).

In contrast to this was the ideological bias which gave men a far superior status in terms of both physiology and religion but also empowered them through the law and education. The hierarchical order of Shakespeare's time set up the father as the head of the family, comparable to the ruler of the realm, a comparison made explicit in the writing and speeches of King James I:

> In the Scriptures kings are called the gods, and so their power after a certain relation compared to the divine power. Kings are also compared to fathers of families; for a king is truly *parens patriae*, the politic father of his people. And lastly, kings are compared to the head of this microcosm of the body of man. (James I)

The father in the Early Modern period enjoyed considerable power vis-à-vis his wife and children. As Theseus says to Hermia in *A Midsummer Night's Dream* about her father Egeus,

> To you your father should be as a god,
> One that composed your beauties, yea, and one
> To whom you are but as a form in wax,
> By him imprinted, and within his power
> To leave the figure or disfigure it. (I.i.47–51)

This passage reinforces the concept of the father as all-powerful and demonstrates the weight attached to his position, especially with regard to daughters. Indeed the father's power is seen in the passage wherein Egeus asks that Hermia be killed if she refuses to accept his choice of a bridegroom for her, and claims that this is provided for "according to our law"(I.i.44). The authority of the father which we see in this instance is also made clear via Lear's treatment of Cordelia's suitors in I.i of *King Lear*; and in plays as diverse as *The Taming of the Shrew*, *Romeo and Juliet* and *Henry V*, in each of which the decision for a daughter's marriage and the choice of bridegroom is based upon the father's will, even when in opposition to the daughter's.

However, when thinking of gender roles during this period it is necessary to understand that the benefits of patriarchy were not available to all men through their entire lifetimes.[4] As children and youth, males were held to be in the process of arriving at manhood and this was not an automatic accomplishment: they had to "grow up" into manhood and then there was the possibility that they would command their households. Thus when Romeo in *Romeo and Juliet*, or young Prince Hal in the two parts of *Henry IV*, leads a riotous life, pursuing pleasurable activities and neglecting their responsibilities, they are yet to arrive at manhood.

While occupations and careers were necessities, men were accounted as such not on the basis of the work they performed but in terms of their honour and reputation. This honour was vested in their ability to keep their word, to be honest and scrupulous in all their dealings, to control their families and to provide for them. While women's honour was nearly always linked to their sexual morality, men's honour covered a range of dealings, in the personal, professional, social and economic realms. Excess was held to be dishonourable and hence detracted from patriarchal masculinity. We see this at work in the two parts of *Henry IV* wherein the youthful excesses of Prince Hal and his boon comrades incur the displeasure of his father. And its counter is seen in *Henry V* (I.i) when the Archbishop of Canterbury and the Bishop of Ely give their account of Prince Hal's abrupt metamorphosis into King Henry, at the death of his father. It is the transformation of "wildness" (27) and "Hydra-headed willfulness" (36) into a "king full of grace and fair regard" (23) that shows us the attainment of perfect masculinity by King Henry V.

Manhood was said, in the conduct books and other literature of the time, to be accompanied by a set of virtues that included "discretion, reason, moderation, self-sufficiency, strength, self-control and honest respectability" (Shepard 9). However, it was also acknowledged that this was rarely achieved in totality, or with any consistency. Indeed the anxieties about manhood that are seen across Shakespeare's dramas (whether early or late, in the tragedies or comedies), play upon this normative ideal that was set up, but that so few measured up to. Thus whether it is Iago questioning Othello's manhood in, "O grace, O heaven forgive me! / Are you a man? have you a soul or sense?" (III.iii.378–79), or Leontes deriding Antigonus on his inability to control his wife, Paulina, in *Winter's Tale*:

> LEONTES. How!
> Away with that audacious lady! Antigonus,
> I charged thee that she should not come about me:
> I knew she would.
> ANTIGONUS. I told her so, my lord,
> On your displeasure's peril and on mine,
> She should not visit you.
> LEONTES. What, canst not rule her? (II.iii.41–46)

they are merely two examples of a host of characters across the plays who are endorsing certain views regarding manhood even as they also mock it, evidence its slippery nature and constantly hold up the ideal to the real. Patriarchal gendered prerogatives were available only to those who, ideally, were of a certain age (past their youth and into the prime of their life), married and belonged to the landed classes, or were substantially well-off tradesmen. In Shakespeare's work these are usually fathers of grown-up daughters, ruling their households, their wives and daughters, brooking no defiance and unable to comprehend it when their authority is flouted. Thus even as Shakespeare shows us the functioning of patriarchy within the family he also attests to its unstable nature, in several of the plays in which he shows us fathers and daughters. It is also important to note that even as daughters come into conflict with their fathers (over their choice of a lover/husband, usually: it is only Cordelia in *King Lear* who challenges his patriarchal authority over an issue not related to the choice of a life partner) their mothers are customarily either missing, silent or supportive of their husbands rather than their daughters. Authority within the family was given to the man, the head of the household, who commanded all and, secondarily, to his wife who commanded the children and the servants. This chain of command is seen particularly in a play such as *Romeo and Juliet*, where Juliet's mother washes her hands off her daughter's concerns even as Juliet pleads against the marriage that has been arranged for her by her father: "Talk not to me, for I'll not speak a word: / Do as thou wilt, for I have done with thee" (III.v.202–03).

Towards the closing stages of life, as old age arrived, men found themselves floundering once again, with patriarchal powers passing to the next generation and their hitherto unquestioned masculinity open to debate. King Lear discovers this when he is told by Regan that he should return to Goneril:

> O, sir, you are old;
> Nature in you stands on the very verge
> Of her confine. You should be ruled and led
> By some discretion, that discerns your state
> Better than you yourself. (II.iv.139–43)

Old age, accompanied by physical weakness, and the failing of one's mental powers, was said to make men child-like or womanly. Thus in *King Lear*, Shakespeare's most sustained examination of old age, Lear asserts that he is ashamed that his daughter has the power to "shake (his) manhood thus" (I.iv.274) and pleads, "And let not women's weapons, water-drops, / Stain my man's cheeks!" (II.iv.272–73). But it is Goneril's comment on King Lear's characteristic imperfections that is particularly apt in this context:

> The best and soundest of his time hath been but
> rash; then must we look to receive from his age,
> not alone the imperfections of long-engraffed
> condition, but therewithal the unruly waywardness
> that infirm and choleric years bring with them. (I.i.293–97)

Goneril indicates Lear's habituated rashness and imprudence (which itself would be seen as not measuring up to the ideals of manliness) and then adds to them those which accompany "the infirm and choleric years" of old age. Lear's patriarchal prerogatives are seen as unsuited to someone who has consistently proved himself to be lacking in all the virtues associated with masculinity.

Thus when we consider Shakespeare's era in terms of gender and gendered roles, what we see is that even as the "rule of the father" was prevalent in society that did not necessarily mean that all men were seen as perfect in their masculinity. While women were generally accepted as "lesser than" men, they learnt to negotiate the tricky social terrain, finding ways and means that empowered them, howsoever marginally and minimally.

Gender in the Everyday

The construction of gendered identity that we have observed in the previous section played out in the material realm, in everyday life and reality for the men and women of Shakespeare's time.

This section will examine gender and family life initially and then move on to a brief account of the ways in which gender influenced and constrained quotidian social life.

Gender and/in the Family

As mentioned above, gendered notions of identity ensured that the family was, in large measure, a patriarchal construct, wherein the father ruled all the others. In addition, women, having been rendered weaker than men and more unstable by the working of science, religion and classical learning, were mostly seen in ways that disadvantaged them, creating stereotypes that were born out of, and fed into, these discourses. Within the family these ways of imagining women affected marital relationships, the education and the marriage of daughters, and also the lives of women after the death of their spouses. Patriarchy also worked in tandem with the concept of male primogeniture to the advancement of the first born son, while younger sons were often left to fend for themselves.[5]

Marriage during this period was not based upon personal inclination as much as it was upon other considerations. This was particularly so among the upper classes and the landed gentry and aristocracy when considerations other than love and liking determined marriage partners. These included the possibility of increasing one's wealth and property via the bride's dowry, but also political alliances (as seen in *Henry V* where Henry desires to marry Katherine of France, a decision which is not based solely upon love and desire, unless it is the love of increasing his kingdom's bounds) and the prospect of future benefits. Also it was not yet the prerogative of the young to choose their own partners: fathers played a significant role in determining the marriage of their children and this was so even for young men, though, of course, more so for young women. Thus in play after play we see Shakespearean fathers trying to determine who their daughters will wed. And in the case of men we only need to listen to Laertes advising Ophelia to steer clear of Hamlet:

Perhaps he loves you now,
And now no soil nor cautel doth besmirch
The virtue of his will; but you must fear,
His greatness weighed, *his will is not his own,*
For he himself is subject to his birth.
He may not, as unvalued persons do,
Carve for himself, for on his choice depends
The sanity and health of the whole state;
And therefore must his choice be circumscribed
Unto the voice and yielding of that body
Whereof he is the head. (*Hamlet* I.iii.14–24; emphasis added)

If considerations of the kingdom were thought to determine Hamlet's choice of a bride, Prospero in *The Tempest* plots a marriage between his only daughter and Ferdinand, prince of Naples, in the hope that this would win him back his kingdom. While daughters might be cosseted and pampered by their fathers, the first signs of rebellion cause them to be reminded of their station in life: thus Lear in *King Lear* describes Cordelia in ways that mark her out as the ideal daughter and begins by claiming that the suitors for Cordelia will receive their answer, depending upon her choice, only to cast her off, labelling her a "little seeming substance" (I.i.199) when she refuses to speak as he desires. Further he strips her of her dower and asks her suitors if they will take her "dower'd with our curse" (I.i.205). Juliet's father initially asks Paris to woo her as his permission for their marriage depends upon Juliet's consent: "And, she agreed, within her scope of choice / Lies my consent and fair according voice" (I.ii.16–17). However, once she speaks against the choice of her father she is coerced into the marriage, even as Egeus in *A Midsummer Night's Dream* attempts to force Hermia. The control of fathers (and, to a lesser extent, brothers) over a young girl has, of course, been most famously depicted in *Hamlet*, where not only is Ophelia asked to distance herself from Hamlet but also used to spy upon him, her will overpowered by that of her father. The family structure that was operative in Shakespeare's time, especially in aristocratic circles, involved daughters who were often used to advance the position of their families at court.[6] Thus their will was of little or no concern, in the choice of marriage partners. The choice rested with the fathers and with the prospective bridegroom and his family but rarely with the girl. An extreme example of this is seen in *The Merchant of Venice* where Portia cannot choose her own husband, even after her father's demise, but is constrained by her father's will (pun intended) which declares that whosoever picks the correct casket will be her husband. The obverse of this, and the class complications inherent in situations such as this, are seen when Maria, Olivia's maid in *Twelfth Night*, can accept a proposal made to her by Sir Toby Belch without checking with family members. We could, of course, argue that in doing so there was the very real possibility of social advancement and hence her acceptance of the proposal is a shrewd move on her part. However, the fact that Sir Toby can do so also speaks of the easier lives that the lower classes of the nobility led as opposed to the monarchy and the higher aristocracy.

An associated concern was that of dowry for the bride, a practice that was normal during this period and often determined the girl's standing in the marriage market. Marriage was as much a monetary transaction as an emotional and social one. While young men and women of the middle and lower classes were expected to wait until such time as they could afford to get married and have their own household, in the upper classes the girl's dowry often determined how many suitors she had. We see this in *King Lear* where the Duke of Burgundy, "great rival" to the King of France for Cordelia's hand (I.i.44), steps back the instant he is told that she is "dowered" with her father's "curse"; while its obverse can be seen in *The Taming of the Shrew* where

Petruchio is willing to marry Kate once he knows the dowry she will bring to the marriage.

While daughters had little or no choice in the matter of choosing their husbands, another aspect of the contemporary discourse led to women being stereotyped as lascivious and sexually intemperate. "Women as easily tempted and prone to fall" was a line of thought that derived directly from the Bible and following from that, their tendency to fall was translated into a sexuality that needed to be restrained for the good of society, the family and the marriage. Thus women's monstrous, bestial appetites were almost a given; and in plays from *Titus Andronicus* through *Hamlet* to *Cymbeline*, Shakespeare builds upon this stereotype of woman as lustful. Indeed, even in plays that do not necessarily feature a woman who appears lustful, Shakespeare put in words to the effect that there can be no certainty about the chastity of women who are possessed of a "riotous appetite" (*King Lear* IV.vi.120). Thus lines such as "strange fowl light upon neighbouring ponds" (*Cymbeline* I.iv.78) and "more water glideth by the mill / Than wots the miller of" (*Titus Andronicus* II.i.85–86) reflect popular opinions of the time regarding women; but Shakespeare complicates these views by putting them into the mouths of characters who are either outright villainous or at best, unreliable.

Marriage was seen as essential during this period "for as much as matrimony serveth as well to avoid sin and offense as to increase the kingdom of God" as it was stated in the "Homily on the State of Matrimony". And it was clear as to who was to obey and who was to control and command between husband and wife. Indeed, homilies and sermons, as also marriage manuals, all reiterated the necessity of order within marriage, an order which required the man to govern the family and household and for the wife "to be an help" (Gouge). But to think of marriage as a particularly oppressive institution during this period is to ignore the other advice that often went along with these injunctions to men and women to command and obey, respectively. The writers of these handbooks and manuals, even as they set out the roles of each party, also exhorted the husband and wife to avoid "perverse dispositions", to "be joint-governors with their husbands," as Gouge does here.

Due to the rise of Protestantism and the fact that many of those writing marriage manuals were Puritans and Protestants, there was a gradual movement towards the making of what was called the "companionate marriage" by Lawrence Stone (325). As opposed to the early system wherein spouses were chosen by the families and there was little personal regard or affection within a marriage, from the seventeenth century there began a gradual change: one characterised by personal affection between the partners and a more equal relationship, not as enmeshed as previously in questions of authority and obedience. While these were models that were prevalent in Shakespeare's time, we see versions of these as well as those that were seen as contemptible and/or subversive of the norm in his plays. Marriages such as that of Leontes and Hermione (*The Winter's Tale*) and the Capulets in *Romeo and Juliet* were traditional in upholding the authority of the husband/father and elevating him as the undisputed head of the family, even when he was making grave errors, which sometimes led to tragedy. In stark contrast to these were marriages such as that of Goneril and Albany in *King Lear* where the wife is seen as the stronger character and is, of course, eventually given her just punishments for usurping the position of the male. Marriages where a husband is unable to control his wife and becomes the butt of mockery include that of Paulina and Antigonus in *The Winter's Tale* where the king himself asks Antigonus, "What, canst not rule her?" (II.iii.46).

While the marriages of the Macbeths and Regan and Cornwall in *Macbeth* and *King Lear* might be seen as evil in their consequences, they are however exemplars of the companionate marriage: the spouses being well-matched, conversant with each other's characters and willing to help the partner to further his or her desires. If these are companionate marriages that bring out the worst in the spouses, the many marriages in the mature comedies give us the obverse: characters such as Orlando and Rosalind in *As You Like It*, Beatrice and Benedick in *Much Ado about Nothing* and Viola and Orsino in *Twelfth Night*[7] evidence the shift in modes of marriage: they grow into love together, even as they also develop a knowledge and understanding of the other which then leads to appreciation and deep-seated affection. If we are to see the beginnings of the companionate marriage in Shakespeare's plays, these would be the examples we need to study.

While men's familial roles are as fathers and husbands (as already seen above), they also play the role of sons and brothers. As fathers and husbands they are usually posited for us in fairly authoritarian roles, domineering and even willfully cruel, on occasion. There is considerable controversy among historians as to how family members interacted with each other and the affective range that could be seen in those relationships, in this period. Thus one viewpoint held to be true for familial relationships is that they were not built upon intense affections, that parents and children, as also spouses and siblings, were not emotionally attached to each other with the force that we now see as "normal". However, this has been disputed by other historians who have claimed that affections tended to be structured around communities and group identities rather than family identity, which was also however, fairly strong and thus affectionate and loving relationships were the norm.[8] What much of the historical work has drawn attention to is that generalisations are not possible as these were class-based distinctions; and this is something that we would do well to keep in mind during any discussion of Shakespearean society and family structure.

While the marital is one relationship that we have studied in some depth as also fathers and daughters, it is necessary to consider the father-son relationship as also the bonds between siblings. While the concept of male primogeniture privileged the first-born son in a family, it also worked to the disadvantage of the other sons. This often led to acrimonious relationships, especially between male siblings, as daughters and sisters were usually provided for by the dowries that were given to them at the time of their marriage (see above). The system of male primogeniture ensured that the first-born son of a family inherited the family property. The consequences of this were often deleterious on family life and relationships: the first-born son had no options other than to wait for his father to die so that he could come into his inheritance; the younger sons had nothing other than what they had been given during the father's lifetime in the way of education or a living. And if the father's death empowered the eldest son, it could pave the way for hardships for the younger sons as the eldest son then had complete power over the estate and property. This is seen in *As You Like It* where Oliver, the elder son, ill-treats Orlando, the youngest, even as he continues to care for their middle brother.

> My brother Jaques he keeps at school, and
> report speaks goldenly of his profit: for my part,
> he keeps me rustically at home, or, to speak more
> properly, stays me here at home unkept; (I.i.4–7)

Orlando acknowledges that "the courtesy of nations" allows the elder to be the "better" (I.i.39–40) of the siblings but that does not necessarily benefit the younger ones, as Orlando discovers. Younger sons, especially of the landed gentry and nobility, were often forced to seek their fortunes in a world where there were few avenues for improving their prospects. Thus Edmund in *King Lear*, both younger and illegitimate, decides to improve his fortunes by doing his elder brother out of *his*. While elder brothers are seen to have unalienable rights over property, with the law as well as custom favouring them, we also see the disputes that surround this custom and law in plays such as those mentioned above, as also in the English history plays where Shakespeare speaks about the rightful heir to the throne who might be the eldest son of an eldest son but is still supplanted by the son of a younger son (*Richard II*).

Schooling within the family is one more area of interest and one which, while not centre-stage in Shakespeare's work, is still glanced at in passing in some of his plays. While Hamlet was, most famously, away at school in Wittenberg, we also see Laertes who also was sent away to school, in *As You Like It* we see the middle brother Jaques away at school, as are sundry other characters. On the other hand, the education of the daughters of the house is rarely mentioned. What we have are occasional lines such as that spoken by Desdemona to her father in the Council Chamber in Venice, "To you I am bound for life and education" (*Othello* I.iii.182), or Prospero's statement about himself and Miranda on the island:

> and here
> Have I thy schoolmaster made thee more profit
> Than other princes can, that have more time
> For vainer hours and tutors not so careful. (*The Tempest* I.ii.172–75)

During Shakespeare's time, while boys received some schooling, most girls were given a minimal education, if at all, and this at home, via private tutors. Again based on class, what we can say is that in aristocratic families boys and men were given a comprehensive education while girls might be tutored privately at home. (Queen Elizabeth was highly educated, knowing many languages, able to converse in Latin, etc., but she was the exception, not the norm.) And among non-aristocratic families, boys would still receive some education whether at the petty schools or the grammar schools (to which they graduated from the petty schools). This we see in one of Shakespeare's most famous set of lines, in *As You Like It* when Jaques speaks of the ages of man and references

> the whining school-boy with his satchel
> And shining morning face, creeping like snail
> Unwillingly to school. (II.vii.144–46)

And as seen, young men, if they showed aptitude and if their families could afford it, could then progress to a university education.

Gendered Roles in Society

The construction of men as superior to women in the physical, mental and moral realms made it possible for men to have a wider range of options and possibilities with regard to occupations and pursuits. While the nobility was always already endowed with a wider range of possibilities with regard to what they could do, Shakespeare's age was also an age of social mobility, a period when it was possible to advance in society, to leave behind the limited social spheres which had constrained men in feudal times and improve their social and economic standing. This is best illustrated by Shakespeare's own life and career trajectory where he begins as the son of a prosperous glove-maker who also held public office in their hometown of Stratford. However, the family suffered some financial misfortunes and Shakespeare's father's attempts to improve his situation failed, but finally through Shakespeare's career and economic success, they moved up the social strata: in October 1596 Shakespeare's father, John Shakespeare, was granted a coat of arms, making him part of the gentry and the very next year, William Shakespeare invested in property and buildings in Stratford.

During this period, men from the upper echelons enjoyed the traditional options of being courtiers, men of letters, soldiers and politicians, but in addition the many discoveries and travels to new lands made it possible for sea voyaging to be added to their list of pursuits. Travel, discovery and settlement opened up new possibilities for those who had the capital to finance new ventures and travel. And while these required capital, it was also possible to sign up for voyages and improve one's fortunes if one was willing to work hard and venture out of the comfort of known spaces and lifestyles.[9] The possibilities were more numerous, in this era, for younger sons and for men of the middle classes and even traditional avenues of employment and improvement such as the court and the Church provided more opportunities as the feudal system of the Middle Ages gradually eroded. Shakespeare is, of course, one of the best known examples but others included Thomas Cromwell, chief minister to Henry VIII, Inigo Jones, son of a cloth worker who became England's first notable architect and even Ben Jonson, stepson of a bricklayer who went on to become the poet laureate of England. The theatre was one more of those avenues which in this age made it possible for men to transcend the circumstances of their birth and fortune, as evidenced by these examples. But the theatre also dramatised this possibility by showcasing men who tried to improve their lot in the world, often to end in failure. Among the best known examples are Bosola and Antonio from *The Duchess of Malfi* but Shakespeare's own plays included characters such as Bushy and Bagot in *Richard II*, who were trying to improve their status via their friendship with the king, and Rosencrantz and Guildenstern in *Hamlet*. However, these are still examples of courtiers who hope to win favour from the rulers, a traditional mode of prospering. More contemporary is the depiction of sailors who hope to make their fortunes by bringing back strange and exotic beings as depicted in Shakespeare's *Tempest* where Stephano and Trinculo, on first seeing Caliban, think of putting him on display back in England as, "there would this monster make a man.; Any strange beast there makes a man:"

(II.ii.28–29). Another less felicitous example of someone who seeks social mobility but is denied it is Iago in *Othello* who, when deprived of promotion vows vengeance, "I follow him to serve my turn upon him", and eventually destroys Othello (I.i.42). The disaffected and the unhappy, often called the "malcontent" during this period, was a stock character in the drama of this period as his attempts to climb the social ladder were thwarted and he was mocked by those above him.

While social mobility for men was possible via many avenues, at least in theory, for women the roles that society provided were still limited to those associated with the family. Given that women could not inherit property, could not own businesses and that there were few professions for them to adopt, the possibilities were limited to either familial roles, helping out in family businesses or working as domestic or farm labourers. In addition, on a daily basis they battled the biases which were inbuilt into the patriarchal model of society within which they lived. While men had, as per Shakespeare in *As You Like It*, seven ages through which they lived, most women had just three: daughter, wife and mother. And in each case these ages were lived in the control, and under the dominance of a man: father, husband and sometimes, the grownup son, in case of the demise of the husband. While their lives were thus restricted and limited by the structures within which they lived, many women found themselves empowered via early widowhood, especially if there were no children or if the sons were young. But widowed women battled against other restrictions: stereotyped as lustful and unable to live without male support, widows were seen as susceptible to the blandishments and advances of men on the make. Indeed, even as women had limited roles within which they functioned, the stereotypes that circulated in Shakespeare's time about them dominated society's perception of women. Thus women could be either virginal and pure, quiet, meek and submissive as the Virgin Mary, mother of

Jesus (Miranda[10] in *Tempest*) or they could be shrews, scolds and nags, uncontrollable, resistant to their men folk (Paulina in *The Winter's Tale*), or lustful and uncontrolled in their appetite (Gertrude in *Hamlet* or the two elder sisters in *King Lear*), etc. Seen in limited ways, these perceptions then shaped and enclosed women's roles and lives. This is not to say that there were no strong positive women figures during this period: Queen Elizabeth was the best example of such a woman. But then these strong individualistic women were seen as possessing the male virtues of assertiveness, courage and self-respect, and this aligned them with masculine virtue even as it negated the traditional shortcomings of the feminine. The "virago", a term used positively (and not just with the now-well-known negative connotation) during this period, was as important a stereotype as the "virgo", the Virgin: the woman who contained within herself all the positive attributes of Mary, caring and taking care of her family, particularly the men folk. Interestingly, in *King Lear,* Cordelia is seen to possess the positive attributes of both virgo and virago, even as Goneril and Regan are seen as the negative stereotypical virago figures.[11]

Stereotypes, roles, constructions of gender which privileged one in opposition to the other: while all these are true of Shakespeare's time as of any other, what should be kept in mind is that these are broad brush strokes that do not give us all the truth. Individual lives and particular families deployed these constructions and roles in particular ways. Thus what is offered here are broad generalisations which were true in large part of Shakespeare's society; but they were not the whole, nor even the only truth.

Works Cited

"An Homily of the State of Matrimony." *Renaissance Electronic Texts 1.2*. Ian Lancashire. University of Toronto. 1994, 1997. Web. 26 February 2014.

Aristotle. *Historia Animalium* or *The History of Animals*. Trans. D'Arcy Wentworth Thompson. *Internet Classics Archive*. Daniel C. Stevenson. n.d. Web. 26 February 2014.

Cox, Catherine S. "'An Excellent Thing in Woman': Virgo and Viragos in *King Lear*." *Modern Philology* 96.2 (1998): 143–57. Print.

Gouge, William. *Domestical Duties: Part I*. 1622. Chapel Library. Mount Zion Bible Church, 2014. Web. 28 February 2014.

James I. "Speeches to Parliament (1609)." *Readings in European History*, 2 vols. Ed. James Harvey Robinson. Boston: Ginn & Company, 1906, 2: 219–20. *The History Guide*. Steven Kreis, 2004. Web. 26 February 2014.

McRae, Andrew. *Renaissance Drama*. New York: Arnold, 2003. Print.

Shepard, Alexandra. *Meanings of Manhood in Early Modern England*. New York: Oxford UP, 2003. Print.

Stone, Lawrence. *The Family, Sex and Marriage in England 1500-1800*. New York: Harper and Row, 1977. Print.

Notes

1. It is essential to remember that Shakespeare's plays do not only reflect contemporary, popular attitudes regarding gender in his time. His plays show a destabilising of accepted, stereotypical gender roles, even as they appear to endorse it, an interrogation of accepted, normative gender roles and attributes. While we cannot claim with certainty that Shakespeare was aware of the debates regarding gendered roles that were in circulation at the time, we can say that his work shows an awareness of how gender played out in reality as opposed to the fixity that writers and commentators on gender prescribed.
2. While Gertrude is castigated as "frail", Cleopatra can well be considered the epitome of "frailty": fickle-minded, tempestuous,

shifting from mood to mood; and yet, Shakespeare transforms this figure of frailty, making her into a woman of utmost charm, passion, courage and strength, a figure who stands as the composite of women's frailties as well as strengths.

3. This is, of course, to elide the creation story in Genesis 1:27 wherein it is stated that "in the image of God he created them, male and female he created them": an earlier creation story which is usually overlooked for the preferable one of Genesis 2.
4. The following discussion draws upon the work of Alexandra Shepard.
5. It must, however, be kept in mind that while this discussion is broadly true of all classes, class distinctions did give rise to variations in family life.
6. A historical example of this would be Lady Jane Grey, daughter of the Duke of Suffolk, married to the son of the Duke of Northumberland and elevated to the throne on the death of Edward VI. However, her reign lasted a mere nine days and eventually she was executed.
7. This last pair is however complicated by Orsino's affection for Viola when she is dressed as his page, Cesario. It can be said that Viola knows and understands the Duke, but the degree of affection, understanding and knowledge that he brings to the relationship is, however, uncertain.
8. For a brief overview of familial relationships and the two contradictory viewpoints, see the discussion in McRae's *Renaissance Drama* 45–46.
9. See chapter 3 for a brief overview of this aspect.
10. Alongside Miranda, it is possible to place Ophelia and even Desdemona: women who are seen as feminine, submitting to the patriarchal system, to the laws of the father and husband, who even when they do attempt to assert agency as Desdemona does, eventually find the inculcated ideology to be stronger, all-consuming.
11. See Cox's essay on the Virgo and the Virago for a fascinating discussion of women's roles and character attributes.

THREE

EXPANDING WORLDS AND NEW PEOPLES

"To seek new worlds for gold, for praise, for glory," said Sir Walter Raleigh in the long poem "The Ocean, to Cynthia" (written between 1590 and 1603), and the phrase neatly encapsulates the motivating factors for those who set out on voyages of exploration and discovery during the Early Modern period. Christopher Columbus's travels in 1492 and the stories he brought back had fuelled interest and impatience in most European countries, a desire to be a part of this exploratory narrative, of discovering new places, new peoples, finding new material resources, etc. This emphasis on the "new" led gradually to the New World and its peopling, then eventually its colonisation and pillage.

We see this awareness of new knowledge regarding newly discovered peoples and spaces in the drama and poetry of the times with poets such as Shakespeare and John Donne speaking of the Americas, the Indies, their material resources and the "savages" who inhabited these spaces. Thus in Shakespeare's *Othello* we have Othello telling Desdemona tales

> of the Cannibals that each other eat,
> The Anthropophagi, and men whose heads
> Do grow beneath their shoulders. (I.iii.142–44)

while in *A Midsummer Night's Dream*, Titania speaks of her friend who "in the spiced Indian air" (II.i.124) kept her company upon "Neptune's yellow sands"(II.i.126). She goes on to speak of the "embarked traders on the flood" (II.i.127) and compares her friend as she returns with gifts for Titania to ships returning, "as from a voyage, rich with merchandise" (II.i.134).

This chapter will consider the expansion taking place in the Early Modern period with respect to geographical knowledge and also how it changed the ways in which the English thought about themselves as a result of this expansion. The first section provides a brief historical account of the expansion of geographical and cultural knowledge through the many voyages. Section 2 looks at other forms of the expansion of knowledge. In section 3 I examine the multiplicity of "outsiders" (about whom knowledge had been obtained through travel) that enabled Shakespeare's England to construct its "insiderness", or cultural identity.

Travel

The first Englishmen in the Tudor era to set out on a voyage of exploration were actually Venetians living in England, John Cabot (c.1450–c.1499) and his son Sebastian (c.1474–c.1557) Cabot, who were licensed to travel by Henry VII as early as 1496 and discovered Newfoundland and Nova Scotia. During Elizabeth I's reign, the English sailor was performing feats of navigation and sailing that transformed the English nation into a contender alongside Spain and Portugal, who had till then been the frontrunners in this race to explore unknown lands and new worlds. Francis Drake's (c.1540–96) circumnavigation of the globe in 1579, a few years later Thomas Cavendish's (1560–92) performance of the same feat, the almost mythic voyages of Walter Raleigh (c.1554–1618), Martin Frobisher (c.1535–94) and John Hawkins (1532–95) paved the way for

Englishmen to travel worldwide and these travels in turn made it possible to establish English settlements and trading posts in lands which fifty years ago were unknown, or if known, feared and considered inhospitable.

While geographical awareness expanded during Shakespeare's time, there was also an exponential growth of knowledge and learning: the world was opening up and new developments took place on a regular basis in many spheres. Thus the earlier geocentric understanding of the universe was challenged by the heliocentric theory of Copernicus and Galileo. Anatomical dissections were revealing secrets of the human body and as the Reformation progressed, the inherent value of knowledge itself was magnified as reading the Bible and other religious texts was no longer only a church activity but also a personal duty. Education spread and with the printing press's arrival in England a revolution was underway. In addition, the seafarers were bringing back new narratives of peoples and goods which were then sent out into the English world via Richard Hakluyt's *Principall Navigations of the English Nation* (1589) and Samuel Purchas's *Purchas His Pilgrimage* (1613), as well as other narratives of travel, exploration and discovery, translated from other European languages. Another kind of, and among the earliest, travel narratives was Thomas More's *Utopia* (1516), which imagines a new land into existence, yet also locates it in the New World and makes of its discoverer a person who might have been an actual traveller and discoverer, a companion of Amerigo Vespucci (1454–1512), the Italian explorer. Writing such as More's heralds a whole new tradition of Utopic and Dystopic fiction, which includes in it texts such as Bacon's *New Atlantis* as well.

Travel in this age was facilitated by advances being made in other forms of knowledge, namely astronomy and cartography. The mapping of the heavens helped mariners in plotting sea routes more accurately and the creation of globes and maps demonstrated the existence of land masses and new lands where hitherto none were thought to have existed. During this period the first atlas of the western world was published: the *Theatrum Orbis Terrarum* (1570) by Abraham Ortelius, the first of many made available to the people so that they could see for themselves the New Worlds that were being discovered.[1]

Many of the travels of the time were set-out-upon with an eye to profiting from trade rather than discovering new lands and new peoples. Indeed, finding a sea route to China and the Indies and all their wealth was the prime motivation for all the Europeans. Improvements in ship design (harnessing the wind rather than using manpower was a Renaissance improvement) and instruments of navigation (the compass was improved during the Renaissance and map making became more precise and refined) helped the Europeans in their travels; and by the end of the sixteenth century, sea routes around the world had been laid out. Henry VIII's interest in the navy and navigation provided Elizabeth I a foundation upon which she built a strong navy for her country, encouraged sea-faring and voyaging, and rewarded those who travelled the seas. Among the many who profited from seafaring during this period were Francis Drake, Walter Raleigh, Martin Frobisher and others. As Drake circumnavigated the globe he laid claim to California for his queen. Raleigh financed an expedition by Amadas and Barlowe, which named a corner of America, Virginia, in honour of their queen, and he tried to found a colony on Roanoke Island in 1595. It is also possible to read these sailors and interpret these activities as a mode of furthering social mobility. In a world where gaining substantial quantities of wealth was possible via trading journeys, where these sailing voyages enhanced the prestige of the nation and the monarchy, sailors such as Drake and Hawkins moved higher in the hierarchic society of the period due to their prowess on their seas, their reputations as privateers and soldiers and their ability to enrich the coffers of the ruling monarch. While they were not originally lower-class men, these were men from the middle classes, men who came of farming or merchant stock and made their way to titles, lands and the position of naval commanders to the queen because of their own abilities. Their stories illustrate a crucial aspect of the Early Modern period: with innumerable opportunities opening up it was possible for men to improve their lot in life, if they had some ability, were willing to work hard and were not bothered by too many scruples. These were men who brought back large quantities of precious metals and other goods (spices such as nutmeg, peppercorns, mace, etc.; fabrics such as silk; plant products such as tobacco, potatoes and corn; even mummified flesh which was valued for its so-called medicinal properties). The profits from these were shared with the queen to whom went the best of the precious stones as also large shares of the gold and silver. In addition, sometimes people from the New Worlds and newly discovered lands were brought back as captives to be exhibited in London, none of them surviving for very long in the Old World. Thus Martin Frobisher brought back Inuits or Eskimos from his travels to Baffin Island in his search for the North-West passage,[2] who were usually dead within a month of their arrival in England. Slaving voyages were also not uncommon. The wealth that could be made on these voyages was from trade (in humans and/as commodities) as well as pirating: though the queen was aware that her sailor-courtiers were also buccaneers, slavers and pirates, that did not deter her from offering them her patronage, knighthoods and even (for Drake, Frobisher and Hawkins) positions of responsibility and command in the royal navy during the battle of the Spanish Armada (1588).

The voyages during Elizabeth I's time which were exploratory in nature moved into a different mode during her last years and in James I's reign: now businessmen and nobles travelled to establish colonies or trading posts in what were just twenty years ago, newly discovered lands. Yet from the earliest voyagers' accounts it is possible to discern a dominant theme/motif about the new worlds: eventually these new lands and peoples were to be subdued and governed by the English and their religion replaced by the true Christian faith. Thus Thomas Hariot, when he speaks of the natives of Virginia in his *Brief and True Report of the New Found Land of Virginia* (1590), admires their ingenuity and their friendly nature even as he observes that they can be easily subdued with the military might of the English, and that because they show excellent sense, "In time they will find that our kinds of knowledge and crafts accomplish everything with more speed and perfection than do theirs." George Peckham in his *True Report of the Late Discoveries of . . . New-Found Lands* . . . (1584) on the other hand advocated that the natives were to be subdued initially with

> . . . benefit, commodity, peace, tranquility, and safety. To further this, and to accomplish it in deeds, there must be presented unto them gratis, some kinds of our petty merchandises and trifles: as looking glasses, bells, beads, bracelets, chains, or collars of bugle, crystal, amber, jet, or glass, etc. For such be the things, though to us of small value, yet accounted by them of high price and estimation, and soonest will induce their barbarous natures to a liking and mutual society with us. (Peckham)

The fascination of the natives for trinkets and things "of small value" was repeatedly remarked upon by these travellers and underlined for them the simplicity and naiveté of the native.

The shift from exploration to possible settlement and definitely trade is evidenced by two documents: the charter issued to the East India Company by Elizabeth I and that issued to the Virginia Company by James I. The "East India Company Charter", issued on the last day of the year 1600, clearly states the reasons why her subjects petitioned her to issue them a charter:

> That they, at their own adventures, costs, and charges, as well for the honour of this our realm of England, as for the increase of our navigation, and advancement of trade of merchandize, within our said realms and the dominions of the same, might adventure and set forth one or more voyages, with convenient number of ships and pinnaces, by way of traffic and merchandize to the East Indies, in the countries and parts of Asia and Africa and to as many of the islands, ports and cities, towns and places, thereabouts, as where trade and traffic may by all likelihood be discovered, established or had. . . . ("East India Company Charter")

Similarly, the "Virginia Company Charter" of 1609 clearly states the purpose of the petitioners in asking James I for a charter: it is "at the humble suite and request of sondrie oure lovinge and well disposed subjects intendinge to deduce a colonie and to make habitacion and plantacion of sondrie of oure people in that parte of America comonlie called Virginia. . ." ("Virginia Company Charter"). These two documents, as also others of the period, document an approach that would eventually lead to the British Empire; and while Shakespeare would not have known the precise words of the charters, he would have been familiar with the spirit of such enterprises as these. The multitude of postcolonial readings of *The Tempest* bears witness to these initial moments in Britain's imperial and colonial history and also to Shakespeare's awareness of the great sea voyages of the time, as well as possible outcomes.

Many were travelling during Shakespeare's time, not just those who voyaged on the seas, seeking new routes and opportunities for trade and commercial enterprise. Among these other travellers were those who travelled for leisure on the continent (caricatured by Ben Jonson in masterly fashion in *Volpone, or The Fox* [1605]); Catholics and Protestants, escaping from religious persecution and looking for a refuge where they could practise their faith; those sent on military and trade expeditions funded by the monarchs, etc. While those who travelled upon the continent encountered some difference, those who travelled the sea routes saw peoples, religions and civilisational practices at stark variance with their home countries. Racial difference was further underlined by differences in terms of dress, eating habits and religion. In addition, social structures were also seen as different and other. The startling practices and appearances of the new peoples were written up in travelogue after travelogue during this period,[3] whether of Ralph Fitch writing about India, Hariot writing about Virginia or Jean de Léry writing about Brazil. These added to the knowledge-base about the new races of humanity, but also underscored racial and cultural *differences*. Travel was therefore instrumental in the expansion of geographical and cultural knowledge, as we see below.

The description of India and Indian customs in Fitch's travelogue of 1599 mentions the religious beliefs and customs of the Indians. He briefly mentions a practice that was to continue to resonate with the English till it was abolished in 1829:

> They have a very strange order among them: they worship a cow, and esteem much of the cow's dung to paint the walls of their houses. They will kill nothing, not so much as a louse, for they hold it a sin to kill anything. They eat no flesh, but live by roots, rice, and milk. *And when the husband dies, his wife is burned with him, if she be alive*. (Fitch; emphasis added)

The practice of *suttee* (what the British called 'widow-burning') was viewed with horrified fascination by English travellers in India and detailed descriptions recur in their travelogues of women committing *suttee* whether voluntarily or under duress. But it is not just *suttee* which they regard with fascination and horror: the descriptions of Hindu sages and holy men likewise betray the ethnocentric viewpoint of the Englishman. A similar perspective is obtained in Jean de Léry writing about Brazilian tribes in *Histoire d'un voyage faict en la terre du Brésil* (1578; translated and made available in English in 1625):

> And surely, they did not only horribly howl, but also leaped forth with great violence, and shaked their paps, and foamed at the mouth, nay some of them (not unlike unto those that are troubled with the falling-sickness) fell down dead. So that I think, that the Devil entered into their bodies, and they suddenly became possessed with the Devil. (de Léry)

The insular outlook of the European traveller, whether Englishman or French, is discernible in all the travel writing of the period. Sir Thomas Roe, writing of the court of Jehangir, in the *Journal of the Mission to the Mogul Empire* (1618), compares it unfavourably with that of James I, remarking upon the disorderly nature of the former and deriding the emperor's fondness for blood sports. The reason this insularity is worth noticing is that it shapes the views of those who read these accounts, confirming for them the superiority of their civilisation and culture and eventually making it possible for them to put into motion the colonial enterprise. Indeed, this is visible in the charters of the East India and Virginia companies too as both Elizabeth I and James I exhort the petitioners to steer clear of any territory that is "the lawful and actual possession of any such Christian prince or state" (EIC) and "nowe actuallie possessed by anie Christian prince or people" (VC). Religion as a marker of difference, as much, if not more so, than race is seen in the "Virginia Charter" where James I speaks of the necessity to propagate the "Christian religion to suche people as yet live in darkenesse and miserable ignorance of the true knowledge and worshippe of God and may in tyme bring the infidels and savages living in those parts to humane civilitie and to a settled and quiet govermente." The idea of religion, as marking difference as much as race, is visible in *The Merchant of Venice* where Shylock's persecution is on the basis of his being a Jew, the opposition between Jew and Christian explicitly foregrounded. Texts such as Bacon's *New Atlantis* (1626), creating a new ideal world, featured Jews as an accepted and honoured part of society. This was unusual in a world where Jews were hated, feared and despised, except that the Jews within this text are rewritten as hating neither Christ nor Christians, but integrally appreciative of the virtues of the world they inhabit and the people thereof.

One particular passage in *The Tempest* speaks of Shakespeare's knowledge of the "objects" often brought back from sea-voyages:

> Were I in England now, as once I was, and had but this fish painted, not a holiday-fool there but would give a piece of silver. There would this monster make a man. Any strange beast there makes a man. When they will not give a doit to relieve a lame beggar, they will lay out ten to see a dead Indian. (II.ii.26–31)

It also speaks of the possibility inherent in Shakespeare's time and world where a "monster" or "strange beast", i.e., a member of a different race, could "make a man". Here, Shakespeare was clearly indebted to travel accounts of other races, species and cultures.

New Knowledge

There was a considerable growth of knowledge in all fields and this expansion helped in drawing Shakespeare's time out of Late Medieval mindsets into the Early Modern.

While European explorers discovered new lands and new peoples, scientific knowledge was also expanding, whether of the human body or the heavenly bodies. Advances in medical learning, a more scientific understanding of the universe and also new methods of learning and gaining knowledge were some of the significant changes of the period, aided by developments which included the gradual evolution of new inventions such as the microscope and the telescope. The change in modes of knowledge production is one of the reasons for the period being called the "Early Modern": it heralds the change to a more scientific, inductive mode of reasoning, one wherein experiments were conducted to determine whether certain ideas were tenable or not. Towards the latter years of Shakespeare's life Galileo Galilei had invented the telescope (1609), inventors in the Netherlands and in England too were working on microscopes which then revealed the secrets of nature, the human body and the universe to those who were interested in studying them.

While medical knowledge was changing, the earlier age's reliance on the elemental theory and the theory of humours continued to hold sway over the practice of medicine. The anatomy of the human body began to be studied, not in the pursuit of medicine but in the pursuit of Art. Painters such as Michelangelo (1475–1564), Leonardo da Vinci (1452–1519) and Titian (c.1488–1576), who wanted more exactitude and accuracy in their painting, advanced the course of anatomy to see how the human body was constructed.[4] Key figures such as Andreas Vesalius (1514–64), William Harvey (1578–1657) and Paracelsus (1493–1541) brought about progress in medical knowledge. Vesalius advocated that the human body was best learned about by dissecting actual bodies; Harvey in 1628 published his discovery about the circulation of blood in the human body; and Paracelsus discovered the use of laudanum as a painkiller. Other advances included the use of catgut as ligatures for surgery and the use of quinine learned from the New World. Several of these new methods were accidental discoveries, stumbled upon by physicians and surgeons. And while the new knowledge was gaining ground, much of the practice of medicine was still in the hands of uneducated, superstitious practitioners who relied on common knowledge, herbals, superstitions and popular practices such as bloodletting and cupping.

That Shakespeare was acquainted with several of these ideas is apparent from his plays. The Friar in *Romeo and Juliet* is someone who speaks about the value of herbs and the properties of various herbs:

Within the infant rind of this small flower
Poison hath residence, and medicine power,
For this, being smelt, with that part cheers each part;
Being tasted, slays all senses with the heart. (II.ii.23–26)

Bloodletting and the need to cool the body by letting blood is seen in *Richard II* when Mowbray says: "The blood is hot that must be cooled for this..." (I.i.51); and eventually, Richard II, in a speech which foregrounds medicines, forbids bloodletting:

Let's purge this choler without letting blood.
This we prescribe, though no physician:
Deep malice makes too deep incision;
Forget, forgive, conclude, and be agreed;
Our doctors say this is no time to bleed. (I.i.153–57)

The knowledge Shakespeare had of illness and the practice of medicine is seen in several plays: thus Lear speaks of "hysterica passio" (II.iv.55), Lady Macbeth speaks of Macbeth as having been afflicted with fits since his younger days (III.iv.52–54), Macbeth asks the physician to diagnose the ailment that afflicts Scotland:

If thou couldst, doctor, cast
The water of my land, find her disease,
And purge it to a sound and pristine health, (V.iii.52–54)

While medical learning and improvement progressed in a haphazard fashion, advances were also being made in astronomy and the study of the heavenly bodies. The earlier Church-endorsed view that the earth was at the centre of the universe was being challenged. The Copernican theory (propounded in the 1540s) proposed that the sun was at the centre of the planets, not the earth, and further proposed that the earth was one among the many planets revolving around the sun. The theory was met with antagonism by Church authorities and for a time Copernicus's book (*De revolutionibus orbium coelestium*, 1543) was banned, even though mariners' charts based upon his theory were immediately in use and proved themselves considerably more reliable than the earlier charts. Copernicus's theory was improved upon by Johannes Kepler (1571–1630) and Galileo Galilei (1564–1642) and these advances were fairly common knowledge; and though it is unclear whether Shakespeare was aware of these new developments, we do know that he was aware of the earlier beliefs regarding the heavenly bodies, speaking of the "heavenly music" in *The Tempest* (V.i.52), and in *The Merchant of Venice* speaking of a heavenly music which mortals cannot hear:

> There's not the smallest orb which thou behold'st
> But in his motion like an angel sings,
> Still choiring to the young-eyed cherubins;
> Such harmony is in immortal souls, (V.i.59–62)

But it was Shakespeare's early contemporary, Christopher Marlowe (1564–93) who evidenced his knowledge of the Ptolemaic versus the Copernican theories regarding the planets in *Faustus*, where Faustus quizzes Mephistopheles as to the nature of the universe and has to sit back resignedly when finally Mephistopheles gives him the old-fashioned viewpoint and indicates that there will be no more explanations forthcoming.

Marlowe's *Faustus* also indicates one other aspect of the new learning: the determination to experiment and determine the truth by the evidence of one's eyes. This is the reason he wishes to fly to see the planets and stars for himself, not able to accept the "known" wisdom of the time. Thus Wagner/the Chorus says of Faustus,

> Learned Faustus,
> To know the secrets of astronomy
> Graven in the book of Jove's high firmament,
> Did mount himself to scale Olympus' top,

Being seated in a chariot burning bright,
Drawn by the strength of yoky dragons' necks
He now is gone to prove cosmography, (Marlowe,
Doctor Faustus III)

This insistence on observation also led to a more accurate depiction of both plant and animal life as it was deemed essential to represent the object of study as itself rather than what it stood for, its symbolic value, etc. Descriptions were thus to be objective and scientific after which they could be invested with symbolic value and significance. Thus when Perdita speaks of the flowers and plants, she speaks in terms of both, their actual physical details as well as the iconic value they possess:

the fairest flowers o'th' season
Are our carnations and streaked gillyvors,
Which some call nature's bastards. Of that kind
Our rustic garden's barren, and I care not
To get slips of them.
....
Here's flowers for you:
Hot lavender, mints, savory, marjoram;
The marigold, that goes to bed wi'th' sun,
And with him rises, weeping. These are flowers
Of middle summer, and I think they are given
To men of middle age. (*The Winter's Tale* IV.iv.81–85, 103–08)

With these new advances in so many spheres of knowledge, accompanied by an education system that made it possible for more people to be literate than in any previous era, and with the establishment of the printing press and consequently a revolution in terms of the reading material that was available, Shakespeare's England was not the England of previous centuries but showed, instead, the fruits of the Renaissance, the rebirth of knowledge and learning.

Insiders/Outsiders

In the section on travel, I noted how the expansion of geographical knowledge enabled a simultaneous expansion of England's knowledge about other races and cultures. The age of Shakespeare is the one that was most radicalised as a result of the cultural encounter with "others". In this section, I shall examine the multitude of racial and cultural "others" or "outsiders" that populates Shakespeare's landscape.

During Shakespeare's time many different people played the role of the outsider to the Englishman's "insider" self. These would have included the Moors, the Ethiopians, the Moroccans, the Indians, the Turks, gypsies, savages, and of course, the Jew. As the horizons of the known world expanded and the English came into contact with more and more foreign lands and the people who inhabited them, they discovered alien ways of life. These encompassed differences in physical appearance, in habits of food and dress, in familial, social and community structures, in religions and religious practices, systems and forms of governance, etc. This encounter with otherness took place in various formats: there was the encounter via the print media, where accounts of the travels of other Englishmen and Europeans were published and circulated, which when read by those who stayed at home showed them stark differences, in terms of landscapes and those who occupied them. They also saw the other in England: whether Jews or Moors, the Turk or the Indian, while some were resident in England, others came as ambassadors and still others were brought as captives and exhibited. With otherness visible all around them, the English during this time classified as "savage" and "barbaric" all that was *different*. Michel de Montaigne, the French Renaissance philosopher, said in "Of Cannibals" that

> . . . every one gives the title of barbarism to everything that is not in use in his own country. As, indeed, we have no other level

> of truth and reason than the example and idea of the opinions and customs of the place wherein we live: there is always the perfect religion, there the perfect government, there the most exact and accomplished usage of all things. . . . (de Montaigne)

and the truth of this can be seen not only in how the English reacted to the foreigner who was racially different, but also how they considered the Welsh, the Scottish and the Irish, not to mention the Europeans who were their near neighbours: in particular, the Spaniards and the Italians.

Yet, difference was not always seen as inimical: Thomas Hariot initially, in his prefatory remarks, speaks of how others saw Virginia negatively because of their mis-/pre-conceptions. Harriot speaks of this when he says that his *Brief and True Report of the New Found Land of Virginia* is different from that of others due to various reasons, one of them being that those who reported the conditions there "could not find in Virginia any English cities, or fine houses, or their accustomed dainty food, or any soft beds of down or feathers: the country was to them miserable, and they reported accordingly." He goes on to call their reports and accounts "envious, malicious and slanderous" and pinpoints the fact that difference is not necessarily demeaning, evidencing a degree of self-reflexivity that is a rare feature. Connected to this is another aspect of several of the travel accounts of the time: even as the explorers and writers showcase difference, they also remark the positive attributes of what they see. This is particularly interesting because it demonstrates a certain willingness on the part of these writers to accommodate difference and even appreciate certain aspects of it. This ambivalence is apparent across English culture in Shakespeare's time and it finds expression in Shakespeare's plays as well, where we are shown the outsider and the alien in all his difference but we are also shown his admirable or sympathetic side.

For the Elizabethan, the alien known most immediately was not necessarily a Moor or a Jew, but a Protestant European, either escaping persecution from his Catholic homeland, or one who settled in England for trade and business opportunities. Interestingly, during Elizabeth's time, cities often petitioned the queen for permission to invite immigrant foreigners to settle there, with an eye to learning new skills, trades and crafts: Norwich was one such example. Immigrants from the Lowlands (including present-day Holland, Belgium and parts of France) were invited to England and eventually settled in London, Southampton and Norwich, successfully working in the textile industry and teaching English apprentices. Eventually, these immigrants integrated into and became a part of English society; but in the initial years, there were restrictions on their movements, their practice of religion, etc.[5] But while the Norwich settlement worked well, others were not so lucky: English men and women were suspicious as to whether the foreigners would take away their livelihood and their profits and even as they petitioned the queen to allow in foreign artisans and tradesmen as immigrants, later they petitioned her to expel them. The Crown's policy about immigration changed frequently in response to the pressures of the rioting English who found the foreigner an easy target to blame for their lack of employment and their losses in the business arena.

Religion and religious practices were often one way of defining the outsider: thus Spaniards and Frenchmen were treated with deep suspicion by the English on account of their Catholic allegiances. Indeed, during Elizabeth's time, the edict by the Pope (1570)[6] which freed her Catholic subjects from owing her allegiance, and almost encouraged them to actively work against her and even assassinate her, made it impossible for Catholics to be seen as loyal and English. It also, in turn, caused English edicts to be issued against Catholics. The Irish who were stubbornly Catholic were thus viewed with distrust and received their fair share of persecution. But even the Welsh and the Scots were not exempt from this distrust and it was only an outside threat that could unite these discrete elements. This is most famously seen in Shakespeare's *Henry V* where the Irish, Welsh and Scottish are ridiculed for their accents and their mutual rivalry is highlighted; and eventually, all of them are united in Henry's famed "band of brothers". The play begins with Henry's council discussing the problem of Scotland: that if they go to France the Scots are likely to invade England

> For once the eagle England being in prey,
> To her unguarded nest the weasel Scot
> Comes sneaking, and so sucks her princely eggs,
> Playing the mouse in absence of the cat,
> To 'tame and havoc more than she can eat. (I.ii.169–73)

and the mistrust and enmity of the neighbours are showcased repeatedly in the play.

If other Europeans and Catholics were often the outsider and the alien, for the Elizabethan, the most consistent alien was the Jew. In theory there were no Jews in England during Tudor times: they had all been expelled in 1290 by Edward I and thus there was no Jewish community in England. However, a small number of Spanish or Portuguese Jews (called Marranos) lived in England, with no possibility of practising their faith openly, calling themselves 'New Christians' and surviving in a world of hostility, hatred and persecution. The most prominent Jew of the time was one Roderigo Lopez (1525–94), physician to Elizabeth I; and though he had access to the monarch, he was convicted for treason in 1594. Accused of having tried to poison the queen, his execution was watched by the English, in the usual atmosphere of cruel hilarity. Poison was seen as a Jew's weapon and popular legends held that Jews were in the habit of poisoning wells and killing people, in addition to various other wicked activities. Marlowe's *Jew of Malta* (1589) showcases this version of the Jew:

BARABBAS. As for myself, I walk abroad a-nights
And kill sick people groaning under walls.
Sometimes I go about and poison wells,
And now and then, to cherish Christian thieves,
I am content to lose some of my crowns
That I may, walking in my gallery,
See 'em go pinioned along by my door.
Being young, I studied physic, and began
To practise first upon the Italian.
There I enriched the priests with burials
And always kept the sexton's arms in ure
With digging graves and ringing dead men's knells.
And after that was I an engineer,
And in the wars 'twixt France and Germany,
Under pretence of helping Charles the Fifth,
Slew friend and enemy with my stratagems.
Then after that was I an usurer,
And with extorting, cozening, forfeiting,
And tricks belonging unto brokery,
I filled the gaols with bankrupts in a year,
And with young orphans planted hospitals,
And every moon made some or other mad,
And now and then one hang himself for grief,
Pinning upon his breast a long great scroll
How I with interest tormented him. (Marlowe, *The Jew of Malta* II.iii)

Shakespeare's *Merchant of Venice*, performed in 1596, would have been watched by some who might also have watched Lopez's execution. The ambivalence remarked upon earlier is seen clearly in Shakespeare's depiction of Shylock: even as we are meant to despise him and enjoy his discomfiture, Shakespeare accentuates his humanity in the famous "Hath not a Jew eyes" speech. Further, when he learns of his daughter's elopement with a Christian, though he mourns the loss of his daughter and his ducats, his grief is magnified because she took with her, and sold, a jewel given him by his dead wife: these touches transform Shylock from the stock villainous Jew to a more realistic representation. We have no idea how the audience reacted to Shylock's "Hath not a Jew eyes" speech but we do know that they would have been pleased with Portia's defeat of his villainous plan and with his forced conversion at the end: he would have remained an outsider but a defeated one.

If the Jew was the most well-known outsider figure in Shakespeare's time, he was closely followed by the figure of the Moor. The term "Moor" itself is problematic as it originally referred to anyone who lived in Mauritania, the Roman lands at the top of North Africa. Later it came to include "black", "Muslim", as well as other meanings. As Kate Lowe, the Renaissance historian, says, "It has resonance but not much substance, and you can hang so much off it" (qtd. in MacGregor 112). In Shakespeare texts the Moor refers to Othello, but also Aaron from *Titus Andronicus* and the Prince of Morocco who comes to the contest in Belmont, for Portia's hand, in *The Merchant of Venice*. How would they have fitted into the popular conception regarding Moors, in Shakespeare's time?

Blacks were not altogether strange to Londoners and the English during this period. Towards the end of Elizabeth's reign the English were already slave-trading, selling blacks from Africa as slaves. But we also know that Elizabeth herself had a black page and an African entertainer, that her father and grandfather had black court musicians and that blacks were part of the English landscape, though not in such large numbers that we can speak of racist prejudice against them. However, as seen in *Titus Andronicus* and *Othello*, the figure of the Moor was already spoken of in pejorative terms: Othello, though a valiant general, is spoken of as having "thick lips", "an old black ram", a "lascivious Moor", and "a thing" (I.i.66, 88, 127 and

I.ii.72); and Aaron in *Titus Andronicus*, though learned and a master strategist, is a "swarth Cimmerian" and a "barbarous Moor" (II.iii.72, 78). Thus the negative rhetoric associated with "blackness" is already in place in these plays foregrounding physical difference, lustful sexuality and barbarity.

The term 'Moor' conflates religion, appearance and geographical region and creates a composite identity of the other, easily recognisable to the then audiences. Yet, in Elizabeth's time, London had been host to an embassy from Morocco and Marrakesh in 1600. The people, especially the court, had seen Moors, recognised their difference in terms of appearance and religion and also gained an awareness of the enormous wealth they possessed. Yet that did not eliminate prejudice. Indeed in 1596, Elizabeth I had issued two edicts expelling "negroes and blackamoors" and in 1601, a merchant was licensed to remove all of them from the country, though by the time of James I's marriage, negroes were once again to be seen in England. The black was already associated with wickedness, savagery and sin and like the Jew Barabas, Shakespeare gives Aaron the Moor a similar speech in *Titus Andronicus*:

> Even now I curse the day—and yet, I think,
> Few come within the compass of my curse—
> Wherein I did not some notorious ill,
> As kill a man, or else devise his death;
> Ravish a maid, or plot the way to do it;
> Accuse some innocent and forswear myself;
> Set deadly enmity between two friends;
> Make poor men's cattle break their necks;
> Set fire on barns and haystacks in the night,
> And bid the owners quench them with their tears.
> Oft have I digg'd up dead men from their graves
> And set them upright at their dear friends' door,
> Even when their sorrows almost was forgot,
> And on their skins, as on the bark of trees,
> Have with my knife carvèd in Roman letters,

'Let not your sorrow die though I am dead.'
But I have done a thousand dreadful things
As willingly as one would kill a fly,
And nothing grieves me heartily indeed
But that I cannot do ten thousand more. (V.i.125–44)

In this recital, Aaron echoes Barabas and yet another figure of otherness, Ithamore, the Turkish slave in *The Jew of Malta* who when asked how he spends his time replies,

Faith master,
In setting Christian villages on fire,
Chaining of eunuchs, binding galley slaves.
One time I was an hostler at an inn,
And in the night time secretly would steal
To travellers' chambers, and there cut their throats.
Once at Jerusalem, where the pilgrims kneeled,
I strewed powder on the marble stones,
And therewithal their knees would rankle so,
That I have laughed a-good to see the cripples
Go limping home to Christendom on stilts. (Marlowe, *The Jew of Malta* II.iii)

These figures combine racial difference and religious difference, becoming figures of unparalleled villainy and wickedness. That this was how the blacks were seen in Shakespeare's time is a matter of conjecture, but we do know that much of the racist stereotyping of later centuries was already in place.

While certain categories such as the Indian, the Moor and the Jew were always already in the position of the outsider, Shakespeare's society was one that made it possible for others also to occupy this position, particularly women who transgressed the codes of the patriarchal society that they lived in. Yet it is not possible to claim absolute alterity for any of these either, as the ambivalence in their portrayals in the drama of the times makes it impossible for them to be one-dimensional. Whether that was a feature of the society or a whim on the part of the playwrights is anyone's guess.

* * * *

As this chapter has demonstrated, Shakespeare benefited enormously from the expansion of knowledge – in geography, medicine, astronomy, and, most of all, culture. Voyages and science enabled the English, and Shakespeare, to understand inner and outer worlds as never before. Of course, this expansion of knowledge – of difference and multiplicity – brought with it considerable anxieties, even as it produced the thrill of the new. Shakespeare's plays with their multiple worlds, races and peoples might be read as responses to this expanded knowledge, which energised the literature and, like England itself, "made it new".

Works Cited

Bacon, Francis. *The New Atlantis*. 1626. From *Ideal Commonwealths*. P. F. Collier and Son, New York. (c) 1901. Oregon State, 1996. Web. 18 June 2014. <http://oregonstate.edu/instruct/phl302/texts/bacon/atlantis.html>.

de Léry, Jean. *From History of a Voyage to the Land of Brazil* (1578). Norton Topics Online: The Sixteenth Century. Prepared by Stephen Greenblatt, George Logan and Philip Schwyzer. n.d. Web. 24 May 2014.

de Montaigne, Michel. "Of Cannibals." c.1580. Trans. Charles Cotton. Ed. William Carew Hazilitt. 1877. *Project Gutenberg*. n.d. Web. 26 May 2014.

"East India Company Charter." 1600. n.p. n.d. Web. 24 May 2014 <http://www.sdstate.edu/projectsouthasia/loader.cfm?csModule=security/getfile&PageID=857407>.

Fitch, Ralph. From *The Voyage of Mr. Ralph Fitch, Merchant of London*. *Principall Navigations*. Richard Hakluyt. 1599. *Norton Topics*

Online: The Sixteenth Century. Prepared by Stephen Greenblatt, George Logan and Philip Schwyzer. n.d. Web. 24 May 2014.

Greenblatt, Stephen. *Marvelous Possessions: The Wonder of the New World*. Chicago: The University of Chicago Press, 1991. Print.

Hariot, Thomas. *A briefe and True Report of the New Found Land of Virginia*. 1590. Roanoke Revisited. n.d. Web. 24 May 2014. <http://www.nps.gov/>.

MacGregor, Neil. *Shakespeare's Restless World*. London: Penguin, 2014. Print.

Marlowe, Christopher. *The Jew of Malta*. Perseus Digital Library. 2001. Web. 28 May 2014.

Marlowe, Christopher. *The Tragicall History of Doctor Faustus*. (A Text). c.1589/1604. Ed. Hilary Binda. Perseus Digital Library. 2001. Web. 28 May 2014.

Peckham, George. *A True Report of the Late Discoveries. . . .* 1584. Norton Topics Online: The Sixteenth Century. Prepared by Stephen Greenblatt, George Logan and Philip Schwyzer. n.d. Web. 24 May 2014.

Raleigh, Walter. "The Ocean, to Cynthia." *Sir Walter Raleigh: "the shepherd of the ocean" selections from his poetry and prose* (1916). Ed. Frank Cheney Hersey. Web. 26 May 2014. <https://archive.org/>.

"Virginia Company Charter." 1609. American History. University of Groningen. 2012. Web. 24 May 2014.

Notes

1. For a fascinating slideshow of maps across time, see <http://www.bbc.co.uk/history/interactive/animations/map_making/index_embed.shtml>
2. See watercolour paintings as well as read accounts of the exhibited Eskimos at <http://www.historymuseum.ca/cmc/exhibitions/hist/frobisher/freng01e.shtml>

3. See Stephen Greenblatt's *Marvelous Possessions* for a very readable and instructive analysis of early American explorers' narratives.
4. See <http://www.bbc.co.uk/schools/gcsebitesize/history/shp/middleages/earlymoderncivilisationrev2.shtml> for an illustration of a public dissection.
5. See <http://www.bbc.co.uk/legacies/immig_emig/england/norfolk/article_1.shtml>
6. See the Papal Bull here: <http://tudorhistory.org/primary/papalbull.html>

Shakespeare and/in the Theatre

FOUR

DRAMA, THE THEATRE AND STAGECRAFT

What were the physical conditions in which Shakespeare's plays were performed? What was the structure of the stage and of the playing companies? What are the features of earlier forms of the drama that we can see in Shakespeare's plays? These are some of the questions that will be answered in the following pages wherein we shall study

- English drama before and leading up to Shakespeare
- the theatre and its structure
- playing companies and their conventions.

ENGLISH DRAMA BEFORE AND LEADING UP TO SHAKESPEARE

Elizabethan/Renaissance/Early Modern drama grew out of early English (and European) drama forms such as the mystery, miracle and morality plays. The mystery and miracle plays were forms of drama that were performed in churches and cathedrals, the former depicting Biblical incidents while the latter dramatised the lives of the saints. The mystery plays developed from plays presented in Latin by churchmen and monks during the Middle Ages, wherein they dramatised incidents from the Bible: initially the Crucifixion and Resurrection of Jesus, but later on many more incidents and events from both the Old and New Testaments. These were presented within the church, all the roles being played by monks and other clergy and they were meant as a form of instruction for the common people who might otherwise have little or no access to, and therefore knowledge of, the Bible. Their repertoire increased, with time, to include plays based upon the lives and miracles performed by the saints of the Church.

The secularisation of the miracle and mystery plays began with the drama being moved out of the church premises to, initially, the churchyard and later on, the village green or square. As the drama moved out of the church it began to be performed on portable platforms or stages, often on large carts which were pulled to new locations within the city, for a different audience to watch. It also involved the shifting away from Latin to the vernacular, for the sake of intelligibility. Finally the parts began to be played by laymen, as well as priests and monks, until eventually the entire exercise was taken over by the trade guilds who shouldered the responsibility for these performances. By the mid-1300s, the plays were presented in cycles, some, such as the York cycle, involving as many as fifty or more plays. The trade guilds (which would be somewhat similar to an association or union today) took on the responsibility of specific plays within the cycle and sometimes there was a particular appropriateness to the plays which were the prerogative of certain guilds, such as the watermen performing the story of Noah and the Flood! The secularisation of the drama also meant that some (often coarse) humour[1] was introduced into what earlier was serious business: thus the story of Noah was enlivened by Noah's wife refusing to enter the Ark and finally being beaten and forced to do so. While Herod was presented as a tyrant, he was imaged as loud and raving, someone who harangued and bullied incessantly: we see the memories of such performances in Shakespeare's *Hamlet*, where Hamlet advises the players: "It out-Herods Herod. Pray you avoid it" (III.ii.12).

The morality plays were latter forms of drama, popular in the fifteenth and sixteenth centuries, which arose out of the earlier Christian miracle and mystery plays and were more secular: instead of Biblical incidents or saintly lives they were allegorical, showing personifications of abstract virtues and vices battling for the life/soul of a human protagonist. Thus the Seven Deadly Sins, or some of them, would proffer temptation to the central figure, a type of Everyman or Mankind, and the play would follow his adventures as he battled with all the attractions of the world, eventually being saved through Perseverance and Repentance. While the moralising of the virtuous characters could be extremely tedious and sanctimonious, the morality plays are relevant because of two significant aspects. Firstly, they offered the writer(s) some independence in plotting the storyline, a freedom unknown in the days of the mystery and miracle plays. Secondly, while the pious platitudes of the virtues could be dull and mind-numbing, the vices offered an opportunity for both, a realistic depiction of the low-life of the times and for some clowning and knock-about humour.[2] *The Castle of Perseverance* (fifteenth century) and *Everyman* (late fifteenth century) are two of the best known morality plays, the latter of which is still staged in contemporary times. While the morality play practice of showing the central character battling temptation survives in Shakespearean plays in the tradition of the protagonist being tempted by various other characters (Macbeth by Lady Macbeth, Brutus by Cassio, etc.), a more obvious example of the effect of the morality plays, which Shakespeare might have watched in his childhood, includes the deployment of Falstaff as a Vice figure in *Henry IV* (Parts I and II), called "that reverend Vice, that grey iniquity" (*Henry IV, Part I* II.v.413), and the use of Time, personified carrying an hourglass, in *The Winter's Tale* (IV.i, the stage direction which begins the scene).[3]

In addition to antecedents such as these, Elizabethan drama also built upon other early forms such as the interludes. The interludes furthered the secular project of the morality plays and were very short plays, humourous to the point of being farcical, or tragic. These were presented in the courts and banquet halls of nobles, and by travelling companies of actors, or sometimes the serving men of a nobleman who were permitted to engage in this activity when not required in the nobleman's service. One of the most well-known interludes was *The Playe Called the Foure P.P.* (*c.*1544), by John Heywood. The figure of the Vice becomes further prominent in this form of the drama and was one of the most popular elements of the form. The Vice can be seen as one of the predecessors to the many clowns, jesters and Fools in Shakespeare's plays. In Tudor times, the interludes began to include music and dance as well as the more farcical and comic elements that had earlier characterised them. This can be seen in the interlude-like sections in Shakespeare's last plays such as *The Winter's Tale* and *The Tempest*.

By the late 1570s and early 1580s, when Elizabethan drama was beginning to flower, it had integrated elements from each of these forms in addition to certain features from Greek and Latin drama traditions. The earliest plays which can be seen as connected to classical drama were Nicholas Udall's *Ralph Roister Doister* (1553) modelled on Plautus's and Terence's comedies, and in the Senecan tragic mould, *Gorbuduc* (1561) by Thomas Sackville and Thomas Norton. The latter gains significance as the first play in English in blank verse, thus setting in motion a trend that would be adopted by later dramatists. Udall's play introduced the figure of the braggart soldier to the English stage. The figure of the vainglorious soldier, a type popular in Latin comedies, was one which would be used by Shakespeare in the creation of characters such as Pistol (the two parts of *Henry IV*) and Parolles in *All's Well that Ends Well*, and perfected in the figure of Falstaff in the two parts of *Henry IV*.

Thus what we know today as English Renaissance drama and Shakespearean drama is actually a composite form incorporating select features from a multitude of dramatic forms which had preceded it.

The Theatre and Its Structure

Before the establishment of playhouses, plays were staged in various spaces: in the homes of noblemen, in courts, in marketplaces, in the courtyards of inns or large rooms inside inns. In England, till approximately the 1570s, plays were staged on temporary stages erected in marketplaces, by placing boards on barrels and trestles. These could be dismantled and taken along to the place of the next performance. Inns were also popular as stages for travelling players as they provided a place for the players themselves to stay, but also had galleries around the yard, thus providing not just a space for the actual performance but also a space for the viewers to stand and view the proceedings. In addition, bear and other animal baiting houses could also be temporarily converted into use as a stage or theatre by actors and travelling players. These were spaces that were, however, governed by the City and town regulations and governing bodies, often by people who had Puritan sympathies, and were thus disapproving of plays, playing companies and the disorder that supposedly attended/marked them.

To escape from the governance of the City Corporation in London, playhouses or theatres were built on the outskirts of the City: the Theatre (1576),[4] the Curtain (1577), the Rose (1587), the Swan (1595), the Globe (1599) and the Fortune (1600). Our knowledge of the playhouses in Shakespeare's time is built upon scanty documentary evidence (which includes the famous drawing by Johannes de Witt of the interior of the Swan, builders' contracts, etc.), architectural excavations since 1989 (of the Rose playhouse and later the remains of the Globe, nearby) and considerable speculation. However, based on these we now have a fair idea of the playhouses, their structure and the associated functions.

The Theatre was built by James Burbage—father of Richard Burbage, the principal player of Shakespeare's playing company, the Lord Chamberlain's Men—on leased land in 1576. Till 1594, however, the theatres were not exclusive to any one company: rather the playing companies (discussed in the next section) played at any available playhouse or other space. This changed in 1594 when a complete ban was imposed on playing at inns and in inn yards: from then on only the authorised playhouses on the City's outskirts were to be used. In addition, the many playing companies were finally whittled down to just two dominant ones, the Lord Chamberlain's Men and the Lord Admiral's Men. The latter played at the Rose, built in 1587 and enlarged in 1592, while the Lord Chamberlain's Men played at the Theatre till its lease ran out in 1596. For two years the Lord Chamberlain's Men rented space for their productions and moved around searching for good locations to present their dramas, but in 1598–99 they devised a scheme which was put into operation in January 1599. The Theatre was dismantled and its materials used to build the Globe, the most well-known today of the playhouses of the time, due largely to its association with Shakespeare.

The Elizabethan playhouses are seen as having been fairly similar in shape and structure: octagonal or polygonal in shape, they were almost circular and large enough to accommodate upwards of 2000 and sometimes nearly 3000 spectators. The circular structure of these playhouses was said to have been inspired possibly by the Roman amphitheatres or by the animal baiting rings of Elizabethan times. These playhouses were open to the skies, relying on natural light and had a stage that jutted out into the yard or arena. Beneath the stage was an area that was used as a "hell", in plays such as Marlowe's *Doctor Faustus* where the devils emerge from underneath. In Shakespeare we see the use of this space in *Hamlet* where the Ghost in I.v speaks from below, as also in *Antony and Cleopatra* where the "music of the hautboys (is) under the stage" is heard as "Hercules, whom Antony loved, / Now leaves him" (IV.iii; stage direction at line 9; 14). Above the stage was a canopy supported on columns or pillars, on the underside of which was painted the sun, the moon and the stars. This partially covered the stage and was occasionally paired with descent machinery, for lowering a *Deus ex machina*, or an Ariel in *The Tempest*, onto the stage.

At the back of the stage were doors, for the actors to make their exits and entrances. It is now assumed that there must have been at least two doors with a possible alcove or another concealed door in between: this would have been the space wherein Polonius hid in Act III, scene iv of *Hamlet*. The number

A copy of the Johannes de Witt drawing of the Swan[5]

of doors is a matter of some dispute, though one of the foremost scholars on the Shakespearean stage, Andrew Gurr, is of the opinion that the possible alcove might also have been used as a tomb, a study (for example Titus's study in *Titus Andronicus*, V.ii), a shop or a cell (149). Behind the stage were the "tiring" (attiring) rooms or the "tiring house" and above these were a series of rooms that are thought to have been private viewing rooms for the wealthy. One of these might also have been used by musicians, playing string and woodwinds, in those plays that required it. By 1608, however, one of the central rooms on the Globe's balcony served as a music room, making it possible for a concert to be played before the actual play began.

These playhouses had three tiers of galleries running around the sides for audiences as also a large central portion, around the base of the stage, where the "groundlings", those who paid the least (a penny), could stand. The spectators could stand in the galleries (for two pennies) or by adding one more penny could then have a seat in the higher galleries from where they would be able to see better. The best seats were however those in the rooms above the stage: though one must remember that while comfortable, they would have offered limited viewing. The rich who sat there would have largely seen the backs of the actors and any action at the back of the stage would not have been visible to them. There is a belief that the most expensive seats were on the stage itself so that a close-up view of the action was enjoyed by those who could afford it. But evidence of this is yet to be found. This practice was, however, extant in the indoor playhouses (often called the private theatres) of the time, the foremost example of which was the Blackfriars.

The indoors theatres were often within the City limits, as for example, the Blackfriars, earlier a Dominican monastery. The monks had petitioned for it to be granted the status of a "liberty", and as such it was outside the jurisdiction of the City authorities, even while it lay within the City limits, geographically speaking. As early as 1576, the first Blackfriars theatre started functioning when a section of the old Dominican monastery was leased to the Master of the Children of the Chapel, a company of boy players, for them to rehearse and perform there, prior to performances at court. Other children's companies performed there as well until the mid-1580s. In the mid-1590s, the pioneering theatre entrepreneur James Burbage bought a section of the old Blackfriars monastery and at considerable expense built and furnished a new theatre there. However, the locals, many of whom were rich and politically well-connected, objected to having a theatre in the neighbourhood, with all its attendant vice, and Burbage was forced to lease it out to children's companies. It was only in 1608, after Shakespeare's company had become the King's Men, that they took possession of the theatre at Blackfriars and began using it.

The theatre at Blackfriars consisted of a large hall, with the stage at one of the shorter ends of the room with the tiring rooms behind it. The structure of the stage was similar to that at the large amphitheatres, with an alcove towards the back, a hell below and heavens above, etc. Around the other three walls were galleries but immediately before the stage were benches: the indoor theatres catered to a wealthier clientele who could afford to pay for comfort and thus there were seats for those who could afford them. The price for standing room in this theatre was sixpence and for the best seats in the house (stools placed around the edges of the stage itself), where one could see, and be seen, they paid twenty-four pence. While the use of lights made it possible to play at the indoor theatres at night, the performances at the large amphitheatres were held in the daytime, usually early afternoon, before dark fell.

While the Globe and the Blackfriars belonged to the playing company to which Shakespeare belonged, who composed this playing company? What else did they need to enact a play? And what were the conventions that marked performances during this time? The answers to these and similar questions will be provided in the next section.

The Playing Companies, Stage Props and Staging Conventions

Playing companies had been staging plays and travelling through England since the fifteenth century; but because players were fairly low down on the social scale and were seen as possible sources of disorder, they had to be under the patronage of aristocrats, who were deemed to be responsible for them. Thus from the 1570s through the 1590s, players grouped together calling themselves by the name of their patron—thus Lord Pembroke's Men, Lord Worcester's Men, the Lord Admiral's Men, etc. These groups were constantly dissolving and re-forming themselves until in the mid-1590s there were just two: the Lord Admiral's Men and the Lord Chamberlain's Men. These two were licensed in 1598, by the Queen's Privy Council, as the only two adult playing companies permitted to play in London. Their success was in large part due to the fact that they were controlled by two powerful theatrical families: the Burbages (father and sons) controlled the Lord Chamberlain's Men, while Philip Henslowe, theatrical entrepreneur and landlord (and father-in-law to Edward Alleyn, the principal actor of the troupe), ran the Lord Admiral's Men. What is known about the Elizabethan stage, its many expenses and practices, is derived, in large part, from the detailed records maintained by Philip Henslowe in his diary.[6]

While James Burbage and Philip Henslowe were important to the survival and advancement of the playing companies, in actual fact the companies were cooperatively owned by a group of about ten shareholders who owned its assets, contributed to its daily running and upkeep and shared the profits. The Lord Chamberlain's Men, to which Shakespeare belonged, had eight shareholders in 1596; this number increased to twelve after 1603 when they became the King's Men. But once a shareholder in a company the person had then to work exclusively for that company: there could be no part-interest. Thus Shakespeare wrote his plays for his own company, Richard Burbage acted only with the Lord Chamberlain's Men, etc. They could also sell out and leave only with the consent of the company. While the shareholders were the core group of the playing company, it was not possible to run a theatre with just that tiny number. Thus in addition to the shareholders, there were hired men and apprentices. All of these would participate in the work involved in putting up a play: from acting in it (the less important roles, maybe), to shifting props, assisting with costumes and music to being gatherers: this last were those who stood at the doors taking the price of admittance and letting in the audience.

The hard work involved in putting up a play was also repetitive labour: prior to c.1600, plays were performed *every day* except on Sundays, during Lent, outbreaks of the plague and major church holidays.[7] Rehearsals were held during the morning and the play was staged in the afternoon. Plays were not repeated too often as this could lead to a waning of their popularity. Thus in a week, all six afternoons would see the staging of a different play. This system also required a new play to be introduced at an average of once a fortnight or once in three weeks. All of this meant that the principal actors had to memorise many different parts and could not afford to muddle them up. In addition, apart from the main actors (such as Richard Burbage and Edward Alleyn) the other actors sometimes doubled roles in the same play, so keeping the lines of two characters in the same play in one's mind was also a necessity. This practice of doubling roles was essential as there were never enough players to play all the roles in any play. Even today, some productions of *A Midsummer Night's Dream* have the same actors play the roles of Titania and Hippolyta, Oberon and Theseus. Shakespeare himself, known to have played older characters, might have played the parts of both Adam and Corin in *As You Like It*.

The fact that the Lord Chamberlain's Men had their own in-residence playwright gave Shakespeare the opportunity to write plays which built upon the acting strengths of those in his company. Many of the tragic Shakespearean roles were written for Richard Burbage, the principal actor, as were the roles of the Fool in *Twelfth Night* and *King Lear* which were meant to exploit the talent of Robert Armin, the actor who, it is assumed, first played those roles. It is also assumed that the significant female roles of the great comedies of the late 1590s and early 1600s (Rosalind and Celia in *As You Like It*; Beatrice and Hero in *Much Ado About Nothing*, Viola and Olivia in *Twelfth Night*, etc.) were written due to the fact of two young apprentices who excelled at playing women. These are "facts" which have been painstakingly derived by Shakespearean scholars and sleuths, from the little evidence that survives from Shakespeare's times but also from reading his plays and noting similarities and differences therein.

If the actors were the principal assets of the companies, the other major assets they possessed and guarded zealously were the playscripts. We know from Henslowe's accounts that a playscript was procured by paying a playwright five to eight pounds (after 1600, the price went up to ten to twelve pounds). Once the payment was made and the script delivered to the company it belonged to the company and not the playwright (intellectual property laws and copyright laws were as yet unformulated): as such if someone made away with the script, the play could as well be performed by another company, with no possibility of legal redressal. Thus scripts (which included the author's "foul papers",[8] the prompt book or the "book of the play" used by the company and the scripts of the lines for individual roles) were among the most important of the company's possessions.

Companies also invested large sums in procuring costumes for their players. Given the preponderance of noblemen/noblewomen's roles as well as those of royalty, the costumes used by the players were of necessity grand and opulent, consisting of velvets, silks, damasks, lace and even fur, with gold and silver embroidery and buttons, etc. Shakespeare gestures towards the opulence of costumes (on-stage and off) when Lear says to his daughter,

> Thou art a lady;
> If only to go warm were gorgeous,
> Why, nature needs not what thou gorgeous wear'st,
> Which scarcely keeps thee warm. (*King Lear* II.iv.262–65)

Sometimes more money was spent on costumes for a play than was spent on the playscript itself, as recounted by Russ McDonald (112). These costumes were also cause for criticism as they were stigmatised as "over-costly effeminate, strange, meretricious, lust-exciting apparel" by critics of the theatre such as William Prynne in *Histriomastix* (qtd. in McDonald 112). The expensive apparel also offended notions of order as actors who were not "noble" dressed up and appeared as "nobility" on stage. If the sumptuary laws of the period decreed who could wear what,[9] the theatre contravened these laws and upset order and decorum in matters of dress and attire (as also in gender roles, more of which later).

While the costumes in all their splendour provided a substantial portion of the spectacle upon the Early Modern English stage, other props were also used and deployed to considerable effect by the actors and companies. Special effects were largely in the realm of sounds but the stage also had several other large and small props, from beds and thrones to handkerchiefs, skulls and daggers, swords and shields. While the Shakespearean stage did not have scenery and backdrops, this did not mean that the stage was utterly bare through the course of the play. Props that were essential to the play were used but the setting of the scene was largely an imaginative exercise performed by the audience, based upon the lines spoken by the actors. So from Rosalind's "Well, this is the Forest of Arden" in II.iv.11 of *As You Like It*, to the Chorus's many speeches in *Henry V*, beginning with

> And let us, ciphers to this great account,
> On your imaginary forces work.
> Suppose within the girdle of these walls
> Are now confined two mighty monarchies,
> Whose high upreared and abutting fronts,
> The perilous narrow ocean parts asunder.
> Piece out our imperfections with your thoughts:
> Into a thousand parts divide one man,
> And make imaginary puissance.
> Think, when we talk of horses, that you see them,
> Printing their proud hoofs i' th' receiving earth;
> For 'tis your thoughts that now must deck our kings,
> Carry them here and there; (I.Prologue.17–29)

it is the speakers in the plays who help the audience to recognise where they are and what they are (imaginatively) seeing. If location and scene were set in place by the opening speeches in a play/act/scene, the rest was not similarly left entirely to the fancy of the audience. Thus actors were equipped with swords and daggers (soldiers and warriors whether in *Macbeth*'s Scotland or *Titus Andronicus*'s Rome); stocks were brought out in *King Lear* for Kent to be imprisoned in them; Desdemona would have been smothered in her bed on stage or in the alcove towards the back of the stage in *Othello*; an ass's head would have been set on Bottom's head in *A Midsummer Night's Dream*; a basket (though without an asp) would have been brought in by the Clown towards the end of *Antony and Cleopatra*; and so on. The final scene of *Hamlet*, as the initial scene of *King Lear*, would have been played out in a king's court, with the monarchs on their thrones, and the gravediggers would have had spades as they dug Ophelia's grave in *Hamlet*. Thus while the imagination would have been the primary method of setting a scene, it would have been aided by some props. Due to the limited nature of the props on Shakespeare's stage some props had been rendered emblematic. Thus their very appearance would send across very particular signals to the audience: a turban was enough to indicate a character from the East, as the wearing of swords and shields signalled that the scene was set out of doors. Certain conventions governed the use of these props too: thus the skull in *Hamlet* while referring to Yorick, the jester, also signified mortality and the temporality of life itself; the handkerchief in *Othello* (which is used by Iago to make Othello jealous) though seen as an exotic item was also emblematic and evocative of a woman's chastity in that era. Even the wigs worn by the boys playing women characters could be used to send across clear signals: untied hair, loose and dishevelled, indicated madness and wandering wits, as seen in Ophelia in *Hamlet*.

The most well-known convention of the Shakespearean stage involves, of course, the use of male actors for all roles: thus no women ever played on the Shakespearean stage. Apprentices, young boys, whose voices had not yet broken, were instead responsible for playing the women's roles on Shakespeare's stage. As mentioned earlier, Shakespeare was fortunate enough to have in his company at particular times apprentices who excelled at playing women's roles: thus there must have been two at a certain point which led to Shakespeare writing a series of plays featuring two significant roles for women. Towards the latter end of his career, there must have been one apprentice who was a particularly brilliant actor, especially at playing slightly older women's roles: it is assumed that this led to Shakespeare creating the roles of Lady Macbeth and Cleopatra in *Antony and Cleopatra*. Indeed, Cleopatra's outraged and unhappy comment towards the end of the play points to this convention even as it mocks it:

I shall see
Some squeaking Cleopatra boy my greatness
I' th' posture of a whore. (*Antony and Cleopatra* V.ii.215–17)

This practice led to a rather limited number of women characters in the plays of the time (rarely exceeding four, of which only two might have large roles), but also led to an exploration of gender/sexual roles and identities in quite a few of Shakespeare's plays. The cross-dressing Rosalind in *As You Like It* and Viola in *Twelfth Night* are perhaps the best known explorations of sexual desire and gender roles as they both play complicated gender roles: the boy actor plays a woman who then disguises herself as a boy and flirts with a man. Contemporary scholarship has unravelled the politics of homoerotic desire and the nuances of this multi-layered playing of gendered sexual roles, but Shakespeare's contemporaries were as aware of the dangers of this kind of roleplaying as is evidenced by critics such as John Rainoldes who castigated drama and the theatre for instigating desire: "The appareil of wemen is a great provocation of men to lust and leacherie . . . A woman's garment beeing put on a man doeth vehemently touch him and moue him with the remembrance and imagination of a woman; and the imagination of a thing desirable doth stirr up the desire" (qtd. in Scott-Warren 116). Transvestism on the Early Modern stage evoked all manner of peril in the minds of the puritans, from the fear that the boys who played the women's roles would be rendered effeminate to the fear that they would arouse transgressive desire on the part of the men and women in the audience. There was also the fear that the players could be, all, guilty of same-sex relationships and liaisons.

****

Shakespeare's plays, as we see them today, performed on stage or in movie adaptations, are at a far remove from the conditions in which they were first performed. However, to gain an understanding of many of the conventions and conditions of the Shakespearean stage it is only necessary to read two of his plays: *Hamlet* and *A Midsummer Night's Dream*. In both of these you have extended discussions and dramatisations of the art and nature of the theatre, playing companies, the conventions of drama and even the composition of the audience and its contribution to drama in the times.[10]

Works Cited

Greenblatt, Stephen. *Will in the World: How Shakespeare Became Shakespeare.* New York: W. W. Norton, 2004. Print.

Gurr, Andrew. *The Shakespearean Stage.* 3rd ed. Cambridge: Cambridge UP, 1992. Print.

McDonald, Russ. *The Bedford Companion to Shakespeare: An Introduction with Documents.* Boston: Bedford/St. Martin's, 2001. Print.

Scott-Warren, Jason. *Early Modern English Literature.* Cambridge, UK: Polity, 2005. Print.

Notes

1. Much of the humour in these early forms of the drama involved a focus on characters from the lower strata of society, sometimes petty criminals and rogues. We can see echoes of this in some of Shakespeare's major tragedies where humorous episodes involving gatekeepers (*Macbeth*) and gravediggers (*Hamlet*) evoke laughter in the midst of serious affairs of state. The best cast of rogues in Shakespeare is seen in the two parts of *Henry IV* where Prince Hal's friends are all petty criminals, from the lower class (apart from Falstaff), forever trying to improve their lot, via foul means or fair.
2. One of the most interesting off-shoots of the morality play is Christopher Marlowe's *Doctor Faustus* which incorporates several of the features of the form and then develops it in new, earlier impossible, directions.

3. For a detailed speculative account of how the morality plays impacted Shakespeare's plays, see pages 31–36 in Greenblatt's *Will in the World*.
4. Usually accounted the earliest though there was, earlier to this, the Red Lion, built in 1567, again by James Burbage.
5. For more images of Shakespeare's stage see <http://workforce.calu.edu/aune/RenaissanceTheater.html>
6. See detailed records at <http://www.henslowe-alleyn.org.uk/essays/henslowediary.html>
7. From 1600 there were injunctions in place as the possible number of performances in a week was restricted to two each by the two companies that now enjoyed a duopoly in the London theatre scene.
8. Dramatists wrote their plays in longhand, and that first manuscript was usually called the author's "foul papers". This was copied out neatly and submitted to the playing company, this second manuscript being the "fair copy" and finally, a member of the playing company made notations in it, regarding theatrical details and such, and this was called "the book of the play", the one from which individual parts were copied out and given to the actors.
9. Details as to who could wear what, in terms of colours, fabrics and such, the suitable length of swords, etc. can be seen at <http://elizabethan.org/sumptuary/who-wears-what.htm>
10. Thus in *Hamlet* we hear the prince being told of the emergence and popularity of the child players in the city: groups of young boys who were then so popular that the playing companies had taken to touring the country side (II.ii.315–30). Further, Hamlet also speaks of the need for a restrained style of acting, rather than loud passionate ranting which might appeal to the groundlings but which would lack "smoothness" (III.ii.1–12).

Five

Shakespeare and His Contemporaries

When we say "Shakespeare" today, do we mean the man who lived and worked between 1564 and 1616? Do we mean the dramatic works he is said to have written between approximately 1590 and 1612? Or do we mean both these but also all that surrounds the man and his work: the myth of being the greatest playwright ever, the many adaptations and retellings of his work, the translations and rewritings that exist in every conceivable language? While "Shakespeare" includes all this and more, in this chapter we are concerned with the life and times of William Shakespeare: the playwright and player who was born in Stratford-upon-Avon and returned there to die, after a long and profitable career in the theatre worlds of London. But even as we speak of Shakespeare, it is not possible to speak of him in isolation: he lived in a bustling world of other players, playwrights and poets.

To talk of Shakespeare's contemporary playwrights is to speak of a motley group of men (only men, yes: there were no professional women playwrights) who lived and worked alongside him through much of the Elizabethan and Jacobean periods. Within this chapter there will be no inventory or listing of all the other literary figures of the age, from Anon to Webster: what the reader will find is a discussion of those whose lives and works touched Shakespeare's life and works, in ways that we can see and recognise. It is when their lives converge upon Shakespeare's that they become relevant to this study of the backgrounds to Shakespeare's work. Thus from Robert Greene through Christopher Marlowe and Ben Jonson to John Fletcher, this chapter will examine the intersections and meeting points of great minds, their influences upon each other and the insecurities and jealousies stirred up by each other's successes.

When Shakespeare began his career as a playwright, in the late 1580s–early 1590s, the theatre was already a vibrant place, enabling a number of writers and poets to find popular and financial success, a privileged position in society and a patron. It was also, ironically, a dangerous space. While today we look back at the world of Shakespeare as a place and time that fostered individual talent and genius, what we frequently forget is that the genius that flourished did so in a world wherein one wrong move could lead to imprisonment, torture and even death. This chapter will initially plot the coordinates of Shakespeare's life and times and in the second section, it will examine his life in conjunction with that of other dramatists of the times. It concludes with a brief section on the publication of drama during this period and the complications which surround the publication history of many of the plays of the time.

Shakespeare's Life

Much of what we know of Shakespeare's life is conjecture: thus stories circulate as to how he fled Stratford for London because he was nearly apprehended for poaching, that initially in London he held the heads of horses as their owners watched plays in the theatres, etc. But we have more accurate knowledge regarding Shakespeare's life than we have of any of the other playwrights of the time, apart from Ben Jonson. Parish records, documents regarding business and other financial transactions, records of performances and theatre activities and the mention made of him in the work of other writers of the period: all these combine to give us a fairly clear and precise picture of the life of William Shakespeare.

The parish records of Holy Trinity Church, Stratford-upon-Avon, Warwickshire, record the baptism of William, son of John Shakspere (sic), on 26 April 1564. Conventionally it is believed that he was born on 23 April as children were baptised within a few days of their birth. But the choice of 23 April is also connected to the fact that William Shakespeare died on 23 April 1616 and by ascribing this as his birthdate a sense of neat proportion is bestowed upon his life.[1] An additional layer of meaning is added by the fact that 23 April is also the day dedicated to St George, patron saint of England, thus transforming William Shakespeare into a representative figure for English national identity too.

The church and parish records at Stratford-upon-Avon tell us that William Shakespeare was born (in a plague year) to John and Mary Shakespeare, the third of their eight children, though the first son, and eventually their eldest living child. John Shakespeare, a glover, was a prominent citizen in Stratford, holding various public offices (including that of ale-taster and bailiff) until financial and associated social misfortune (records state that he was in debt and failed to attend church) came upon him around 1577. His recovery is believed to have been at least partially because of William's intervention: the latter's prosperity helping his father to regain lost ground and even apply for a coat of arms, thus making him part of the gentry. Little is known of Mary Shakespeare, other than that she was born an Arden, part of the family that gave its name to the nearby Forest of Arden, immortalised in Shakespeare's *As You Like It*, where Charles, Duke Ferdinand's wrestler, speaks of it as a mythic place: "They say he is already in the forest of Arden, and a many merry men with him; and there they live like the old Robin Hood of England. They say many young gentlemen flock to him every day, and fleet the time carelessly, as they did in the golden world" (I.i.99–103).

Though we have no documents or records of Shakespeare's schooling, it is possible to say with a fair degree of certainty that Shakespeare would have received his initial education at the petty school, where he would have learnt his letters with the help of a hornbook, and then gone on to attend the grammar school, the King's New School which was established in 1553, in Stratford. The records of the King's New School show that the schoolmasters during the period when Shakespeare might have studied here were all university degree holders: this would have ensured that the education Shakespeare received was of a reputable standard, with an emphasis on Latin. The school day was nearly twelve hours long: beginning at six or seven and going on till five or six every day except the Sabbath. The long day stretching ahead, looked at in the light of Shakespeare's "whining school boy . . . creeping like snail unwillingly to school" (*As You Like It* II.vii.144–46), can be seen as a reflection of his own early mornings, as a school boy. Schooling was also structured in set ways: learning by rote, the use of the cane and an emphasis on reading the Latin classics, so Ovid, Plautus and Cicero would have been part of the curriculum. We see some of this reflected in Shakespeare's work: the reliance on Ovid's *Metamorphosis* is blatant as both plot device and as part of the plot in *Titus Andronicus*; Plautus is the source for much of *The Comedy of Errors*, for instance. Thus Jonson's remark about Shakespeare's "small Latine and lesse Greek" has to be seen in the context of an age when many were well versed in both Latin and Greek, when a university education was primarily in those two languages and when a grammar school education might have provided some knowledge of the languages and their literatures but would not have been seen as comparable to those who had a certified education. Indeed, Shakespeare's education remains more a matter of conjecture than certain knowledge, to this day, as no records survive of his schooling and we do know that he did not go to university. Indeed, even his schooling might have been cut short with the onset of his father's financial problems.

The next clear mention we have of William Shakespeare is the confusing record of his marriage: two records survive, and in each the name of the bride is different. Thus one (dated 27 November 1582) records the granting of a marriage license for the marriage of William Shakespeare to Anne Whateley, the second (28 November 1582) speaks of the posting of a bond for the marriage of William Shakespeare and Anne Hathaway. Today it is assumed that the name of the bride in the first was the result of a clerical error and we do know that William Shakespeare, at the age of eighteen, was married to Anne Hathaway, a twenty-six-year-old, who was already pregnant when the marriage took place. Their first daughter, Susanna, was born six months later in May 1583, and in 1585, twins were born to Anne and William Shakespeare: Hamnet and Judith. After this we next hear of William Shakespeare in 1592, in London. The intervening years are usually called the "lost years", as there is no mention of what Shakespeare did during those years.

The first we hear of Shakespeare after this is the mention made of him in Robert Greene's *A Groats-worth of Witte* (1592) wherein he says, "Yes trust them not: for there is an vpstart Crow, beautified with our feathers, that with his *Tygers hart wrapt in a Players hyde,* supposes he is as well able to bombast out a blanke verse as the best of you: and beeing an absolute *Iohannes factotum,* is in his owne conceit the onely Shake-scene in a country" (Greene). That the reference was to Shakespeare is clear because of the punning "Shakes-scene" but also because of the line "Tyger's hart wrapt in a players hyde": a line that has its genesis in *Henry VI, Part 3* wherein Shakespeare wrote, "O tiger's heart wrapped in a woman's hide"

(I.iv.138). While today the Henry VI plays are comparatively little read or performed, we can gain an understanding of the success that was Shakespeare's by the inclusion of this line in Greene's satirical and angry outburst against playwrights who were not as educated as the University Wits but whose output was still popular, arguably more popular than that of Greene himself who died in poverty and relative obscurity shortly before *Groats-worth of Witte* was published. The reference in Greene's pamphlet caused some uproar and was responsible for a public acknowledgment of Shakespeare's worth by Greene's friend, Henry Chettle, who had initially seen to the publication of Greene's *Groats-worth of Witte*.

Several assumptions can be made based upon Greene's statement: for one, by this time (1592) Shakespeare was an accepted part of the London theatrical scene, well enough for other playwrights and players to recognise him and feel aggrieved against him. Secondly, the line attributed to him indicates a measure of popularity to his work which helped in identifying him. Thirdly, his work while popular, was seen as lacking in erudition and as not measuring up to the standards set by the University Wits and the more educated playwrights of the time (calling him an "upstart crow", speaking of his verse as "bombastic", etc.). Finally, the rancour and ill will against the young William Shakespeare is visible in the overall tone as well as the specific insults being heaped on him by Greene. So what had Shakespeare been doing to cause Greene to hold him in such distaste?

Given the accepted chronological sequence of Shakespeare's work, we know that by the time Greene wrote his acerbic indictment Shakespeare had already written the three parts of *Henry VI*. In the following two years (by 1594) he had added at least another five plays to the number, including *Titus Andronicus*, *Richard III*, *The Comedy of Errors* and *The Taming of the Shrew*. In addition, he had also written and published two long narrative poems: *Venus and Adonis* and *The Rape of Lucrece*. Shakespeare's prolific writing was matched only by his experimental drive: history plays, comedies, tragedies *and* poetry were all part of his monumental output during these years. In addition, we have a record from March 1595 which tells us that William Shakespeare, with Will Kempe and Richard Burbage, was paid twenty pounds by the Treasurer of the Royal Chamber for a performance they had presented before the queen the previous Christmas. This document[2] helps us to understand several facts: that by this time Shakespeare was part of the playing company, the Lord Chamberlain's Men; that his playing company was highly regarded, so much so that they presented performances at the court itself; that he alongside Burbage and Kempe was a principal sharer in the company and that he was accounted as such by the authorities. One must acknowledge that these were no mean achievements given he had come from the country and was still finding his feet in London. Also to be factored in is the truth that he had no formal education as such and was thus, in a very real sense, living by his wits, in a world wherein many of those who were in the same profession had university degrees.

By the time we are at 1595 there is no looking back for Shakespeare: he continues in London, playing an active part in the world of the theatre till 1612 when finally he retires and returns to his hometown. So what did Shakespeare do in these intervening seventeen years? For one, as scholarship has demonstrated repeatedly, he *wrote*: busily, swiftly, often superlatively, sometimes in a pedestrian fashion but he was, nearly always, writing. In addition, he was also part of the Lord Chamberlain's Men, after the ascension of King James, renamed the King's Men. As a principal sharer in one of the foremost companies of the time (the other being the Lord Admiral's Men), he participated in performances, was responsible for the daily activities of the company, from rehearsals to maintenance of the costumes and all this, in addition to writing for his company's players, approximately two plays every year, sometimes more. Today when we speak of Shakespeare as having written between thirty-six and thirty-eight plays, when we revile the pedestrian verse in one and the borrowed plot in another, what we tend to forget is that Shakespeare was not crafting great literary masterpieces during his years in London. The work of the playwright in Renaissance England was not seen as "literature": it was entertainment and the playwrights of the time were aware of that fact. They wrote to fulfil a need for a new play every two weeks or so and in the process several pedestrian plays were written, served up to the ever-eager audiences and consigned to the dust heap. In the years between 1576, when one of the first London theatres (unimaginatively named The Theatre) was built, and 1642, when the theatres were closed with the ascendance of the Puritans, many men found their livelihood within the theatre, whether as players, managers or playwrights. However, within this period, the golden age of Renaissance drama could be said to have existed from approximately 1585 to 1625, when the largest number of new plays were written and performed. By the 1620s the playing companies and theatres had a large corpus of successful plays to fall back on. It has been estimated by Maus and Bevington that "a mere twenty two men wrote over half of the twelve hundred plays of which we have any records from the period" (xx). That one playwright contributed thirty-six to thirty-eight plays of those twelve hundred, which have lasted in performance and print, speaks for the quality of the work, and the genius of the writer.

The years between 1595 and 1612 are usually divided into periods which are seen as reflective of his early maturity, then the period at which he was at the height of his powers and the final stage wherein he was approaching retirement. In the period of his early maturity (which stretches till approximately 1600), we see Shakespeare exercising his talents in a versatile manner:

comedy, tragedy, tragicomedies and history plays were all written and performed and Shakespeare was gaining a reputation as an undisputed master in every genre. The best proof of this is seen in the words of Francis Meres, who in *Palladis Tamia, Wit's Treasury* (1598) speaks of Shakespeare as rivalling Plautus and Seneca in comedy and tragedy respectively. He also lists many of Shakespeare's tragedies and comedies, a particularly valuable listing as it helps in the dating of Shakespeare's plays. Another index of Shakespeare's increasing stature is the documented fact of his material prosperity: in 1597 he bought New Place, one of the largest properties in Stratford. He is also supposed to have been instrumental in procuring the coat of arms for his father that made the Shakespeares gentry.[3] However, tempering this success was the death of Hamnet, Shakespeare's only son, in 1596. This period saw Shakespeare writing *Romeo and Juliet*, *The Merchant of Venice*, *A Midsummer Night's Dream*, *Richard II*, the two parts of *Henry IV*, *Henry V*, *Julius Caesar*, the great romantic comedies (*As You Like It*, *Much Ado about Nothing* and *Twelfth Night*), and finally, *Hamlet*, among the greatest tragedies of all time. And with *Hamlet* the period shades into the next stage in Shakespeare's career: the period of his darkest vision when he wrote tragedies and problem plays.

The prosperity that had begun in the latter half of the 1590s, as seen in the purchase of New Place, was now well established: Shakespeare could afford to purchase property and land in Stratford and he did so. Between 1601 and 1605 he bought cottages, land, half interests in leases and made other such investments. This becomes particularly interesting as William Shakespeare thus is not just a playwright and player but also a man of shrewd financial dealings, someone who invested the money he earned from his London career in the small town where he was born and to which he returned. The usual image of the mythical Shakespeare: a transcendent genius, far above the mundane concerns of the everyday, is given the lie to by these financial transactions, which show that he was a hard-headed businessman. His career in London was not just that of the principal playwright of the Lord Chamberlain's Men (from 1603, the King's Men) but also that of an actor who played the roles of older men, small character roles such as that of Adam in *As You Like It* or the Ghost in *Hamlet*. It is easy to forget that Shakespeare acted not just in his own plays but also in those by other playwrights, including Ben Jonson, who also wrote for the same playing company and lists William Shakespeare as both "Principall Comœdian" and "Principall Tragœdian" in the published versions of his plays. It is also during this period that Elizabeth I died and King James ascended the throne, an event that was of particular significance to Shakespeare's company as with the King's patronage they were now the foremost company in the land, their prosperity assured. And yet when we examine the plays of this period, we see in them a vision of humanity that is darkly disturbing. Even as order appears to be restored in plays such as *Othello*, *King Lear*, *Macbeth*, *Antony and Cleopatra*, *Measure for Measure* and *Coriolanus*, we are also left with a stinging realisation of the depths to which humans can descend, the cruelties they can so thoughtlessly inflict upon each other and the tenuous and fragile nature of familial bonds and human affections. It is difficult to reconcile the huge success of this period in Shakespeare's career with the bleak vision of humanity that pervades the work he did during those days.

In the last period of Shakespeare's active London career we see him writing a set of plays now commonly called the romances, plays that melded elements of tragedy and comedy, bringing the characters close to disaster and then eventually, sometimes after many years, helping them along to a happy ending featuring repentance, forgiveness and reconciliation. The dire vision of the tragic period is now overlaid with a happier, sunnier hopefulness, that though disasters might come, eventually joyous endings were possible. Belonging in this group are plays such as *Pericles*, *Cymbeline*, *The Winter's Tale* and *The Tempest*, written between the years 1608 and 1611. By this time, the King's Men were performing on a regular basis before the royal court: evidence exists of thirteen plays performed during the Christmas season of 1609 as also of six of Shakespeare's plays performed during the wedding festivities of King James's daughter in 1613. Also, in these years many of Shakespeare's plays were being published in Quarto editions. Additionally, many records exist of Shakespeare's financial transactions and land deals, the court cases which involved him, as also records of a marriage, births and deaths within his family, all of which work together to give us a complex picture of a man who was doing well in his professional and personal lives.

It is an accepted fact that Shakespeare retired from London to Stratford sometime in 1610–11. This is not to say, however, that after that he had nothing to do with either his playing company or other London matters. We know that he continued to write till nearly 1615. While *The Tempest* is the last known play that he authored by himself, he is known to have collaborated with John Fletcher on three plays: *Henry VIII*, *The Two Noble Kinsmen* and the lost *Cardenio* of 1612–13. It is assumed that *The Two Noble Kinsmen* was the last play that Shakespeare worked upon, in his long and prolific career. *Henry VIII* is particularly interesting as during one of its first performances, in 1613, the firing of a cannon led to the Globe burning down. (An index of the prosperity of the King's Men was that in 1614 the Globe was rebuilt and was once again the performance space for the company.) During this period of retirement, Shakespeare did not only write and collaborate with Fletcher but he also played the role of wise investor and businessman, continuing his astute management of his monetary matters. Proof of his business acumen and further proof, if any is needed, of his prosperity and success, is found in his will. It records his bequeathing money and objects to his sister, her sons, his second daughter (by her own name), and the majority of his "barnes stables orchards gardens landes tenementes & hereditamentes" as also "All the Rest of my goodes chattels leases plate jewels & household stuffe whatsoever" to his eldest daughter, Susanna.[4] This is also where people have encountered the strange bequest of the "second best bed" to his wife, giving rise to much speculation, as to the character of their marriage. Shakespeare died on 23 April 1616 and was buried on 25 April. His gravestone was inscribed with the words:

> Good friend for Jesus sake forbear
> To dig the dust enclosed here!
> Blest be the man that spares these stones,
> And curst be he that moves my bones.[5]

SHAKESPEARE'S PEERS

Who were, or are Shakespeare the playwright's peers and contemporaries? If we were to read Ben Jonson's poem on Shakespeare, titled "To the Memory of My Beloved the Author, Mr William Shakespeare", included in the prefatorial material of the First Folio, we come across one listing of his contemporaries, as in those who lived and worked alongside William Shakespeare. But interestingly, Jonson, himself a contemporary of Shakespeare, then gives us a second list of names: the Greek and Latin dramatists whom Renaissance England knew and revered.

> For if I thought my judgment were of years,
> I should commit thee surely with thy peers,
> And tell how far thou didst our Lyly outshine,
> Or sporting Kyd, or Marlowe's mighty line.
> And though thou hadst small Latin and less Greek,
> From thence to honour thee, I would not seek
> For names : but call forth thund'ring Aeschylus,
> Euripides, and Sophocles to us,

Pacuvius, Accius, him of Cordova dead,
To life again, to hear thy buskin tread
And shake a stage:

By providing us with two parallel listings Jonson raises an interesting question: are contemporaries those who inhabit the same time ("judgment were of years") as the person concerned or is it a question of temperament, talent and a reckoning of equality in those terms ("call forth . . . to life again")? While Jonson compared Shakespeare to his long-dead peers we are here concerned with those who inhabited and worked in the same spaces, at the same time as Shakespeare did, influencing his work in some way. Thus his contemporaries, or peers, for our purposes are Thomas Kyd (1558–94), the University Wits and Christopher Marlowe (1564–93) and also in the latter half of Shakespeare's career, Jonson (1572–1637) himself as also John Fletcher (1579–1625).

The Spanish Tragedy is the one play of Thomas Kyd's that survives today and still finds a place in university curricula, mainly because it is seen as the inaugural play (believed to have been produced between 1584 and 1589, though published later) for the great outpouring of dramatic art that took place in Early Modern England from about 1585 to 1625. Yet on reading it what strikes one is the excessive violence and bloodshed that is an integral part of it as well as several passages of florid and pompous poetry, today often considered laughable. The reason it continues to command our interest is because Kyd's *Spanish Tragedy* is the earliest revenge tragedy of the era and it and a now-lost play by Kyd himself, tentatively called the *Ur-Hamlet*, are said to be the precursors for Shakespeare's revenge tragedies, the early *Titus Andronicus* and the accomplished *Hamlet*. *The Spanish Tragedy* also marks an interest in the often indistinguishable nature of justice and revenge, which continued to inform several plays well into the 1600s. This early tragedy of blood brought into fashion a dramatic style wherein characters went mad, and mutilation and murder were committed onstage, thus providing enough thrills for the audience. Hieronymo's madness as also the deaths of Horatio, Pedringano, Lorenzo, Balthazar, Bel-Imperia, etc., and the biting out of Hieronymo's tongue are all on-stage in this play and Shakespeare's indebtedness to this tale of excessive violence and bloodshed can be seen in *Titus Andronicus* wherein he has mutilations, murders and cannibalism take place on stage. By the time we get to *Hamlet* this delight in gore is somewhat subdued but we do see several murders taking place on stage, as also Ophelia's madness and Hamlet's real or pretended madness. But subtler echoes of Kyd's *Spanish Tragedy* are seen in Hamlet's agonising over his delay in avenging his father's murder, strongly reminiscent of Hieronymo's puzzlement and distress that his son's murder goes unavenged by him. Additional evidence of Kyd's influence is seen in the parallels Shakespeare sets up in *Hamlet*, of sons losing their fathers and needing to avenge them, one initiated by Kyd in the episode wherein Hieronymo meets Don Bazulto, who also has had his son murdered and is seeking justice. Given these, Shakespeare's debt to Thomas Kyd can hardly be underestimated.

Our first mention of William Shakespeare in London comes in the Greene extract from his *Groats-worth of Witte* (quoted earlier) wherein the slighting reference to Shakespeare indicates the familiarity and fame that Shakespeare had already achieved in theatrical circles. At about the time Greene was writing, the main playwrights in the London theatre were the so-called University Wits, each of whom has contributed to the making of Shakespeare in varied ways. The University Wits, famous in their time, though not as well-known now, included John Lyly (c.1553–1606), Robert Greene (1558–92), Thomas Nashe (1567–c.1601) and Thomas Lodge (1558–1625), George Peele (1556–96) and the most famous of them all, Christopher

Marlowe. The collective name derives from all of them being university educated, men of learning who nonetheless chose to write for the stage. To understand the significance of that statement, one requires an understanding of what theatre and the stage meant in these years. While the theatre was indisputably entertainment it was also seen as a lowly form, catering to a large populace, often "exciting them to lust and violence" (as stated by Maus and Bevington xvi; but also seen in McRae who speaks of the theatres as sites of "disorder and immorality" [13]). The opposition to the theatre was intense and based upon various factors: those who objected to the plays being staged based their criticism on the belief that these incited rebellion, sedition and sin. The staging of plays, in playhouses which accommodated between two and three thousand people, caused criticism of the gatherings and the variety of corrupt immoral practices that flourished in the crowd, from pick-pocketing to fornication and same-sex love. The theatre was an easy target for all manner of criticism and thus play-writing as an occupation was looked down upon. The plays themselves were seen as slight, labelled "baggage" by Thomas Bodley (qtd. in Maus and Bevington xvii) when he was founding his library at Oxford in 1602, when he excluded plays from the library on the basis of their trivial nature.

It is in this atmosphere of disdain that the previously listed poets began to write for the theatre. Their innovations were many and in several areas, predominantly in language and plot structure. Though there was no unity or even sustained interaction among them, they are seen as predecessors to Shakespeare, especially as several of them have contributed to Shakespeare's own work. John Lyly, for instance, wrote plays for child actors mainly, performed at the royal court, in addition to prose romances. Today remembered for *Euphues, or the Anatomy of Wit* (1575), Lyly in this play inaugurated a prose style which derives its name from the title. To be "euphuistic" is to use language that is elaborate and employs parallel structures as well as excessive ornamentation. While Shakespeare parodies Lyly's style in his plays, he learnt from Lyly's dramatic output,[6] as also that of George Peele, to have multi-layered plots, ones wherein the lower classes and servants mirrored and parodied the actions of the main plot, itself something observed in Roman comedies. (A similar construction can be seen also in Marlowe's *Dr Faustus*.) But another influence that Lyly might have exerted over Shakespeare is with regard to the pattern of male friendship that is a visible thematic device in Lyly's work: seen in works such as *Euphues* and *Endymion* (1586–87). This was a popular element in Renaissance culture and elevated male friendship and companionship far above the love of a man for a woman. We see this being played out over and over again in Shakespeare's plays, from as early a play as *The Two Gentlemen of Verona*. But where Shakespeare departs from the prevalent creed is in examining the friendship and often demonstrating its limitations, not merely endorsing it, as is seen in the late play *The Winter's Tale*.

George Peele, another of the University Wits, is sometimes considered to have been a potential rival to Marlowe, the greatest of the University Wits. However, he distinguished himself by leading a scandalous and reckless life and died early. It is often speculated that Peele collaborated with Shakespeare in the writing of *Titus Andronicus*, or revised it considerably. In addition, Peele's chronicle play *Famous Chronicle of King Edward the First, sirnamed Edward Longshankes, with his returne from the holy land. Also the life of Lleuellen, rebell in Wales. Lastly, the sinking of Queen Elinor, who suncke at Charingcrosse, and rose again at Pottershith, now named Queenehith* (1593), though rambling and often discrete, is seen as an improvement on the earlier chronicle plays, showing the ways in which history would be treated in the theatre in days to come. Of the remaining University Wits, Thomas Lodge is remembered today for his *Rosalind: Euphues' Golden Legacy* (1590), which is the main source for Shakespeare's *As You Like It*, contributing not only plot elements but also characters and even the title. Robert Greene, as we have already seen, is immortalised as the first commentator to specifically name Shakespeare and speak of him, though in an adverse, critical manner. However, Greene's other associated-with-Shakespeare-claim-to-fame is as the author of *Pandosto, or the Triumph of Time* (1588), a prose romance in which Shakespeare found the entire plot of *The Winter's Tale*, and most of the characters too!

Christopher Marlowe, the last of the University Wits, can hardly be contained within that group or limited by that label. While he was accounted one of them, was acquainted with Thomas Nashe and Robert Greene (both of whom made disparaging comments regarding him), roomed with Thomas Kyd on occasion, and was associated with the Lord Admiral's Men, not much else is known of Marlowe's life in London's theatre world. While the scandal associated with his death is grist for gossip mills, as also the scurrilous details of his free thinking ways and his life as a spy, his reputation today rests upon four undisputedly great plays written between 1587 and 1593, the year of his untimely death. The contention that but for his early death Marlowe's work would have rivalled, if not surpassed, Shakespeare's is not something that we can debate here, though it is again undisputed that when Shakespeare's work of the same period is compared to Marlowe's, the latter's is usually acknowledged as far superior. Given that Marlowe was playwright for the Lord Admiral's Men, the rival company to Shakespeare's, we can imagine that the two were acquainted with each other. Jonson in his poem prefixed to the First Folio speaks of "Marlowe's mighty line" and that is the greatest debt owed by Shakespeare to Marlowe. When Marlowe wrote *Tamburlaine* Parts I and II, he changed the way the world looked at verse and its use in drama. Indeed, he explicitly references it in the opening speech of *The First Part of Tamburlaine the Great* when he speaks of leading the audience away from "jigging veins of riming mother wits" to the "stately tent of war" where we will hear Tamburlaine "threatening the world with high astounding terms" (Prologue). That promise is kept as the two parts of *Tamburlaine* present us with blank verse of an exceptional standard, hitherto unknown on the English stage. Further, as Marlowe went on to write plays such as *Dr Faustus* and *Edward II*, his poetic gifts only showed greater maturity and power, as witnessed by the last speeches of Faustus, especially the one beginning

> Ah Faustus,
> Now hast thou but one bare hour to live,
> And then thou must be damned perpetually.
> Stand still you ever moving spheres of heaven,
> That time may cease, and midnight never come;
> Fair Nature's eye, rise, rise again, and make
> Perpetual day, or let this hour be but a year,
> A month, a week, a natural day,
> That Faustus may repent, and save his soul.
> Olente, lente, curritenoctisequi.
> The stars move still, time runs, the clock will strike.
> The devil will come, and Faustus must be damned. (xiv)

The significant achievements of Shakespeare were possible only because of his predecessor, Marlowe, who showed him the possibilities and beauties of the English iambic pentameter.[7] It was not only the use of English blank verse that Shakespeare learned from Marlowe. Character types and characteristics, the crafting of characters who while fallen and evil nonetheless evoked sympathy and fellow feeling in the audience: these were some of the other elements in which Marlowe can be said to have influenced Shakespeare. The Jew Barrabas and Ithimore the Moor in Marlowe's *Jew of Malta*, Dr Faustus, the scholar from Wittenberg and Edward II are all precursors to some of Shakespeare's greatest characters: Shylock (*The Merchant of Venice*), Aaron (*Titus Andronicus*), Hamlet, who is also a scholar from Wittenberg, Richard II, etc. Even in terms of form Marlowe influenced Shakespeare: *Edward II*, Marlowe's history play, moves further away from the older chronicle play tradition and shows the way to Shakespeare who in the decade of the 1590s perfected the history play in England, learning from and bettering the example set by Marlowe.

While it is more difficult to mark the influence Ben Jonson had on Shakespeare's work, it is undoubtedly true that Shakespeare and Jonson were not just contemporaries but also colleagues: they were both playwrights affiliated with the Lord Chamberlain's Men (later the King's Men) and Shakespeare is listed in the "Principall Comœdians" of the performances of Jonson's hugely successful *Every Man in His Humour* (1598) in the version he published in his *Works* in 1616. Given this, alongside the fact of Jonson's exemplary tribute to Shakespeare in the First Folio, we can understand that the two had more of a relationship than did the other contemporaries we have listed thus far. Jonson presents us with several interesting facts which become pertinent in understanding Renaissance drama. For one, when he spoke of Shakespeare's "small Latin and lesse Greek" ("To the Memory of My Beloved. . .") he was gesturing towards a condition of the Early Modern: with the new grammar schools and the consequent spread of education, many in Elizabethan England were acquainted with Latin and Greek. Jonson, an erudite and scholarly man, convinced of his own talent, if not genius, was contemptuous of the lesser learning of contemporaries such as Shakespeare. At the same time, his generous temperament made him acknowledge the genius and success of the latter, so much so that he offered him the highest praise he knew, in comparing him to the greatest Greek and Roman dramatists. Jonson's own plays, written during their time together in London, illustrate the different trajectories of the drama in the time: his early comedies based upon the theory of humours were witty and satirical but also displays of knowledge and learning. His tragedies such as *Sejanus, His Fall* (1603) were again exercises in demonstrating his wide and deep knowledge of the technicalities of classical drama as well as his knowledge of ancient history. Written with a careful adherence to the rules of classical drama, observing the unities and not mixing the tragic and the comic, these were nonetheless not as successful as Shakespeare's less learned and more loosely constructed dramas. In addition to writing full length plays, Jonson was engaged from 1605 in writing masques for the royal court, in which venture he collaborated with Inigo Jones. At the same time, he was also writing the satirical comedies upon which his reputation rests today: *Volpone, or the Fox* (1605), *The Alchemist* (1610) and *Bartholomew Fair* (1614). The comedic trajectory taken by Jonson's plays is at sharp variance with those of Shakespeare's. While the latter wrote romantic comedies, with love and marriage as a significant theme and plot device, the former worked at exposing the foibles of a range of characters, presenting exaggerated portraits of particular character types and demonstrating repeatedly the follies of mankind. This was done through characters such as Corvino in *Volpone* who is willing to be cuckolded so that he may win Volpone's fortune or Tribulation Wholesome in *The Alchemist* who dabbles in alchemy for riches, even while denouncing the world and worldly attachments. Portraits such as that of Malvolio in *Twelfth Night* show Jonson's influence upon Shakespeare.

During the last decade of Shakespeare's active career life in London, after the ascension of King James I, numerous playwrights were practising their craft in the city, and they must all have been known to each other, working together, collaborating with each other but also being competitive. The main among them, as accounted today, were George Chapman (c.1559–1634), John Marston (1576–1634), Thomas Middleton

(1580–1627), John Ford (1586–c.1640), John Fletcher (1579–1625) and Francis Beaumont (1584–1616) and John Webster (c.1580–c.1634). Several of these have Shakespeare connections in one form or the other. Thus to speak of Middleton is to also consider his contribution/revisions to *Macbeth* and *Measure for Measure*, to see the resemblance between *Macbeth* and *The Witch* (1613?), and to keep in mind that in the last few years *The Revenger's Tragedy*, earlier attributed to Cyril Tourneur, has been claimed as a Middleton play. John Webster is said to be almost Shakespearean in his two greatest plays, *The White Devil* (1612) and *The Duchess of Malfi* (1612–13) with their interesting gender and familial dynamics and the impossibility of assigning easy characteristics or motives to the main female characters. It is likewise impossible to speak of most of the playwrights of the era without finding some Shakespearean echo or connection in their work and the borrowings and echoes are never one-sided. To speak of Shakespeare's contemporaries is to also note that towards the end of his career he was engaged in collaborative work for the stage, with John Fletcher. Working together they wrote *Henry VIII* and *The Two Noble Kinsmen*, though the collaborative nature of *Henry VIII* has been disputed, some claiming that it is Shakespeare's own work. Interestingly, Fletcher is responsible for one of the first sequel-adaptations of Shakespeare's work: *The Woman's Prize or The Tamer Tamed* (1611?) in which Petruchio, the tamer of Shakespeare's *Taming of the Shrew* is finally tamed and quietened.

FROM THE STAGE TO THE PAGE

Today when we speak of Jonson's or Shakespeare's plays, many of us are usually speaking of the texts of the plays, this being especially so in education: school or university syllabi teach the plays of the period as "words on a page". In the process the idea of the play as drama, performance, is usually forgotten or ignored. This is particularly true of the literature student and academic who analyses the words on the page for thematic and literary devices, studies language in detail, picking bare the bones of the text, all the while not even reading it aloud to hear what it sounds like, while when first written it was meant, not just to be read aloud, but to be acted, performed on a stage before a large audience and lines, and action and dialogue were changed accordingly.

During Shakespeare's time, the dramatist's first rough drafts were called the "foul papers", which were then transcribed, maybe by the playwright himself, maybe by a scribe into the "fair copy" of the play from which was made the "book" of the play, which was held by the company. This "book", which could also be the prompt book, was held by the book-keeper, a trustworthy member of the company, and he would have used the prompt book to make the individual actor's rolls (roles): the script for the dialogues for each character, as no actor was given the entire playscript. We have a mention of this in *A Midsummer Night's Dream* when Quince gives out the "parts" to each player and asks them to "con them" (I.ii).

The fact that several of Shakespeare's plays exist in multiple versions is an indication of the different copies of the play that were in circulation: published editions could be from foul papers, fair copies, the book of the play or even from the rolls of individual actors, combined and with a reliance upon the memory of the actors themselves.[8] While the playwright himself did not hold the legal copyright of the play, once it had been sold to the company, the company did have rights over the playscript. When unauthorised versions of the plays were published, the company would then have an authorised version published with the corrections and additions that had been incorporated into, say, the foul papers. To add to this, often plays were revised at a later date by hands other than the original playwright's. The near-impossibility of claiming that a Shakespearean play as it exists today is the product of only Shakespeare's work should be apparent at this juncture. And the same holds true for the work of many of the other playwrights of the time. Ben Jonson stands out in this era as the only playwright who deemed his work worthy of publication and thus published his *Works* in Folio[9] in 1616, while most other playwrights wrote for the stage rather than for publication.

****

The late Elizabethan, early Jacobean era was a vibrant, bustling time in terms of the theatre and drama in London. While we now speak of it as the "Shakespearean era", it is wise to remember that there were several others who were writing then whose works are as impressive and interestingly nuanced as Shakespeare's are now considered to be. This is evidenced by the fact that plays such as those by Marlowe, Jonson, Middleton and Webster continue to enjoy revivals on British stages. In addition, several of the plays of the time are also available as films and continue to be produced in ever newer versions. Thus to posit Shakespeare as unique is to overstate the case: Shakespeare was, maybe, the best among many good and great writers, all working away at entertaining London audiences.

Works Cited

Greene, Robert. *Greene's Groats-worth of Wit, Bought with a Million of Repentaunce*. 1592. Transcribed by Rita S. Bear for *Renascence Editions*, University of Oregon, 2000. Web. 21 May 2014.

Jonson, Ben. "To the Memory of My Beloved Master William Shakespeare, and What He Hath Left Us." *The English Poets*. Ed. Ward, Thomas Humphry. New York, London: Macmillan and Co., 1880–1918; *Bartleby.com*, 2013. Web. 22 May 2013.

Marlowe, Christopher. *The First Part of Tamburlaine the Great*. 1605. Ed. Alexander Dyce. (n.p; n.d) *Project Gutenberg*, 2008. Web. 23 May 2014.

——. *The Tragicall History of Doctor Faustus*. (A Text). c.1589/1604. Ed. Hilary Binda. Perseus Digital Library. 2001. Web. 23 May 2014.

Maus, Katherine Eisaman and David Bevington. "General Introduction." *English Renaissance Drama: A Norton Anthology*. New York: W. W. Norton and Co., 2002: xiii–lvii. Print.

McRae, Andrew. *Renaissance Drama*. London: Arnold, 2003. Print.

Notes

1. See <http://internetshakespeare.uvic.ca/Library/SLT/life/childhood/childhood.html> and <http://internetshakespeare.uvic.ca/Library/SLT/life/retirement/death.html> for an image of the baptism records, as also the parish register records of his death and burial.
2. See it at <http://internetshakespeare.uvic.ca/Library/SLT/life/youth/accounts.html>
3. Both these facts are illustrative of the empowering nature of the theatre: a glover's son now owned the second largest property in Stratford. The theatre made this rise in social hierarchy possible.
4. See his will's transcript at <http://internetshakespeare.uvic.ca/Library/SLT/life/retirement/will+1.html>
5. See an image of his grave at <http://www.poetsgraves.co.uk/shakespeare.htm>
6. It must be kept in mind that though we attribute a particular element to one or the other Shakespearean contemporary, several of these were becoming conventions in the theatre of the time. They are thus visible in a range of plays of the period with variations and alterations, depending upon the use being made of them.
7. While Shakespeare's use of the English language and the many words he contributed to it are worthy of an entire chapter to themselves, a brief overview is provided in the Introduction.
8. For a discussion of the difficulty of determining which of the multiple extant texts is more authentically Shakespearean, see chapter 7.

9. The words "Folio" and "Quarto" refer to the size of the page as it appeared after publication: a Quarto was a Broadside paper folded twice leading to four leaves, and eight sides that could be printed while a Folio was only folded once and hence had two leaves and four sides. These were then either stitched together or bound to make a book.

Six

The Forms of Shakespearean Drama

> The best actors in the world, either for tragedy, comedy, history, pastoral, pastorical-comical, historical-pastoral, tragical-historical, tragical-comical-historical-pastoral, scene individable or poem unlimited. (*Hamlet* II.ii.379–82)

Polonius's words to Hamlet, announcing the arrival of the players in Elsinore, also introduce us to the subject matter for this chapter: the forms of the drama in England in Shakespeare's time and what he made of them. It is necessary to keep in mind that the forms of *Shakespearean* drama discussed in this chapter were not forms exclusive to Shakespeare: indeed, he took on the forms that were already available in the period, forms such as the revenge tragedy and the chronicle play and so on. That he made something new of them is debatable: he remains in one sense, just one more Early Modern playwright, using the same forms and technical devices that his other peers were using. Variations and improvements upon the common forms are not specific to him alone and thus what follows can also be seen as an introduction to the forms of English Renaissance drama, with specific reference to the work of William Shakespeare.

While the term "genre" is usually used to distinguish between poetry, fiction and drama, the word is also employed, somewhat loosely, to classify subgenres within each category. What we are talking about in this chapter is in essence, the categorisation and classification of Shakespeare's plays, a process that was begun by Shakespeare himself when he titled his plays, continued by the editors of the First Folio and continues to this day in the efforts of academics and scholars. The last-named, interested in models of classification, work to isolate features within sets of plays that can then be seen as unifying and which, taken together, can describe a particular set.

What we today think of as the tragedy of *King Lear* was titled the "True Chronicle Historie of the Life and Death of King Lear. . ." in the Quarto of 1608, while the history play *Richard III* was titled "The Tragedy of King Richard the Third. . ." in the Quarto of 1597. The First Folio editors, John Heminges and Henry Condell, worked with three categories, dividing up the thirty-six plays it included into tragedies, comedies and histories, and these continue to be the broad categories within which Shakespeare's plays are still categorised. However, the problems inherent in Heminges and Condell's classification system are easily apparent: for one, the number itself: thirty-six? Today in addition to the thirty-six listed in the First Folio, editors include *Troilus and Cressida* and *The Two Noble Kinsmen* as well. Further, the broad classification can be disputed and debated: thus *Cymbeline*, listed in the First Folio as a tragedy, is no longer considered such, while *The Tempest* and *The Winter's Tale* are no longer seen as comedies, though listed as such. Indeed, these alongside *Pericles* are today accounted to be romances, one of the newer classifications for Shakespeare's plays. Included in this bracket are also the Shakespeare-John Fletcher collaborations, *The Two Noble Kinsmen* and the lost play, *Cardenio*. In addition, the category of history plays is sometimes divided into English history and Roman history plays, while sometimes the Roman plays are classified as just that (Roman plays) without adding the label of history plays to them. In addition to tragedies, comedies, histories and romances, a fifth classification used in contemporary times is that of the problem plays or the tragicomedies, which defy easy classification and seem to teeter on the edge of tragedy before finally achieving a somewhat comedic ending.

The brief discussion of classificatory models above should have indicated the difficulty inherent in trying to divide Shakespeare's plays into sub-genres. Given this difficulty a good question to ask at this juncture would be "why bother?" The answers to that are several, though we might dismiss the query by saying that it is part of human nature to classify and categorise. For one, the plays themselves, by demonstrating some unifying features, separate into distinct categories. Two, the idea of genres is something that Shakespeare himself was familiar with and worked within, as seen in the titles of several of his plays. This is further seen also in the plays themselves where Shakespeare sometimes comments on the forms of drama (as in Polonius's words, cited above, among others). Three, genres were integral to the Early Modern literary and dramatic imagination as they were familiar with classical work on the concept but also were revising and thinking about it further (see Philip Sidney's *Defense of Poesy* [1595] where he writes on both comedy and tragedy). In addition, if we take into account the pre-eminent position of Shakespeare's plays within education systems, classifying them helps both students and teachers to read and understand them better, or at least minimally so.

In the following sections we shall look at Shakespeare's plays in terms of the sub-genres of comedies, tragedies, histories, romances and the problem plays.

SHAKESPEARE'S COMEDIES

Shakespeare's comedies are usually termed "romantic comedies" but if we read them looking for uproariously humourous dialogue and situational comedy of the farcical, slapstick variety we will be disappointed. So then why are they called comedies at all? Comedy requires *a movement towards a happy ending* and that movement will ideally lead to an *affirmative appraisal of human nature and life*. If viewed in the light of this formula, Shakespeare's comedies are indeed comedies: most of them end in at least one marriage, some in several (most notably *As You Like It*). Yet Shakespeare's romantic comedies are not just about marriage and love, though that is inescapably one of the significant themes and plot devices. Comedy, as defined by Philip Sidney in *The Defense of Poesy,* also indicates a form that points to "the common errors of our life" holding them up to ridicule and scorn. And even as lovers wend their way towards marriage, Shakespeare also demonstrates to us the follies and intemperate nature of the world and the actors therein.

Shakespeare's romantic comedies are usually held to include *The Comedy of Errors, The Two Gentlemen of Verona, The Taming of the Shrew, Love's Labour's Lost, A Midsummer Night's Dream, The Merchant of Venice, Much Ado About Nothing, The Merry Wives of Windsor, As You Like It* and *Twelfth Night*. These were all written by about 1601, by which year Shakespeare had moved into the phase of his career when he concentrated on tragedy. And though he returned to the genre later, towards the end of his career, those plays are no longer classified as comedies but as romances now.

Most comedies present us with at least one pair of lovers: a pair who though they may love each other, is unable to unite in marriage due to some obstacle in their path. Thus romantic desire and its fulfillment, and the barriers in the way of that fulfillment are one of the chief elements of a Shakespearean comedy. We see this playing out in *Twelfth Night* where at the beginning, Orsino languishes for love of Olivia and is thwarted by her vow to observe mourning for her brother's death:

> The element itself till seven years' heat
> Shall not behold her face at ample view;
> But like a cloistress she will veilèd walk. . . . (I.i.25–27)

A Midsummer Night's Dream presents us with Hermia and Lysander who love each other but are prevented from marrying because of Hermia's father's determination to wed her to Demetrius; Portia's liking for Bassanio has to be held at bay because she is constrained by "the will of a dead father" (*The Merchant of Venice* I.ii.21–22); and in *Much Ado About Nothing*, Hero and Claudio's love cannot progress to marriage because of the schemes and machinations of Don John. Smoothening the path of true love and making it possible for the lovers to unite in marriage brings us to the end of comedy after comedy. The obstacles that arise in the path of love and marriage are often of as much, if not greater, interest than the love story itself and contribute not only to a better understanding of societal structures, norms and practices but also human nature.

While romantic love is central to the comedies, it is however presented to us with considerable complexity: nowhere is it premised to be supremely valuable and/or absolutely essential. Indeed, even as Shakespeare builds play after play upon the premise of romantic love he also undercuts its importance in those very plays. Thus in I.i of *Midsummer Night's Dream* when Lysander and Hermia swear everlasting love to each other, it is done in terms and phrases that are picturesque and contrived, and we know that Demetrius who has Egeus's favour, and who claims to love Hermia, likewise "made love to Nedar's daughter, Helena" and then turned "spotted and inconstant"(I.i.107,110). But the most well-known send-up of romantic love was put into Rosalind's mouth in *As You Like It* where Rosalind laughs at Orlando for saying that he will die if Rosalind will not have him:

> No, faith; die by attorney. The poor world is almost six thousand years old, and in all this time there was not any man died in his own person, videlicit, in a love-cause. Troilus had his brains dashed out with a Grecian club, yet he did what he could to die before, and he is one of the patterns of

> love. Leander, he would have lived many a fair year though Hero had turned nun if it had not been for a hot midsummer night, for, good youth, he went but forth to wash him in the Hellespont and, being taken with the cramp, was drowned; and the foolish chroniclers of that age found it was Hero of Sestos. But these are all lies. Men have died from time to time, and worms have eaten them, but not for love. (IV.i.81–92)

Thus to claim that Shakespeare's comedies are unalloyed in their presentation of romantic love is to be in error: they are built upon the idea that "the world must be peopled" (*Much Ado About Nothing* II.iii.213–14) but even as they posit a world wherein lovers enjoy the delights of falling in love, they also mock the notion of romantic love, pointing to its constructed nature, presenting it as an imagined state of mind, one built upon fancy and changeable.

While all plays whether tragedies or comedies contain a conflict and work towards its resolution, in comedies that resolution is arrived at by overcoming the obstacles and blocks that otherwise impede the smooth progression of the plot. We have already seen the obstacles that arise in the way of true love but in Shakespeare's comedies the "path of true love" is not the only path there is. There are usually several plots and narratives each with its own obstacles and blocks and the richness of Shakespeare's comedies comes from the fact that these multiple strands are each given their own satisfying resolution. Thus in *The Comedy of Errors* not only do the Antipholus twins discover each other but Aegeon, their father, finds his lost wife, is saved from execution by the Ephesians and has his family united. In addition, the Dromio twins are united and Antipholus of Syracuse finds a bride. Similarly in *As You Like It,* Oliver, elder brother to Orlando, is reconciled to him, Duke Senior has his dukedom restored to him, and four marriages take place! What usually happens is that with the romantic and sometimes multiple marriages at the end of these plays, the reader/viewer loses sight of the other happy endings that accompany these marriages. But intricately woven into the love stories are other stories: of fraternal enmity and viciousness, of strife between fathers and daughters or between husbands and wives, stories of debt and repayment, etc. The eventual "happy ending" depends on all of these stories finding a happy resolution, with forgiveness and pardon, affections restored and families reinstated to the satisfaction of most of the characters.

While most of the characters find their happy endings, Shakespeare also showed the impossibility of happiness for all concerned: there is usually one character who is excluded from the merry festivities at the end. This exclusion tempers the ending with a realistic note as we are reminded that it cannot be that everyone achieves happiness and contentment. Thus in *Twelfth Night* we see the sailor Antonio, who saved Sebastian, reduced to the status of an onlooker as Sebastian maries Olivia, while Malvolio marches off huffily rather than stay on where he has been mocked and scorned. Similarly in *The Merchant of Venice,* even if we discount Shylock's misery, the merchant, Antonio, whose friendship made Bassanio's marriage to Portia possible, is left single at the end, his friend now a husband. Punishment awaits Don John in *Much Ado About Nothing*, and Jacques prefers to keep company with the "convertite" Duke Frederick rather than return to the court with Duke Senior, in *As You Like It*.

While thus far we have been focusing on the resolution and conclusion of Shakespeare's comedies, the process by which that conclusion is arrived at is also worth taking note of. Comedies show us characters who achieve happiness at the end, yes, but they suffer misunderstandings, chastisements, confusion and unhappiness before they get to their festive conclusion. It is this matter that produces amusement and humour to the audience: the comedy guarantees that there will be no irrevocable harm visited upon the characters and thus one is enabled to read/view with the assurance that all the problems will be eventually solved. In the process the characters learn valuable lessons but also provide matter for the amusement of the reader/viewer and also the other characters within the play. One only has to think of Jacques in *As You Like It* or Malvolio in *Twelfth Night* to understand the truth of this statement. By virtue of his melancholy and his discontentment Jacques amuses not only Duke Senior and his other courtiers but also Rosalind in the Forest of Arden. Similarly, Malvolio provides amusement to Sir Toby Belch, Maria, Sir Andrew Aguecheek and Feste but also to the audience which enjoys his gulling. These characters, as most of those in Shakespeare's comedies, show us the failings of humanity at large, its pettiness, selfishness and foolishness. But even as we recognise these traits we are asked to laugh at them, be amused by the fallout that these traits cause and rest assured that eventually even these characters will achieve some measure of happiness, or/and understanding. However, the fact of their shortcomings and failures makes it possible to read these plays as possessing the kernel of tragedy, one which is not exploited but which can well be, and is, in some productions. Thus, most famously, Katherine in *The Taming of the Shrew* is usually played at the end as having achieved an amicable, even loving, relationship with Petruchio. But it is possible to see the end as one wherein Kate has been cowed into submission, patriarchal privilege reinstated and financial advantage taken by male power which works to the disadvantage of the free-thinking, independent woman.

Shakespeare's comedies are distinguished by other features as well, namely witty dialogue, wordplay and humour, an element of disguise and deception, and often times a setting which is other than England. While the comic in Shakespeare's comedies is often caused by situations and characters who are inherently humourous, Shakespeare also delighted in witty wordplay and some inventive and snappy word games. Among the most noteworthy examples of wit are the dialogues between Beatrice and Benedick in *Much Ado About Nothing* where neither can resist a pun or a joke at the other's expense:

> BENEDICK. Only foul words, and thereupon I will kiss thee.
> BEATRICE. Foul words is but foul wind, and foul wind is but foul breath, and foul breath is noisome, therefore I will depart unkissed. (V.ii.42–45)

We also see witty wordplay and humorous crosstalk as the clowns speak in plays such as *Twelfth Night* and *As You Like It*. Indeed, the jesters in Shakespeare's comedies are worthy of special attention as they point out the shortcomings of humanity at large but also mock conventions and customs, point out the follies of self-important personages and also sing poignant songs, play practical jokes and turn the accustomed order topsy-turvy. The element of the carnivalesque and the inversion of order is seen, in varying degree, in several of the comedies, and even in some of the tragedies, especially in *King Lear* where the Fool is the only one who can speak to Lear about the immensity of his folly. Whether it is the elevation of Bottom to the Fairy Queen's loved one in *A Midsummer Night's Dream* or Feste turning into Sir Topas the curate in *Twelfth Night*, we see the routine order of class and status being juggled with, and though the order is reinstated at the end, that temporary shuffling accords a space and time wherein there is freedom from decorum and the possibility of a different order.

Other varieties of humour are also seen, such as in the taming of Kate which includes puns and bawdy humour, in the character of Jaques in *As You Like It* who specialises in melancholy humour and Touchstone in the same play who combines bawdy humour with courtly mockery and satire.

Disguise and cross-dressing were often identified as integral to Shakespeare's comedies and we see it in *The Two Gentlemen of Verona*, *The Merchant of Venice*, *As You Like It* and *Twelfth Night* in each of which it is important to the development of the plot and at the same time adds to the humour of the play. The dressing of young boys as women who then dressed up as men and flirted with their lovers gave Shakespeare endless scope for merriment and wit but also caused him to create some of his strongest female characters who even disguised as men, still retained their femininity. Thus when Rosalind in II.iv of *As You Like It* says, "I could find in my heart to disgrace my man's apparel and to cry like a woman. But I must comfort the weaker vessel, as doublet and hose ought to show itself courageous to petticoat; therefore, courage, good Aliena!" (3–6), she offers a comment on masculine and feminine stereotypes even as she also laughs at them and shows herself to be strong and determined, not in being fearless but in working to overcome fear and tiredness. Rosalind and Viola in their male disguise are among the most fascinating of Shakespeare's female characters and never more so than when dressed as men and constantly reminding the reader/audience that they are women dressed as men!

Mistaken identity and all the havoc it causes, while central to the plot in *The Comedy of Errors* and *Twelfth Night*, was also seen in plays such as *A Midsummer Night's Dream* where the interchangeable nature of Demetrius and Lysander and Hermia and Helena brings about confusion and merriment even as it also underlines Puck's comment, "Lord, what fools these mortals be!" (III.ii.115).

While Shakespeare's comedies evoke laughter and bring about a festive merry conclusion, they do so by employing some characteristics of unpredictability, sudden inexplicable transformations and an almost supernatural intervention in the life of the mortals. While *A Midsummer Night's Dream* has the fairies who intervene and sort out the relationships in the wood outside Athens, in the other plays there are sudden transformations which help to bring about the desired ending. Thus in *As You Like It* Oliver, who has consistently persecuted

Orlando, undergoes a miraculous transformation when he enters the Forest of Arden; in *Twelfth Night*, Orsino, in love with Olivia, suddenly finds himself proposing marriage to Viola (dressed as Cesario), and Egeus, Hermia's father, at the end of *A Midsummer Night's Dream*, has to accept Hermia's marriage to Lysander with a good grace.

If in the comedies happy endings are seen to be arrived at and harmony achieved, it is by ignoring certain dimensions of the plays. Thus while strong positive women characters might be seen as having substantial roles and enjoying a degree of agency, it can only be so up to a point. By the end of the play these strong women are also silenced, or made complicit in the patriarchal society they inhabit; female friendships are replaced by heterosexual bonds and the patriarchal norm is restored. The movement from disorder to order and a restored social circle is also a movement which privileges the status quo. Shakespeare's brilliance lies in making this possible even as we see the price that is paid, and by whom, for the restoration of that order.

Shakespearean Tragedies

If the comedies present us with a world wherein order seems happily restored, the tragedies offer us worlds wherein upheavals are stilled but the question of whether this will lead to a restoration of order and a fruitful peace is left open. So while the more optimistic reader might decide that with the death of Macbeth and the coronation of Malcolm, Scotland will once again flourish, the cynic might go with Roman Polanski's (twentieth-century) vision of Donalbain who is on his way to the three witches to find out what the future holds for him! The possibilities contained in the endings of the tragedies are possibilities for good and evil and these throw open the gates for fresh tragedies. This section will examine the features of Shakespeare's tragedies, remarking commonalities with earlier versions of tragedy and the work of Shakespeare's predecessors such as Thomas Kyd and Christopher Marlowe. The identifiable tragedies are *Titus Andronicus, Romeo and Juliet, Julius Caesar, Hamlet, Othello, King Lear, Macbeth, Antony and Cleopatra, Coriolanus* and *Timon of Athens*, written between 1592 and 1609, by which time Shakespeare had begun to move into the phase wherein he wrote the great romances.

In Shakespeare's time tragedies were held to demonstrate one of two primary views. The first, stemming from the medieval worldview, was that a tragedy occurred because of the fickle nature of Fortune, so that the wheel of fortune turned and the rich and powerful lost their position and wealth. It is best expressed in Chaucer's words in "The Monk's Prologue" where he says,

> Tragedie is to seyn a certeyn storie
> As olde books maken us memorie,
> Of hym that stood in greet prosperitee,
> And is yfallen out of heigh degree
> Into myserie, and endeth wrecchedly.

This medieval conception of tragedy was built on the idea that individuals, while they may contribute minimally to their own tragic fates, were more akin to counters moved about by Fortune and this movement was cyclical, so that having touched the highest point in the circle the downfall was both imminent and inevitable. Thus Lear when he meets Cordelia says that he is "bound upon a wheel of fire" (IV.vii. 46–47); Edmund after being defeated by Edgar says "The wheel is come full circle" (V.iii.173); and Kent, dispossessed, exiled and disguised, asks Fortune to "smile once more; turn thy wheel!" (II.ii.165). The second foundational view regarding tragedy, based to a certain extent on the Aristotelian definitions and descriptions, was that tragedies resulted from the character of the protagonist. A somewhat reductive version of the classicist viewpoint regarding "hamartia" and "hubris", it was connected to errors in judgment, overwhelming pride and extreme character traits, which were held responsible for the character's tragic end. In addition to these two principles Shakespeare's world also believed in the corrective effects of tragedy (as they did also in that of comedy), as given to us in Sidney's *Defense of Poesy*: that tragedy "maketh kings fear to be tyrants ... teacheth the uncertainty of the world, and upon how weak foundations gilden roofs are builded".

While these principles might have influenced Shakespeare's own views regarding tragedy, his plays help us to list and understand the elements of a Shakespearean tragedy. These include a protagonist of high stature who falls from prosperity and some happiness to adversity, eventually death, involving not just *himself* (and Shakespeare's tragedies *are* gendered) but others as well in that tragic fall. If Shakespeare's comedies end with marriages or the promise of marriage to come, his tragedies end with death, with corpses scattered on the stage, including the protagonist's but also those of others. Thus at the end of *King Lear* both Lear and Cordelia are dead on stage, Edmund has been carried off to die, while Goneril and Regan are also known to be dead, as also Gloucester, Oswald and a servant or two. Othello dies on stage with Desdemona and Emilia having died moments ago, on stage as well. While *Macbeth* has only Macbeth's death in the final scene and Lady Macbeth's death is only reported to us, in *Antony and Cleopatra* we watch Antony die and then we see Cleopatra and her serving maids die in the last scene. Thus it should be easy enough to say that Shakespeare's tragedies involve death. But is it only death that makes for a Shakespearean tragedy? Or is there more to it than that?

Most Shakespearean tragedies begin with the protagonist in a relatively successful and assured state *but* one wherein the germs of his downfall are already perceptible. (The exception to this is *Hamlet,* where the play opens with Hamlet already dispossessed, his father dead, his mother re-married and his life a shambles around him, as also *Antony and Cleopatra* where Antony's greatness is a thing of the past in the first scene itself.) In plays such as *Macbeth*, *Othello*, *Julius Caesar* and the others we see that the protagonist is, at the beginning, in a situation wherein his virtues are recognised and lauded, his prosperity and power is assured and everything appears to augur well for him. The shift from that mood of prosperity and success through conflict and despair to a resolution which, while it offers release and peace, also epitomises waste and tragic failure is the usual trajectory of a Shakespearean tragedy.

To go back to Aristotelian ideas regarding hamartia, hubris and catharsis, while useful minimally, these cannot explain or do justice to the complexity that is contained in Shakespeare's tragedies. The idea of hamartia was long translated (loosely) as a flaw when it originally meant an error in judgment. Hubris is usually translated as pride but was often, according to Linda Woodbridge, just an "outstanding quality or conspicuous behavior that brings one to the attention of the jealous gods" (213). If considered in this context, we can see that to analyse characters such as Othello or Hamlet in terms of his fatal flaw (jealous pride and over-sensitivity respectively) might be simplistic, reductive and might well be doing a disservice to the play itself. Similarly, the concept of catharsis raises more questions: the idea that we feel pity and fear on viewing/reading these plays works well enough but that we are purged of these emotions is to imply that tragedies allow us a safe channeling of these affects which then renders them safe.

The tragic hero's exalted stature is of particular relevance in our consideration of tragedy because it helps us to see the fall in more stark terms: the height from which the fall occurs makes the extent of that fall even more tragic and devastating. But the hero belonging to the upper echelons of society also makes it possible for the tragedy to be not only personal but also that of an entire social group, a society, even a nation. Thus when Macbeth takes the crown of Scotland, rendering himself sleepless and despairing, Scotland is also laid waste:

> . . . Each new morn
> New widows howl, new orphans cry, new sorrows
> Strike heaven on the face that it resounds
> As if it felt with Scotland and yell'd out
> Like syllable of dolour. (IV.iii.4–8)

Hamlet shows us a Denmark which is in the shadow of war and revolt (see I.i and ii for external threats and IV.v for threats of rebellion and revolt from within). When the tragedy of *Antony and Cleopatra* unfolds, it does so on a stage which ranges from Rome to Egypt, and shows us a world in disarray. The standing and importance of the heroic figures determines the stability of their world and when they fall the crash resounds through their universe. The restoration we see at the end of the play is a re-establishment of the world to a state wherein the consequences of the fall of the protagonist can be dealt with, overlooked and crossed over: the personal is glossed over in favour of a restoration of a stable society. Thus stature refers to the protagonist's larger-than-life personal stature *and* his leading position in society.

So, can it be said that the tragedies are concerned with both the personal and the political? And to what extent do these plays plot the narrative of a man of high stature, his personal shortcomings and his public role? While criticism prior to the twentieth century and even in the first decades of the twentieth century saw these plays as political *and* personal, labelling only *Othello* a domestic drama, these classificatory models are no longer seen as the only ones available to us. Each of these plays demonstrates the tragedy of a *man in society*, a society which is, in some part, responsible for the tragedy that ensues. A play such as *Othello* is now seen to be tragic not only because of Othello's character traits but because of the society in which he lives, which with its racist and misogynist ideology makes it impossible for both Desdemona and Othello to survive. The world of *Macbeth*, a world predicated on masculinity defined in terms of violence, makes it inevitable that finally there can be only violence and death.

While it is impossible to separate the political from the personal and social in the tragedies, it is also necessary to think of the tragedies as explorations of an individual's private and personal self. The tragedies, especially Shakespeare's major tragedies, show us the ethical and moral selves of their protagonists: we see their individuality, their interiority. We do not read the tragedies without seeing characters such as Brutus, King Lear, Hamlet, even Antony as individuals who ponder their own selves, their desires, their agency or lack thereof. This dwelling upon the protagonists' selves makes the tragic form, as practised by Shakespeare, an examination of personality types and an assessment of fully developed characters who are possessed of a degree of interiority which compares to that of real-life individuals. One of the techniques by which Shakespeare does this is, of course, the soliloquy: the use of the soliloquy by the tragic protagonists (and sometimes by the antagonists, as Iago in *Othello* I.iii and II.iii) reveals them to us in all their complexity and the wide range of their moral and ethical dilemmas. While Hamlet's use of the soliloquy is well known, it should be noted that Macbeth also reveals himself in his soliloquies as do both Iago and Othello, and Edmund and Edgar in *King Lear*. This revelation of the self which takes place in most of the major tragedies makes it possible for us to "know" the characters in considerable complexity.

The gendered nature of Shakespeare's tragedies has come in for some criticism and while the heroes have been admired and looked up to over the centuries, it has taken much re-visioning in the latter half of the twentieth century for the women in Shakespeare's plays to be seen as other than stereotypical.[1]

While mothers and wives are flawed, daughters are no less culpable and the women in the tragedies fall easily into set types. There is the good woman: submissive and quiet, best described by Lear, speaking of Cordelia (but after her death): "Her voice was ever soft, / gentle, and low, an excellent thing in woman" (V.iii.271–72), and Brabantio, speaking of Desdemona before he discovers her perfidy in loving Othello:

> A maiden never bold,
> Of spirit so still and quiet that her motion
> Blush'd at herself; (*Othello* I.iii.94–96)

The best example of this would be Ophelia: while the others assert themselves at crucial junctures, Ophelia falls in line with the orders given her by her father, signing her self, her mind, away. And then there are the lustful women: given to lasciviousness, voluptuousness and the pleasures of the flesh (Desdemona as imaged by Iago and believed to be so, in the latter part of the play, by Othello, and Gertrude who is said to "prey on garbage" (I.v.57), as also Cleopatra and of course, Tamora of the Goths in *Titus Andronicus*). And finally there are the scolds and the viragos: Lady Macbeth, Goneril and Regan and the strong woman emasculating her warrior son, Coriolanus's mother Volumnia. Interestingly, all the tragedies, except *Coriolanus*, end with all the women characters killed, ensuring barren landscapes, unpeopled worlds in the days to come.

While Shakespeare may be held by some to build upon Aristotelian concepts such as those cited above, one realm in which he breaks free of the classical models is in including some comic elements within his tragedies. Called comic relief by the early critics these are the scenes that involve some wit and humour in the midst of the darkness that tends to appear overpowering. Scenes such as the gravediggers in *Hamlet*, the Fool's witticisms in *King Lear* and the Porter scene in *Macbeth* are all held to provide the readers/audience with a little relief from the unmitigated gravity and sombre mood that otherwise prevails. While these comic interludes are humorous, they still retain a thematic link to the tragedy, pointing out aspects which might otherwise have been missed. Thus the Porter in Macbeth speaks of himself as the Porter of Hell and metaphorically we are introduced to the idea that Macbeth's castle has indeed become a Hell. In *King Lear* when the "all-licensed Fool" (I.iv.175) mocks Lear and calls him a fool he points out what the courtiers could not, and what Lear himself cannot see. Thus even as the comic scenes might be funny, causing laughter, they are also part of the tragic texture of the plays intensifying the gravity even as they also point to crucial aspects of the theme.

What is more valuable vis-à-vis the tragedies is the question as to what we feel for the tragic protagonist: do we sympathise with him, see him as suffering undeservedly, see him as a scapegoat for/in a society wherein he carries the punishment for what so many others do? Shakespeare raises this question repeatedly in tragedy after tragedy, beginning with the early *Titus Andronicus* and continuing through plays such as *Macbeth* and even *Coriolanus*. What makes this particular problem even more interesting is the fact that, in the later plays, the heroic figures are less attractive, less easily liked: on his best day Coriolanus remains a "mama's boy" and a war machine; King Lear is petulant, given to self-aggrandizement; Macbeth a petty murderer, even if he does speak some magnificent poetry, etc. Yet what is it about these and the others who people Shakespeare's tragedies that causes us to feel pity, sympathy and sorrow? It can hardly be claimed that we are enthused by fellow feeling: the affect captured in the phrase "there but for the grace of god, go I". These are characters who are larger than life, their sufferings colossal, their actions such that they change worlds by them. The answer lies somewhere in that immensity and grandeur: their sufferings are so terrible that we are awed by it, both by the capacity to cause such pain and to suffer it. Even as we acknowledge that they are the authors of their own fate, to some extent, we also see the enormity of their potential, a wasted potential; we see their descent into a suffering that might lead them into madness and that sense of scale and magnitude and the overwhelming sense of dissolution, of an individual and his world cast adrift, is what works to create and underline the tragic effect. When Aufidius addresses Coriolanus as "thou boy of tears" (V.vi.103) in the final scene of the play and Coriolanus breaks down, reminding himself and the others of how

> Like an eagle in a dove-cote, I
> Fluttered your Volscians in Corioles.
> Alone I did it. 'Boy'! (V.vi.115–17)

we, the readers and viewers, know full well the enormity of the fall he has suffered and that for him death is the only way out: a death died with dignity, even as Macbeth's is, even as we recognise the truth when Antony says

> Bid that welcome
> Which comes to punish us, and we punish it,
> Seeming to bear it lightly. (*Antony and Cleopatra* IV.xv.134–36)

It is in these deaths, and in the words that each of the tragic protagonists speaks before they come to their death, that we see them achieve their greatest glory and transcend the errors and misjudgments that have nonetheless made it inevitable that they should die.

HISTORIES

While the First Folio itself gives us "Histories" as one classification for Shakespeare's plays, the history play was in its initial stages of evolution during Shakespeare's time. Ten of Shakespeare's plays are considered English "Histories" as opposed to the Roman history plays. The English history plays have their origins in earlier forms of the English drama, such as the interlude and the chronicle play. The interludes, according to Stephen Greenblatt were, "in effect, staged dialogues on religious, moral and political themes. . . . The structure of such plays reflects the training in argumentation that students received in Tudor schools, and, in particular, the sustained practice in examining all sides of a difficult question" (32). The same mode, of examining all sides of a "difficult question", is apparent in Shakespeare's history plays. Other forerunners of the history plays included the English political-morality play, in which, often enough, tyrants and their ill effects upon kingdoms were presented and where the focus was on the kingdom and the body politic: examples include one of the earliest dramas of the Elizabethan stage: Sackville and Norton's *Gorboduc* (1562). While Shakespeare's history plays are the best known (and still revived and popular of the history plays of the period), others such as Marlowe's *Edward II* and Thomas Heywood's *Edward IV* were also popular doing the period. While some of these were called "chronicle" plays, the line dividing chronicle and history plays is slight and depends upon interpretive strategies as much as the plays themselves. Chronicle plays are held to be more episodic in nature, united by characters rather than a thematic, as opposed to history plays which are (supposed to be) more plot and theme oriented.

Shakespeare's English history plays include the seven Henry plays (*Henry VI*, parts I, II and III; *Henry IV*, parts I and II; *Henry V* and *Henry VIII*), *Richard II* and *Richard III* and *King John*. These are usually divided into the two tetralogies: chronologically, historically, the first comprises *Richard II*, the two parts of *Henry IV* and *Henry V* (often called the Great Tetralogy), while the second includes the three parts of *Henry VI* and *Richard III* (usually called the First Tetralogy as it was written earlier than the Great Tetralogy). The history these plays recount gives us the story of the rise of the Lancastrian line, the

Wars of the Roses and eventually the rise of the Tudors. While it is perhaps possible to read these as straightforward narratives of the reigns of the English monarchs, to do so is to elide the complexity that characterises them, not in terms of plot lines as much as in terms of characterisation and the themes that can be deduced. In addition, it is well to bear in mind that Shakespeare may or may not have written these plays as a cycle, as they are received and read today. While we speak of the English history plays of Shakespeare, it should also be kept in mind that Shakespeare also wrote the so-called Roman history plays, *Julius Caesar*, *Antony and Cleopatra* and *Coriolanus*, not forgetting that record of youthful enthusiasm and excess, *Titus Andronicus*. While the last named is not strictly speaking a history play as much as a Roman play, the others do treat of incidents and characters from Roman history, using the accepted historical narrative to explore issues related to the nature of power in the realm of politics, relationships, etc.

The features of the English history plays include, initially, the focus upon the reign of an English king and the events during that reign. In the eight plays which together comprise the two tetralogies, Shakespeare does not merely focus on the events which take place within the time frame of the play but he also looks ahead to what is to come (as in the two parts of *Henry IV*, where we are asked to look forward to the reign of Henry V) or ponders on the glories of what has been, or will soon be lost (as in the three parts of *Henry VI*). This feature which adds a certain resonance to the plays also transforms them from being mere recitals of events and incidents, mostly war-like, into depictions of an age with all its attendant hopes and worries and troubles, and their consequences. Thus in *2 Henry IV*, after the death of Henry IV when Henry V is first seen in public, he himself reminds the audience of both his youthful excesses and his proposed trajectory in the future as monarch:

Presume not that I am the thing I was,
For God doth know, so shall the world perceive,
That I have turned away my former self;
So will I those that kept me company.
When thou dost hear I am as I have been,
Approach me, and thou shalt be as thou wast,
The tutor and the feeder of my riots. (*2 Henry* IV V.v.54–60)

Another common feature of the history plays is that most of them end with the death of the eponymous monarch, except significantly *Henry V* which ends with a proposed marriage, that of the king to the daughter of the defeated king of France. This feature should lead us to ask a question regarding the generic properties of the histories: if most of them end in the death of the protagonist, can they be categorised as tragic histories? And in that case, is *Henry V* a comedy? Following from this we should then be able to ask further if each of these history plays, in its entirety, contains the elements of tragedy too?

Where the histories deviate from Shakespeare's tragedies and comedies is in their meld of the tragic and the comic, best seen in the two parts of *Henry IV*. While the primary narrative of the *Henry IV* plays remains that of the rebellions against the Crown, the parallel narrative gives us the humorous subplot of Falstaff and Prince Hal, a subplot which has in it slapstick, practical jokes, witty banter and lewd humour. However, what distinguishes the history plays is that these do not remain strictly differentiated: the narrative of the rebellion, especially in *1 Henry IV* where Hotspur is the leader is also distinguished by flashes of wit and humour, especially as we watch Hotspur grow incandescent in his anger and vigour, in his sparring with Glendower, in his keeping his wife at arm's length, etc. Simultaneously, Falstaff's antics and those of his party are also imbued with an overtone of sadness at the recognition of extreme waste. That Falstaff with all his talents should be thus is what strikes one and by the time we come to the end of *2 Henry IV* and Prince Hal, now the king, rejects his drinking friend, we are conscious of the terrible nature of what transpires: as Falstaff realises that his Hal is his no longer, but is now Majesty, we see the tragic counterpoint to the comic sequences of the two plays. Thus the histories present us with the tragic and the comic inextricably woven together, in historic detail.

The history plays, even as they present history with its extensive complexity, also examine the nature of kingship, power and its effects and also the dynamics of a court and its politics. It must be kept in mind that the history plays largely work with history in the old accepted form: top-down. While there are episodes and events where the common man figures, the history plays present a world of royals and nobles and their concerns and worries. The troubling and troubled quality attached to kingship is something that surfaces again and again in the history plays: kingship is never presented as unadulterated joy; indeed, Shakespeare points us to the disquiet that attaches to being a king. This can be seen, most easily, in *2 Henry IV*, where the king speaks that now-clichéd line: "Uneasy lies the head that wears the crown" (III.i.31). It is however also reiterated in play after play as Shakespeare presents us with the troubled times of the kings of England, each of whom, even as he believes in his right to rule, also claims to be deeply troubled by his condition. Indeed, the history plays give us no easy uncomplicated portraits of kingship: it is shown to be a state that inspires envy, causes disquiet and leads to betrayal and treachery, ending most often in violent death:

> For God's sake, let us sit upon the ground,
> And tell sad stories of the death of kings
> How some have been deposed, some slain in war,
> Some haunted by the ghosts they have deposed,
> Some poisoned by their wives, some sleeping killed,
> All murdered. For within the hollow crown
> That rounds the mortal temples of a king

Keeps Death his court; and there the antic sits,
Scoffing his state and grinning at his pomp,
Allowing him a breath, a little scene,
To monarchize, be feared, and kill with looks,
Infusing him with self and vain conceit,
As if this flesh which walls about our life
Were brass impregnable; and humoured thus,
Comes at the last, and with a little pin
Bores through his castle wall; and farewell, king. (*Richard II* III.
ii.151–66)

The plays also help us to think about the cost of kingship: that even if the king is firmly ensconced in his kingdom and on his throne, the power that he has to exert to keep him thus is one that exacts a price of him in both physical and moral terms. In other words, the cares that accompany kingship are such that they corrupt kings and blur ideas of right and wrong. This has a particular resonance in the entire Great Tetralogy as the kings and their generals seem to have little hesitation in breaking their word, changing their minds or in obfuscating the truth, all done to keep their kingdom intact and their country strong. Thus in *2 Henry IV*, we see the rebels surrendering on the basis of Prince John of Lancaster's word:

ARCHBISHOP OF YORK. I take your princely word for these redresses.
PRINCE JOHN. I give it you, and will maintain my word;
And thereupon I drink unto your grace. (IV.i.292–94)

only to be betrayed and sent to his execution a few lines later, and the justification is a quibble, a playing with words:

ARCHBISHOP OF YORK. Will you thus break your faith?
PRINCE JOHN. I pawned thee none:
I promised you redress of these same grievances
Whereof you did complain; which, by mine honour,
I will perform with a most Christian care.

But for you rebels, look to taste the due
Meet for rebellion and such acts as yours.
Most shallowly did you these arms commence,
Fondly brought here, and foolishly sent hence.
Strike up our drums, pursue the scattered stray.
God, and not we, hath safely fought today.
Some guard these traitors to the block of death,
Treason's true bed and yielder up of breath. (IV.i.337–49)

Examples of such corruption on the part of the king and his closest friends multiply through the history plays, underlining for the reader/viewer the corruption wrought by power.

Another theme that recurs across the plays is that of succession and who might be considered a rightful king.[2] Thus from the first part of *Henry VI* through practically all the history plays the question of who has a claim to the throne and can rule is asked and answered over and over, usually involving bloody uprisings and violent death. Read in conjunction with the contemporary ideological positions regarding kingship, we see an interplay between bloodlines, male primogeniture and of course the backing of the nobility and clergy which trumps the divine right theory every time. Indeed, having once ascended to the throne, usually by eliminating the previous incumbent, each king claims divine sanction and providence as having been the reason for his victory and coronation. Thus in *Richard II* the final scene begins with Richard dead and Bolingbroke crowned as Henry IV and his courtiers speak of his "sacred state" (V.vi.6). Similarly, Richmond's victory at the end of *Richard III* is hailed: "God and your arms be praised, victorious friends! / The day is ours. The bloody dog is dead" (V.viii.1–2).

Thus divine sanction and support is claimed once the throne has been seized and the previous monarch deposed and (preferably) dead. The issue of having a rightful claim, via blood and lineage, depended upon the ability to enforce that claim and this, in turn, depended upon the support of the powerful nobles. Shakespeare's careful negotiation of this tricky terrain only failed once: when a 1601 staging of *Richard II* was taken exception to by Queen Elizabeth, as it was staged on the request of Essex's supporters, immediately prior to a rebellion that he had planned.

While questions as to the accuracy of Shakespeare's facts and dates have always been raised and debated, historical, factual veracity is not the only criterion used in debating the "truth" of Shakespeare's history plays. The plays often alter history, in minor and major ways: incidents and events are invented, as are characters (notably most of Prince Hal's low-life associates in 1 and 2 *Henry IV*), some characters collapse two or more historical figures into one character, events and characters are moved around to provide a tighter plot line and so on. Thus Prince Hal and Hotspur, seen as contemporaries in the two parts of *Henry IV*, were actually separated by twenty years or more in actual historical fact. Other historical facts that are changed include the fact of the surrender of France after the Battle of Agincourt in *Henry V*: France surrendered five years after the defeat at Agincourt! The "truth" factor in the history plays of Shakespeare does not adhere in factual accuracy but in the truth embedded in the larger questions that these plays raise: questions which are instrumental in understanding both history and politics but also the role of memory in the writing of history. While Shakespeare's historical accuracy can be questioned, his understanding of the nature of power, the necessity of adopting Machiavellian ways, the corruption and vice that attends upon the courts of kings and the tensions and stresses of being a king, are all relevant even today. While monarchy may no longer be relevant in today's democracies, Shakespeare continues to speak to those who seek to understand the nature of power, particularly, political power. If read from this viewpoint, it might well be "more profitable to think of these texts as political rather than 'historical' plays" as Michael Hattaway pointed out in his introduction to Shakespeare's history plays (14).

The popularity of history plays in Shakespeare's time has been a source of some curiosity. The most popular view is that which sees the plays as feeding upon a growing English nationalism which required a historical basis; but there are other views regarding this phenomenon as well. Thomas Nashe spoke about how dramatising history made it possible for great English heroes to once again find a place in the popular imagination: that plays revived and revivified "our forefathers valiant acts" and "raised (them) from the Grave of Oblivion" (qtd. in Howard 135). By focusing on great heroes and heroic actions playwrights inspired the viewers with patriotic feelings towards their country and its past. They further consolidated the nation building that was already in process in Elizabethan England by making it possible for the common theatre-goer to familiarise her/himself with a history that would otherwise have been unavailable to him/her as it was only available in the *Chronicles* of Holinshed or Edward Hall. While Shakespeare (and other dramatists) drew upon historical accounts such as Raphael Holinshed's *Chronicles of England Scotland, and Ireland* (1587) and Edward Hall's *The Union of the Two Noble and Illustre Famelies of Lancastre and York* (1548) for their plays, the ordinary person depended upon the dramas of the time to give them a sense of the history of England.

ROMANCES

If the classificatory model of the First Folio were to be employed, the forms of Shakespearean drama are only three: the comedy, the tragedy and the history play. However, it has become the norm to include at least one more classification when talking about Shakespeare's plays and that is the romance. In contemporary times, *Pericles*, *Cymbeline*, *The Winter's Tale* and

The Tempest (all written towards the end of Shakespeare's career) are classified as romances, though initially the editors of the First Folio included *The Tempest* and *The Winter's Tale* among the comedies and *Cymbeline* among the tragedies while *Pericles* was not included in the First Folio. Recent critical work has created one more classification: the so-called "problem plays" or "dark" comedies, which include plays such as *Measure for Measure*, *All's Well that Ends Well*, *Troilus and Cressida* and *The Merchant of Venice*.

The last plays of Shakespeare, now called "romances", are often also called "tragicomedies". Written between 1608 and 1611, they share common features and themes and show a movement away from the tragic phase of Shakespeare's career. The term "romance" connects them to a genre that was familiar to the English from Chaucer's time, if not earlier. Romance indicates a world dominated by chance, not character, and customarily included wandering heroes, near disasters, strange coincidences and eventually near-miraculous reconciliations and reunions. Medieval and Early Modern romance was a prose or verse form detailing the adventures of a hero, in episodic form with no particular shape to them. These were popular in English as tales of chivalry or as folk tales, in forms as disparate as Spenser's *Faerie Queene* (1590) and Robert Greene's *Pandosto* (1588). Shakespeare's use of the form involved a mixing of many modes as well as a reworking of the classical notions regarding drama, that were often employed in any discussion of theatre in his time.

The alternative label of "tragicomedy" indicates to the reader the modes of the romance as practised by Shakespeare, as also the collaborators, Beaumont and Fletcher, who also wrote tragicomedies such as *Philaster* and *A King and No King*. These included the following features as indicated by Giambattista Guarini, in his *Compendium of Tragicomic Poetry* (1601):

> He who composes tragicomedy takes from tragedy its great persons but not its great action, its verisimilar plot but not its true one, its movement of the feelings but not its disturbance of them, its pleasure but not its sadness, its danger but not its death; from comedy it takes laughter that is not excessive, modest amusement, feigned difficulty, happy reversal, and above all the comic order. (qtd. in Foakes 250)

In this description is the essence of the form, particularly in phrases such as "its movement of the feelings but not its disturbance of them" and "happy reversal and above all the comic order". The former indicates how close the form comes to tragedy, exciting similar feelings while not carrying it through to its logical conclusion, instead reversing that conclusion and affirming the comic order, as the latter phrase indicates.

A defence of the genre was also issued by John Fletcher, after *The Faithful Shepherdess* failed, in which he speaks about how the romance blends elements of tragedy and comedy into a new whole in which it would be impossible to separate the two. Speaking of tragicomedy, he says it

> . . . is not so called in respect of mirth and killing, but in respect it wants deaths, which is enough to make it no tragedy, yet brings some near it, which is enough to make it no comedy, which must be a representation of familiar people, with such kind of trouble as no life be questioned; so that a god is as lawful in this as in a tragedy, and mean people as in a comedy. (qtd. in Forsyth)

In each of Shakespeare's romances the characters are brought to the edge of disaster before things come right again, often enough by chance, coincidence or the intervention of the Gods. As in the tragedies the romances are peopled by rulers and their children, people of high degree who suffer misfortunes of an extreme nature. Thus in *The Winter's Tale* Leontes loses both his children and his wife due to his intemperate, suddenly ignited jealousy; Imogen in *Cymbeline* is almost a victim of both rape and murder, while her father Cymbeline, who lost his sons twenty years ago, now loses his daughter too; Pericles is separated from his daughter and wife; while Prospero in *Tempest* is exiled from his kingdom, a survivor on a desert island for twelve years. These misfortunes come about suddenly and to characters who are ill prepared for them. The element of chance thus is part of the plot from the beginning itself. The routine and quotidian is held in abeyance in the world of the romances, replaced by the unexpected, often enough the horrific, and the miraculous.

But if the tragic events are sudden and unexpected so too is the reversal that occurs and the happy ending that results: when everything appears to be heading towards a disastrous ending, miracles occur, the lost are restored to those who still grieve that loss and there is forgiveness, restoration and renewal.[3] In fact the miraculous is portrayed as the work of divine intervention in plays such as *Cymbeline,* where Jupiter descends on to the stage on an eagle, in the final scene, or *Pericles* wherein Diana, the goddess, appears to Pericles as in a vision. The Gods and Goddesses point the way ahead to the characters and pave the way for the final reconciliations. So at the end of *The Winter's Tale* Leontes is reunited with his wife and long-supposed-dead daughter; Cymbeline discovers that the sons he thought dead are alive and well as is his daughter; Pericles regains Marina and also Thaisa, his wife; and Prospero is restored to his kingdom, his daughter marries Ferdinand, the prince of Naples, and all ends happily. What Pericles says in the final scene of the eponymous play, regarding the plot's tortuous and torturous events, is true of all the romances: "No more, you gods. Your present kindness / Makes my past miseries sports" (xxii.62–63). Further his speech to Thaisa in the final scene

> Now do I long to hear how you were found,
> How possibly preserved, and who to thank
> Besides the gods for this great miracle. (xxii.79–81)

is the norm for the characters at the end of each of the romances as they marvel at the events that have transpired, try to comprehend how they came about and eventually are thankful to the Gods and those who have helped in the restorations and reunions that eventually happen.

While the emotions evoked by the romances are extreme, these plays also demonstrate other extremes, in the matter of both space and time. To bring about these startling and excessive movements from near disaster and death to reconciliation and happiness Shakespeare employs a time frame which transcends the classical model and instead involves the passage of many years. So we see Cymbeline loses his sons twenty years before the beginning of the play and re-discovers them at the end of the play; in *The Winter's Tale* sixteen years elapse between Act III's ending and the beginning of Act IV; the plot in *Pericles* involves the passage of fourteen-odd years, etc. (*The Tempest* of course is famous, among all of Shakespeare's plays, for observing the unity of both time and place.) These long periods of time which elapse are seen as a necessity as the affect that the plays evoke and endorse are impossible to engender in an action that is restricted to a short period of time. Further, the reconciliation that features at the end of these plays is one that is built upon a sense of acceptance, repentance and the willingness to endure further sorrow as penance for the guilt of having injured the innocent. These are emotions that require time to evolve and hence the sweep of time that features within these plays is seen as a dramatic device that Shakespeare employed for the furtherance of his plays' plot lines.

In the romances or tragicomedies there are also significant shifts in location: the characters in the plays traverse tremendous distances, travel through countries and shift from courts to pastoral locations. In *The Winter's Tale* two countries are seen, Bohemia and Sicilia, the courts of two kings as well as the pastoral setting wherein we first meet Perdita and the Prince of Bohemia, Florizel. Similar shifts in location are seen in both *Cymbeline* (from Rome to Britain to Wales) and *Pericles* (which locates its scenes in Antioch, Tyre, Tarsus, Ephesus and other locations too), though *The Tempest* locates all its action on Prospero's island. The spread of geographical location, as also the many years that are necessary in bringing the action to an ending which promises happiness to all the principal characters, are both indicative of the genre's affinity to the genre of the prose romance, a genre which made it possible for many adventures to occur in unspecified or specified locations, and which happened in a loosely episodic fashion over a period of time that was left uncertain.

More than any other feature, however, what this particular genre builds upon is the close affinity between tragedy and comedy, where tragedy is averted narrowly and in the end marriages are either re-made or young lovers are about to unite in marriage. Hence in *The Winter's Tale* and *Tempest* the young lovers await marriage, but in the former Leontes and Hermione are also given a chance to renew their marriage; as also in *Pericles*, where Thaisa and Pericles are reunited; and *Cymbeline* where Imogen and Posthumus are brought together once again.

However, while most of Shakespeare's plays can be conveniently slotted into one genre or the other by itemising their features, there are some that resist easy categorisation. These include the immensely popular and problematic *The Merchant of Venice*, *Measure for Measure* and *All's Well that Ends Well*, and sometimes *Troilus and Cressida*. These are plays that present us with the traditional comic ending of lovers united or about to be so; but they also leave us uncertain as to whether these are indeed lovers or whether one of the partners is compelled to take on the role of a lover. We see this in *Measure for Measure* where the Duke wishes to marry the chaste Isabella, whose one desire is to enter a nunnery, and in *All's Well That Ends Well* where Bertram is given no option but to remain married to

Helena as she fulfils the conditions he had set for her. While *The Merchant of Venice* ends with husbands and wives united and happiness reigning, it is difficult to shake off the memory of the punishment meted out to Shylock and to rejoice without reservations. *Troilus and Cressida* presents a far worse conundrum as it ends with the death of Hector, Cressida in the Greek camp, and a disillusioned Troilus grieving the death of his brother and the loss of his lover. These plays evade easy classification, presenting the reader/audience with the problem of a complex plot which does not end conventionally, generically. Thus, even as Shakespeare's forms and genres enable one to understand the plays, they do not provide easy definitions or answers as to how to read them.

Works Cited

Chaucer, Geoffrey. "The Monk's Prologue." *The Canterbury Tales*. 1476. *The Geoffrey Chaucer Page*. L. D. Benson. Harvard, 2000. Web. 10 February 2014.

Foakes, Reginald. "Romances." *Shakespeare: An Oxford Guide*. Ed. Stanley Wells and Lena Cowen Orlin. Oxford: Oxford UP, 2003. 249–60. Print.

Forsyth, Jennifer. "*Cymbeline*: Introduction." *Internet Shakespeare Editions*. University of Victoria. 6 April 2013. Web. 16 February 2014. <http://internetshakespeare.uvic.ca/Annex/Texts/Cym/intro/GenIntro/section/Genre>.

Frye, Northrop. *A Natural Perspective: The Development of Shakespearean Comedy and Romance*. New York: Columbia UP, 1965. Print.

Greenblatt, Stephen. "General Introduction." *The Norton Shakespeare*. Ed. Stephen Greenblatt et al. 1997. New York: W. W. Norton, 2007. 1–78. Print.

Hattaway, Michael. "The Shakespearean History Play." *The Cambridge Companion to Shakespeare's History Plays*. Ed. Michael Hattaway. Cambridge: Cambridge UP, 2002. 3–24. Print.

Howard, Jean E. "Other Englands: The View from the Non-Shakespearean History Play." *Other Voices, Other Views: Expanding the Canon in English Renaissance Studies*. Ed. Helen Ostovich, Mary V. Silcox, Graham Roebuck. New Jersey: Associated University Presses, 1999. 135–53. Print.

Polanski, Roman, dir. *Macbeth*. Caliban Films and Playboy Productions, 1971. Film.

Sidney, Philip. *The Defense of Poesy*. 1581(?). *English Essays: Sidney to Macaulay*. Vol. XXVII. The Harvard Classics. New York: P.F. Collier & Son, 1909–14; *Bartleby.com*, 2001. Web. 8 February 2014.

Woodbridge, Linda. "Tragedies." *Shakespeare: An Oxford Guide*. Ed. Stanley Wells and Lena Cowen Orlin. Oxford: Oxford UP, 2003. 212–23. Print.

Notes

1. See chapter 7 for a brief discussion of how women characters from the tragedies have been re-visioned in contemporary times.
2. See chapter 1 to gain a better understanding of this aspect.
3. An interesting way to think about them is to use the Northrop Frye line of argument in *A Natural Perspective* which sees the romances as a logical extension and culmination of the comedies, where the movement from death to life is made more explicit than it is in the comedies which nonetheless contain it in an implicit fashion.

Shakespeare Ever After

Seven

Shakespeare Adaptations

Adaptation, rewriting, retelling, spin-off, condensation, abridgment, revision, spoof, revisiting, variant, appropriation, parody: the list can go on and each label moves the focus of what is meant by a degree or two in some direction, whether in terms of length (condensation and abridgment), in terms of style (parody and spoof), in terms of the degree of fidelity and the degree to which it is a new work (appropriation, variant), etc. Involved in the understanding of these terms is the extremely rudimentary concept that a prior, existing work is reworked, period. When distilled in this manner what should immediately strike any Shakespeare student is that Shakespeare himself was in the same business: he was an adapter, a rewriter, a revisionist! Thus *The Comedy of Errors* is a rewriting of the *Menaechmi* (a Roman comedy by Plautus), *King Lear* revisits *The True Chronicle Historie of King Leir* (an anonymous play of about 1590), *Hamlet* rewrites a now-lost play, probably by Thomas Kyd, which is based on Belleforest's *Histoires Tragiques* which tells a story drawn from the *Histoire Danicae* of Saxo Grammaticus: the list can be added to endlessly and only demonstrates what every student of Shakespeare knows, that Shakespeare borrowed his plots from a wide range of sources. Thus to speak of Shakespeare adaptations is to immediately be faced by a problem: are we speaking of Shakespeare's adaptations of his source texts? Or, are we speaking of those who came after him who adapted *his* works? Given the fact of Shakespeare's pre-eminent role in world literature and the layers of critical commentary regarding his original genius, his unsurpassed (and unsurpassable) talent for making all things new, we usually do not think of Shakespeare as part of the "adaptation industry". Indeed, to speak of Shakespeare adaptations is to speak of a range of texts that have borrowed from, played with, rewritten (hacked?) and revised Shakespeare's original plays and poems. It is to speak of the original and the derived, the source and the variant, the parasite and the prey, etc., wherein Shakespeare's own work is always privileged over the adaptation, where the latter is seen as preying parasitically upon Shakespeare's greatness and his great works.

In this chapter we study Shakespeare's influence: those works that have in some sense been derived from Shakespeare's plays reworked into various media and genres: their forms altered, their plots, language and characters re-visioned in accordance with other, newer contexts, in keeping with changes in cultural backgrounds,[1] in accordance with the politics of the authors or adapters, in keeping with the target audience, etc. We briefly examine the new area of literary and cultural studies called "adaptation studies"; we move on to pre-1900 adaptations of Shakespeare's work and then we study the range of Shakespeare adaptions available today, examining form, genre and media. In the concluding section we look at the motivation that brings about an adaptation: what causes people to adapt a Shakespeare play?

Through all of this it is wise to keep in mind Linda Hutcheon's pithy formulation of what Shakespeare himself did, so as to avert value judgments regarding the lesser worth of the adaptations: "Adaptations are obviously not new to our time, however; Shakespeare transferred his culture's stories from page to stage and made them available to a whole new audience" (2).

Adaptation Studies

Before examining the huge body of work that can be encompassed under the title of "Shakespeare adaptations", it is necessary to speak of the new and still developing area of literary and cultural study called "adaptation studies". Till nearly the end of the twentieth century the word "adaptation", in the non-biological and non-evolutionary realm of culture, referred in large part to print-to-film remakes, which were referred to derogatorily as "betrayal", "deformation", "perversion", "infidelity" and "desecration", a list put together by Robert Stam (qtd. in Hutcheon 2–3). But in the last two decades, adaptations have received a less prejudiced press, their virtues noted and new theories used to understand them as not only derivative and plagiarised but as *new* and *different*. Maybe it is only with the advent of postmodernism that such a change could have been possible, in a theoretical climate that foregrounded and privileged plural voices, multiplicities and an abundance of narratives rather than claiming almost divine sanction for one overarching narrative. Originality, earlier seen as essential to genius, and fidelity to the original which was the hallmark of a "good" adaptation were suddenly not as necessary as they had been. Theories and concepts such as intertextuality, palimpsestuous texts, citation and allusion have all made it possible to think of adaptations not just in terms of their fidelity to the so-called "original" but as *texts in their own right*. Thus movies such as *Ten Things I Hate about You* (1999) and *William Shakespeare's Romeo + Juliet* (1996), while adaptations of Shakespeare's *Taming of the Shrew* and *Romeo and Juliet* respectively, by their referencing of other Shakespearean plays gain an intertextual nuance, incorporating as they do several details from the Shakespearean canon. Adaptations such as these, while they build upon earlier texts, are not just aiming at blindly replicating them in a new medium or form but are making something *new* of them: exactly as Shakespeare did with his source materials. Thus Robert Browning's "Caliban upon Setebos" (1864) even while it does not have the plot of *The Tempest* nor its range of characters, can be seen as an adaptation as it reworks the relationship between Caliban and Prospero into a meditation of gods and the nature of divinity: one minor strand of *The Tempest* gaining a new focus and form.

Implicit in this new approach is also the acceptance that an adaptation is not just from printed word to film or image. Now, in adaptation studies various genre and media are included: the more traditional opera, ballet and film coexisting side-by-side with comic books, manga graphic art, poetry, short and long fiction, some of it fan fiction, drama itself but also hypertexts, video games, paintings and songs. The purview of adaptation studies tends to be almost all-encompassing and the question is often raised as to what can be termed an adaptation? Are only those texts that announce themselves to be adaptations to be considered so? Thus Baz Luhrmann's *William Shakespeare's Romeo + Juliet* must be an adaptation because it says so, right in the title itself, while *The Lion King* need not be, or is it not because there is no mention of Shakespeare, not even in the end credits? Hutcheon, as far back as 2006, defined an adaptation as "an announced and extensive transposition of a particular work or works" (7), but also went on to speak of adaptation as a process, both of creation and reception. If so *The Lion King* would then be an adaptation of *Hamlet* for a person familiar with Shakespeare's play. As she put it, "we experience adaptations (as adaptations) as palimpsests through our memory of other works that resonate through repetition with variation" (8). Thus an adaptation involves some degree of repetition but it is a *repetition* that does not *replicate*. It is also necessary to remember that a text might strike one reader/viewer as an adaptation but might have no such resonance with another who is unfamiliar with the source material. Adaptations are thus, both process and product; both announced as such (by the creator) and recognised as such (by the audience/viewer/reader); they can be media adaptations (from print to film, or from film to graphic novel, etc.) but also genre adaptations (from print to print, in terms of genre and form, etc.); they might move the setting of the text in terms of time and location, in terms of the gender, ethnicity, sexual orientation, nationality or age of the characters: any of a hundred different ways of rewriting, watching or reading might then give rise to an adaptation.

Early Shakespeare Adaptations

Given the post-Romantic emphasis on the importance of the solitary author figure and his imaginative, creative genius, any work that could be called derivative obviously would garner negative criticism in the main. But Shakespeare adaptations were in the market long before this: in fact the earliest Shakespearean adaptation was a sequel to *The Taming of the Shrew*: *The Woman's Prize, or The Tamer Tamed* (c.1611) by John Fletcher. Records exist which show that both plays were performed as an evening's entertainment for Charles I where while Shakespeare's play was "liked", Fletcher's was "very well liked" (qtd. in Fischlin and Fortier 25). Another instance of an adaptation which gained greater popularity than the Shakespeare play which it rewrote was the version of *King Lear* (1680–81) written by Nahum Tate. Tate had earlier collaborated with another adapter of Shakespeare, John Dryden, who rewrote *Antony and Cleopatra* and *Troilus and Cressida*, the former in 1677, the latter in 1679. Tate adapted three Shakespeare plays: *Richard II*, *King Lear* and *Coriolanus*, of which only *The History of King Lear* was successful. The success of the play was such that it was the only version that was produced and performed in theatres in England till the early 1800s. Other drastic adaptations, albeit also for the stage, included the 1723 Charles Johnson's version of *As You Like It*, called *Love in a Forest* which included the "Pyramus and

Thisbe" staging from *A Midsummer Night's Dream* and also the death of Oliver as a moral ending! Popular taste also changed *The Winter's Tale* into Macnamara Morgan's *The Sheep-Shearing: or Florizel and Perdita* (1754) which eliminated the Leontes–Hermione plot line with its tragic overtones and shifted focus to the young lovers. Most of the adaptations of this period retained the dramatic form but shifted focus in terms of the plot and characters, adding, eliminating, changing and reworking endings and plot lines.

The nineteenth century saw several adaptations of Shakespeare's plays, notably Thomas Bowdler's *Family Shakespeare* (1818) and Charles and Mary Lamb's *Tales from Shakespeare* (1807). Both of these represent a new trajectory in Shakespeare adaptations: they both sought to rewrite Shakespeare's plays so that they would be suitable as reading matter for a particular audience. In Bowdler's case, it was the family and the Lambs wanted it to be "easy reading for very young children" and for "young ladies" who might not be permitted to look into this "manly book" as early as their brothers, as they stated in their "Preface". Victorian poets revisited Shakespeare's plays as starting points to explore their own concerns: Tennyson's "Mariana" (1830) and Browning's "Caliban upon Setebos" being just two examples. Adaptations of Shakespeare were also being produced in Europe: Alfred de Vigny adapted *Romeo and Juliet* (1828), *Othello* (1829) and *The Merchant of Venice* (1830); Alexander Pushkin wrote a narrative poem, *Angelo* (1833), his version of the plot of *Measure for Measure*. One of the favourite ways of adapting the plays for the stage was by adding spectacle and grandeur, *Antony and Cleopatra* being one of the best examples. In the words of Rebecca Brown, performance history expert, writing for the Royal Shakespeare Company,

> In 1849 at Sadlers Wells, Samuel Phelps devised an impressive procession to accompany Antony as he returned in triumph to Alexandria, complete with numerous officers, ranked in fours,

> followed by 21 troops, three abreast. His Cleopatra entered with two sets of guards, one Egyptian and one Amazonian. Spectacle reached its zenith (or nadir, depending on your point of view) in Chatterton's production at Drury Lane in 1873, in which Shakespeare's long play was reduced to no more than 12 scenes. These scenes, of course, still took a long time to be enacted since there was so much on display for the audience's pleasure. Chatterton produced realistic galleys for the battle of Actium, a ballet, 30 choirboys and an Amazonian procession to mark the marriage of Antony and Octavia, plus a full-blown representation of Cleopatra's first meeting with Antony on her barge on the river Cydnus. (Brown)

Most of the productions of Shakespeare's plays in Victorian times were interesting more in terms of the acting, and the emphasis on pageantry and grand spectacle than in terms of adaptations involving additions, changes, emendations and cuts. But as the nineteenth century drew to a close there began appearing adaptations of Shakespeare's works that were at the vanguard of the twentieth century's impressive lineup of adaptations, in print, on film and in every possible media and genre.

What is a Shakespeare Adaptation?

Is an *edition* of a play, say the Arden edition of *Hamlet*, edited by Harold Jenkins, an adaptation? What about a stage performance, even a reading, as those advertised by the Royal Shakespeare Company (RSC) in England and the *Hamlet* reading by Samhaara in Hyderabad, my home city? A film such as the Michael Almereyda *Hamlet* (2000)? A TV show such as the BBC TV Shakespeare's version of *Hamlet* or the *Simpsons* version of *Hamlet*: "Do the Bard, Man"? Vishal Bharadwaj's three Hindi films, *Maqbool* (2003), *Omkara* (2006) and *Haider* (2014), based on *Macbeth*, *Othello* and *Hamlet*?[2] A novel such as Lisa Klein's *Ophelia* (2006) which retells *Hamlet*? Or Margaret

Atwood's short story "Gertrude Talks Back" (1994)? What about Wole Soyinka's poem "Hamlet" (1972)? Or Shel Silverstein's rap version of Hamlet (1998)? Or the Book-a-Minute version of *Hamlet* (n.d.)? Or, from Victorian times, the John Everett Millais painting of Ophelia drowning (1852)? Which of these qualifies as an adaptation and which cannot be called as such?

Scholarly editions of Shakespeare's plays, whether the Norton, the Oxford, the Arden, whether *Complete Works* or editions of individual plays, or those edited and compiled for the general reader, with neither detailed notes nor substantial introductions, are not included under the title of adaptations. Editions are based upon the plays as they were published in the late sixteenth and early seventeenth centuries: plays which might have been in Quarto or Folio format, which might have been based on performances or on the playwright's foul papers, or as transcribed in a "prompt book" and published. Editorial interventions are many, picking and choosing between variants for a word, a line, sometimes larger decisions such as choosing between various versions of the same play: say for example the two versions of *King Lear*. But these are choices which are still governed by what is available and how it best represents Shakespeare's own work: these are not governed by personal inclinations, politically motivated choices. They remain interventionist, yes, but also remain attempts to deliver Shakespeare, his work to the reader, in as close a form to the sixteenth-seventeenth century version as possible. To illustrate this consider the Oxford *Complete Works* (1986, 2005) upon which is based *The Norton Shakespeare* (1997). While earlier editions were based on the editors' tastes and on previous editions by other editors[3] rather than the Quartos from Shakespeare's time and the First Folio, in the late Victorian period these ideas changed. As Laurie Maguire says about the Oxford Shakespeare, it was "based on two beliefs: (1) Shakespeare revised; (2) staging does not sully a play. Thus the editors preferred texts adapted from stage production – versions printed from playbooks rather than from the author's longer original drafts; they provided two texts of *King Lear*; they valued stage directions from the short quartos. . ." (591).[4] What this meant was that editors did not impose their own preferences on the plays; through the editorial process they kept it in mind that the play text was meant for dramatic performance and as such there was value in the stage directions and cues given in the early editions; they did not conflate different available versions such as Q1 *King Lear* and the Folio *King Lear*, preferring to provide both versions so that the integrity of neither was damaged. While these were decisions taken keeping in mind new knowledges and new ways of thinking, the attempt was to retrieve, as far as possible, the plays as they had been produced and performed in Shakespeare's time, always holding on to the basic but earlier forgotten idea: Shakespeare wrote plays for the stage, not dramatic texts to be read, loved, taught, etc.

Performances on stage, which retain as far as possible the Shakespearean text and directions for playing it, are usually not considered adaptations either, unless they incorporate new elements, change the plot lines, drop characters or add some, etc. Thus Nahum Tate's version of *King Lear*, hugely popular in its time, is an adaptation but RSC productions of Shakespeare's plays are not. Readings (as in the plays being "read aloud") are not adaptations either as they follow the text of the play as Shakespeare wrote it. However, if the lines were to be moved around, the order changed and thus a new plot imposed upon the same play, it would become an adaptation: Charles Marowitz is one of the foremost exponents of this form of adaptation. Fischlin and Fortier speak of him creating "collages" of the plays, cutting them up "into pieces and reassembl(ing) them with no adherence to the original narrative development" (189). Thus the plot might become something completely unfamiliar, while the language remains the same, even though the speeches might be spoken by different characters from those in the

Shakespeare text. *Measure for Measure* is the most well-known of the adaptations of Marowitz though he has an entire collection: *The Marowitz Shakespeare* (1978).

Among the earliest texts to be called adaptations were those plays and novels which were made into films. The shift from the printed word to the image on screen was the most recognisable form of adaptation. This recognition, of course, always worked with the assumption that the shift was from a superior medium to an inferior one. Thus film adaptations of Shakespeare were seen as inferior to the plays, particularly as the plays were seen as print texts rather than plays-in-performance. The earliest Shakespeare film in existence is a short scene from *King John*, made in 1899, in which the king is shown signing the Magna Carta. It becomes significant not just because it is the first film adaptation but because it shows a very specific adaptation technique: it adds to the play an event that is *not* included in the Shakespearean text. Through the silent movie era Shakespeare texts were made into films though they were largely films made of staged productions, not strictly speaking movies in their own right. The first feature length sound movie of Shakespeare was *The Taming of the Shrew* with Mary Pickford starring as the shrew (1929). Again it achieves significant import because of one crucial moment: Katherine winks at Bianca at the end of her speech of submission to Petruchio, thus subverting the entire speech.[5] A clear demonstration is made of the power of cinema to add to, subvert and provide a different interpretation to the (older) written/spoken word.

The power of cinema is demonstrated over and over again in the case of Shakespeare adaptations: till the 1970s most Shakespeare films were more or less straight adaptations of the plays, adding depth to the words on the page by introducing lavish settings, renowned actors and actresses, but also made with target audiences and particular aims. One of the earliest Shakespeare films to be made with a specific intention was the Laurence Olivier *Henry V* of 1944. Made by Olivier at the request of the British government, it used Shakespeare's play as wartime propaganda, showing how a small number of British soldiers could take on and defeat their continental foes. In a different vein, Franco Zeffirelli's *Romeo and Juliet* (1968) was opulent and lavish but also meant to appeal to younger audiences with a lead pair who were closer in age to the ages of the plays' protagonists than previous lead couples. Directors from various nations such as Grigory Kozintsev, Akiro Kurosawa, Roman Polanski and Orson Welles, all established the extra advantage that cinema could give to Shakespeare's plays from the 1950s through to the 1980s.

Towards the end of the century Shakespeare film adaptations became more edgy and innovative. Settings changed and the contemporary found a place alongside movies with a more traditional setting. But it was not only the contemporary that was found suitable for Shakespeare's worlds: the Loncraine-McKellan *Richard III* (1995) took the play out of the fifteenth century and set it in 1930s London with a fascist background, decadent and corrupt. Baz Luhrmann's *William Shakespeare's Romeo + Juliet* (1996) used the Shakespeare words but moved the action into a youthful world of beaches, drugs, violence and fast cars. Kenneth Branagh's Shakespeare productions retained a largely traditional ambience and mode, but productions such as Michael Almereyda's *Hamlet* (2000) shifted the play out of medieval castles into a New York corporation called Denmark, into a world of moving images, videos, cameras and surveillance. There were also several Shakespeare films that can be called derivative rather than adaptations, especially the teen films of the 1990s and 2000s. Films such as *Ten Things I Hate About You* (1999), *O* (2001), *Get Over It* (2001) and *She's the Man* (2006) (based loosely on the plays *The Taming of the Shrew*, *Othello*, *A Midsummer Night's Dream* and *Twelfth Night* respectively) were all teen flicks, set in high schools, with sport and other school activities forming an integral part of the plot. Other interesting adaptations include the Julie Taymor *Tempest* (2010) with Prospero replaced by Prospera, the upcoming queer small-budget *Iaga* (2014), the soon to be released more traditional *Romeo and Juliet in Harlem* and several more:[6] all of which goes to prove that Shakespeare is alive and well in the film world.

The world of British television saw Shakespeare on the menu soon after telecasting started in 1936, mainly onstage performances transmitted live, an instance of using Shakespeare to give to a new medium respectability and the appearance of sophistication. The BBC from the 1950s has invested in filming Shakespeare in various versions for television audiences. Thus Shakespeare's English history plays were made into *An Age of Kings* (1960), while a similar attempt involving the Roman history plays was comparatively unsuccessful: *Spread of the Eagle* (1963). The BBC's most ambitious venture was to make TV versions of each of Shakespeare's plays: the BBC Television Shakespeare project (1978–85), which succeeded financially, though some of the productions were bland and insipid, lacking the energy and verve that are usually associated with Shakespeare. Other Shakespeare adaptations have included the 2005 ShakespeaRe-Told series which shifted the Shakespeare plays into modern settings: *Macbeth* played out in a Glaswegian restaurant, *Much Ado About Nothing* in a TV studio, and so on.

Far more popular has been the incorporation of Shakespeare plays, characters, themes and quotations into popular TV series. Among the earliest was the *Star Trek* series (1966 onwards) which used Shakespeare effectively in their episodes, whether as titles, in plot elements or as tongue-in-cheek references, for example to "Shakespeare in the original Klingon"! But *Star Trek* is only one of the stars in the Shakespeare universe: the *Simpsons* have more than twenty episodes referencing Shakespeare, British series *Black Adder, Monty Python* and *Dr Who*, all have Shakespearean episodes, some of them adaptations. Several

American TV series too present characters rehearsing and playing in Shakespearean dramas, in series such as *Moonlighting, Happy Days, The Famous Adventures of Mr Magoo, Malcolm in the Middle, Gilligan's Island*, etc. While Shakespearean references (to plays, characters and quotations) are common, several of these present actual plays, shortened and adapted in some form or the other: thus in *Moonlighting*: *Atomic Shakespeare* the show's lead characters act the parts of Petruchio and Katherine in a version in which some of the original dialogue is retained and much more farcical slapstick comedy introduced.[7]

What do the Lambs' *Tales from Shakespeare* (1807), *MacB* by Neil Arksey (1999) and John Updike's *Claudius and Gertrude* (2000) have in common? These and countless others are print adaptations of Shakespeare's plays, rendered into the genres of the novel and short story. These rank alongside texts such as Atwood's short story "Gertrude Talks Back" and Gareth Hind's graphic novel adaptation *King Lear* (2009), all of which deploy Shakespeare's dramas with a focus that shifts slightly so that we see the same events, on the whole, but see them from a different viewpoint or with a different emphasis. Thus the Lambs wrote their tales with a view to familiarising young audiences with the plots of Shakespeare's plays; *MacB* shifts *Macbeth*'s action to schoolboy football and replaces Lady Macbeth with MacB's mother, exploiting the familiar figure of possessive, pushy mothers who place a weight of expectation on their children, forcing them into terrible actions and expecting them to bear up under the relentless pressure. If these are instantly recognisable as Shakespeare adaptations, what can we say about poems such as Soyinka's "Hamlet", Miroslav Holub's "Polonius" (1991) or C. P. Cavafy's "King Claudius" (1961)?

When reading print reworkings of Shakespeare's plays (as is the case with all reworkings) we need to be able to distinguish between texts that only reference incidents, characters or quotes, from those which make a sustained intervention in the

Shakespeare text, addressing different concerns, positing a new twist, creating a new character or ending, etc. P. G. Wodehouse is famous for a liberal sprinkling of Shakespearean tags through his works, but that cannot be called an adaptation. A poem such as Holub's "Polonius", or Ted Hughes's "Prospero and Sycorax" (1982), takes a character and speculates on his or her motivations, working at a critical assessment of the character, Derek Walcott's "Goats and Monkeys" (1964) analyses the relationship between Desdemona and Othello; but none of these are adaptations of the Shakespeare plays in their entirety, or even, in large part. Taken in that sense, the Cavafy poem comes closest to an adaptation of *Hamlet* as it walks the reader through the events of the play, albeit from the perspective of Claudius. The case of Shel Silverstein's Rap Hamlet is somewhat similar as he relocates the Shakespearean into a Rap version, with rhythm and profanity, making *Hamlet* a street-smart version of the philosophical play, one in which the old king has "Gertrude Forever" tattooed on himself, where Ophelia and Hamlet are involved sexually and where there are no restrictions on what can be said.

Print adaptations involve one more subset: drama that adapts Shakespeare's plays. While not strictly *only* print adaptations, as they are meant for performance, the fact that they are issued as print texts as well moves them into this category. Beginning with the very early *The Tamer Tamed* and Nahum Tate's *King Lear*, we can draw a trajectory which includes Bertolt Brecht's *The Resistible Rise of Arturo Ui* (1941), Tom Stoppard's *Rosencrantz and Guildenstern are Dead* (1966), Edward Bond's *Lear* (1971), Welcome Msomi's *uMabatha* (1972?), Paula Vogel's *Desdemona: A Play about a Handkerchief* (1987), etc. All of these, among others, are *announced* adaptations of Shakespeare plays, in various forms of theatre. Theatre adaptations of Shakespeare's plays are innumerable given that each culture translates and transposes the English drama form into its own native theatre forms: thus Shakespeare has been done in Kathakali, Huiju and Noh, in Kabuki and Kuttiyattam, in Xiqu and Commedia dell'arte, in ballet and opera, in First Nation art forms, etc. These plays remain recognisably Shakespeare even as they are freshly rendered into a different culture's art forms with its accompanying modifications and alterations.

Print is also the medium for yet another adaptive mode: the comic book or in its new, updated version, the graphic novel. Comic book Shakespeares are a comparatively old phenomenon: the early 1940s saw the rise of Classics Illustrated which brought out comic book versions of several of Shakespeare's plays as also of other classics of world literature. These comic books retained Shakespeare's words, adding to them illustrations and images which brought the words to life, in vivid, if sometimes rather strange ways. (Their *Macbeth* featured the eponymous hero wearing a Viking style helmet with wings at each side!)[8] From those beginnings, today the comic book industry has a large footprint in the Shakespeare adaptations market: there are the relatively recent Manga Shakespeares; graphic novels by Gareth Hinds which are more "high art" than "comic"; No Fear Shakespeare, a series from SparkNotes which makes Shakespeare easy; online three-panel comics which provide easy access to all of Shakespeare's plays:[9] the list is long and entertaining.

A special mention has to be made of one special set of Shakespeare comic books: those brought out by Classical Comics. What they say under the link "Education" regarding their Shakespeare range is illuminating:

> **Shakespeare Range**
>
> In order to be true to the Bard's works, our Shakespeare titles feature the entire script, unabridged, in the original setting. That is our starting point – the "**Original Text**".

> Our research revealed how the complex Shakespeare language can deter many readers, especially those coming to a play for the first time. To cater for that, we publish a translation into plain English (from the entire script) that we call "**Plain Text**".
> We took this process a stage further to create our third reading level, "**Quick Text**", that features reduced and simplified dialogue for younger and reluctant readers. This version is also ideal for students where English is not the first language, and also for a quick introduction to the play for even mature students.[10]

If originally comics were meant to entertain, this firm has, like No Fear Shakespeare, worked at making Shakespeare accessible for all students. However, their innovative ideas take it one step further: for schools they have created a set of "Interactive Motion Comics" which while meant for use on a computer, provide the user not just with graphic visuals and texts but also a voiceover so that you can hear the dialogues even as you read them. In addition, as the text plays out on your screen, by moving the cursor over the highlighted words you can also see the annotations you need to achieve a better understanding of the words. Thus this version of Shakespeare is a meld, an adaptation of many modes, media and forms: it is a graphic novel or comic book but also an annotated textbook, while it also provides you with audio-visuals. The difference that computers make to Shakespeare adaptations is well illustrated by a case such as this.

There remains the range of Shakespeare adaptations that have flourished with the advent of the internet. These include those that belong to all the above media and genres, now available either freely or for a price, on the WWW, but there are also the new hypertexts and internet gaming (there is now an online game, *Kill Shakespeare*[11] featuring characters from several of the plays, as well as other online games directly based upon one or the other play), both of which are new areas for Shakespeare Studies. The hypertext begins with the text of a Shakespeare play but that is not all. As the *Internet Shakespeares* site explains on the page titled "Plays and Poems: Help":

> Modern editions of our texts contain two levels of annotative notes. The first level provides a brief explanation of words and phrases. The second level provides a more in-depth discussion of the issues the passage raises.
>
> To view the annotations, select "Show notes on the text" from the left-hand toolbox. All annotated words and phrases in the text will be underlined. Select an underlined word or phrase to open a pop-up window with the annotation. For your convenience, the pop-up windows can be dragged around the page, and enlarged or shrunk. . . .

In addition,

> To access a collation of the text (one which shows all the variants), select "Show variants" from the left-hand toolbox. Words or passages with variants will be underlined. To see all the variants side-by-side in the text itself, select "Display variants inline" from the Toolbox. Different versions of the text will be distinguished by color. In either view, click on an underlined or colored phrase to open a pop-up window that lists all the variants and their sources.

The *Internet Shakespeares* edition of *As You Like It* comes with additional links to supplementary material, critical commentary and the possibility of reading it in at least its modern edition and its First Folio avatar: does this then qualify as an adaptation? The jury is still out on this question!

The Politics of Adaptations, or Why Adapt a Shakespeare Play?

If you were to actually answer that question your short, slightly flippant, answer might be: "To cash in on Shakespeare's name!" and there is a definite truth in that statement which remains valid: the monetary, economic advantages to working with an already successful text are undisputed. It is good to remember that though this section asks questions about the reasons for adapting a Shakespeare play, the answers are similar for the question, "Why adapt an already available, and popular, text?" When a film studio or a director decides to film a Shakespeare play, they are working with the assurance of a certain cultural capital that is bound to accrue with the Shakespeare name: that name is saleable and respected, his plots are known and the success of previous ventures in the line encourages them to pursue the project. Especially in cases of print-to-film adaptation there is the additional benefit of upward mobility: the power of the word (especially Shakespeare's words) is such that the project gains a degree of respectability that other projects may not.

If the short answer to "Why adapt?" is based on the definite possibility of financial and cultural capital, it still does not explain other factors that impact an adapter and her adaptation: there remain the casual charges of derivative lazy work, of a lack of respect for the genius of the "original", of an uninspired, boring yet unfaithful adaptation, etc. As Hutcheon asks, "What motivates adapters, knowing that their efforts will be compared to competing imagined versions in people's heads and inevitably be found wanting? Why would they risk censure for monetary opportunism?" (86) The answer to that question, which clearly foregrounds the perils of adaptation, is what this section is concerned with. A person might adapt a text to comment critically on some feature within it; to make a political point about it; to pay homage to the prior text/author/originator; to ensure that a larger audience is able to enjoy the work, or engage with it, etc. These reasons do not function in isolation and an adapter might choose to adapt Shakespeare's work because of several of these reasons working together.

Several of the adaptations of Shakespeare's plays are made as a way of paying homage to arguably the "greatest playwright" of all time. The BBC TV series which adapted all the plays for television can be seen as one such example. The originator of the project, Cedric Messina, and the several directors who worked at creating the series were all foregrounding a resource they deemed essential: that Shakespeare's plays, thirty-seven of them, should be available as televised versions and now in DVD form. The dissemination of the collection, across schools and other learning centres and libraries, often makes it a young person's first introduction to the works of Shakespeare. But the conditions laid down for the series are what frame it as an almost-reverential act, designed to further elevate Shakespeare's status. As Michael Brooke put it, "the productions (were to) be traditional interpretations of the plays in appropriately Shakespearean period costumes and sets." These conditions caused many of the more avant-garde directors (such as Peter Brook) to opt out of the production as the scope was limited by the project conception itself. But even as the BBC project sought to present TV adaptations of thirty-seven plays, they were also concerned with both monetary benefits and the desire to reach a larger audience. Thus the BBC tied up with an American partner so that they would have access to the US market as well, and thus be able to break even, if not make a profit. Interestingly, they were turning a profit before all the plays were filmed: a testament to the saleability of Shakespeare's name and his plays.

While the adaptation-as-tribute is one response to the question "why adapt", another is an extension of this reason: believing that an author's works are eminent enough to deserve a wider audience which they might otherwise not reach. An adapter might move the works out of their own genre and form into other media, genres and forms which reach a range of people who might otherwise never encounter this particular author or his work, or might be resistant to it. The case of Shakespeare illustrates this particularly well: given the language, especially the blank verse, and given the canonicity and eminence conferred upon it. Young people are often taught Shakespeare as part of their school syllabi and are sometimes in awe of his language and reputation or averse to reading texts that, to them, seem outdated and archaic. This resistance to Shakespeare is targeted by the makers of Shakespeare teen flicks: Shakespeare's *Othello* is moved out of Venice and Cyprus to an American boarding school, Othello as a basketball player, Desdemona the daughter of the school's Dean; *The Taming of the Shrew* shifts from Padua, Italy, to an American town and high school; in *Get Over It* (2001), loosely based on *A Midsummer Night's Dream*, the school drama club and basketball team take centre stage. The comfort of a recognisable idiom and familiar activities allows the Shakespearean allusions, quotes and other tags to slip in, in "acceptable" and "non-threatening" ways. In addition, some of these movies do not only work with the basic plot outline of one of the Shakespearean plays, they also introduce other elements from Shakespeare's life and his other works so that there is a strong intertextual component to the whole. Thus in Luhrmann's *William Shakespeare's Romeo + Juliet* there are quotations from other Shakespeare plays: "Such stuff as dreams are made on" is used to advertise a drink called Prospero in the film and the pool club in the film is called the Globe! For the Shakespeare aficionado there is usually far more in these films than what brings in the teenage audience.

Graphic novels and comic book adaptations of Shakespeare are sometimes done with a similar motivation: people, especially young students and teens who might not read the word-intensive text of a play are more than likely to read a word-image text, especially one which gives a simpler version of Shakespeare's Elizabethan English, as the Classical Comics or No Fear Shakespeare graphic novel versions of Shakespeare's texts do. Interestingly, the Oxford Shakespeare Project also endorses this approach as they are now reprinting the Classical Comics editions under the Oxford imprint. Even other graphic novel versions are aimed at specific audiences: the Manga Shakespeare is one such example. Easily accessible to youngsters who love Japanese manga comics, they reinvent the Shakespeare plays in terms of locations and style. The Early Modern is replaced by America in the eighteenth century, as *King Lear* becomes the *Last of the Mohicans*. They retain the Shakespearean language, his words, but place it in exciting, imaginative new settings: *Macbeth* is in the world of the Samurai warriors but it is also a future post-nuclear world with mutants.[12] Shakespeare is de-familiarised but made accessible, and though it is arguable how much the new setting contributes to an understanding of the nuances of the Shakespeare text, there can be no argument that it does win over people who are otherwise resistant to Shakespeare.

Thus Shakespeare fans remake Shakespeare into their own languages, place him in their own regional/national/linguistic contexts, adapt him into art forms that are accessible to their own people/groups, and so on. Examples of this reason for adaptation proliferate, whether in the film world, or in theatre forms that are native to certain areas, languages or peoples. Kathakali Shakespeare versions of *Lear* (1999) from India, Noh performances such as that of *Lear* (1997), operatic and balletic versions of the plays are all adaptations which move English theatre into other theatrical forms, languages and thus give to Shakespeare a greater reach and visibility. A glimpse of the amazing variety and richness of this particular form of adaptation was seen at the Olympic Games in 2012: all thirty-seven plays were produced, each in a different language, including Yoruba, Maori and Mandarin, even British Sign Language. An online Open Access MIT project showcases this variety and richness offering video and performance archives from across the globe so that we can all experience the flexibility with which Shakespeare's plays move across languages and cultures.

Even though reaching Shakespeare to a larger audience, a more various audience, remains one of the principal reasons for

Shakespeare adaptations, equally, if not more important is the fact that many adaptations are called into being because the adapters wish to critique a particular aspect of Shakespeare's work. Feminists, Marxists, blacks, queers, the postcolonials, have all used Shakespeare's plays as a vehicle to voice a perspective that is sometimes an extension of, sometimes at a tangent to, or a counter to, a viewpoint seen in Shakespeare's plays. The politics of Shakespeare's plays and contesting that political view by engaging with it, via adaptation, is what has motivated authors as diverse as Bertolt Brecht, Jane Smiley, Julius Lester and Lisa Klein, to randomly name some authors.

Brecht's reworking of *Coriolanus*, called simply *Coriolan* (1952), shifts the focus from the Roman war hero to the collective, the people of Rome, and thus gives a makeover to Shakespeare's "rabble", now transforming them into a group guided by reason. If the aristocratic hero was seen in Shakespeare's play as exalted and tragically ill-equipped to cope with the Roman mob, a view point which Nahum Tate further built up in *The Ingratitude of a Common Wealth, Or the Fall of Caius Martius Coriolanus* (1682), Brecht created a new version of the mob, and the play, one which is replete with Marxist beliefs and built upon certain notions regarding class. As much as Shakespeare's play and the later Tate version are a product of their times, so is Brecht's a product of a Marxist viewpoint and a belief in the common people. Thus politically motivated adaptations of Shakespeare give us a contemporised, ideologically updated version which might then itself be rewritten in a few decades. The fact that Nahum Tate removed the ambiguity from Shakespeare's version, highlighting the aristocratic Coriolanus's heroism, and that Brecht rewrote it keeping in mind a dedicated consciousness of class, points to this aspect of adaptations. Class consciousness and the rise of the ordinary has also in part been the reason behind *Rosencrantz and Guildenstern are Dead* and *Lear* by Tom Stoppard and Edward Bond, respectively. Showcasing the lives of the marginal, the dispossessed and the disempowered in opposition to the royalty and the patrician upper classes, has been a feature of both plays, both fiercely political and class conscious once again.

If class is one category that causes certain kinds of adaptations, gender concerns also fuel adaptations, especially of the tragedies which are often seen as misogynist to a large extent, with portrayals of women which range from the cruel and depraved (Lear's daughters and Lady Macbeth) to those possessed of a naiveté which is never enough for them to sustain themselves (Desdemona and Ophelia). Thus Ophelia, long seen as an archetypal adolescent girl, sheltered and cossetted to the extent that she cannot deal with the pressures of the world when deprived of male protective figures, is reinvented and adapted by young adult (YA) fiction writers into a fiesty young girl who can make her own way (in Lisa Klein's *Ophelia*) or into someone who flounders initially but eventually takes on the world and learns to cope (in Ray's *Falling for Hamlet*). Goneril and Regan, Lear's elder daughters, are given convincing back stories which go a long way to explaining why they treat their father as they do in Jane Smiley's Pulitzer Prize winning *A Thousand Acres* (1991). Gertrude in Atwood's short story presents her side of the story, amusing but also revelatory, fleshing out in a few short paragraphs her life as wife to Hamlet Sr and mother to Prince Hamlet. Politically motivated adaptations have always found enough material in the tragedies, especially for gender and in the case of *Othello*, for race. While Murray Carlin used *Othello* as the frame for his *Not Now, Sweet Desdemona* (1969), a tale of miscegenation and interracial sex, Djanet Sears's *Harlem Duet* (1997) focused on an Othello who was already in a long-standing relationship with a black woman, and then abandons her to marry a white woman. Others have explored the difficulty of sustaining celebrity status given the relentless pressure (Mal Peet's *Exposure* [2008]) while Julius Lester tried to demonstrate the difference that might have been possible if Iago and Emilia had also been black, in *Othello: A Novel* (1995).

The postcolonial has found particular riches to mine in Shakespeare's *Tempest*, with colonialism, Ariel, Caliban and Prospero to draw upon to make their political points, as evidenced by just two examples: Aimé Césaire's Caribbean *Une Tempête* (1969) and Raquel Carrió's Cuban *Otra Tempestad* (1999). Suniti Namjoshi in her Sycorax poems (2006) works with the figure of Sycorax from *The Tempest* but uses the character to explore not just postcolonial but also gender concerns. But postcolonial writers have not drawn upon only *The Tempest*: Rushdie has appropriated *Hamlet* in his short story "Yorick" (1995); Derek Walcott re-works *Antony and Cleopatra* in part in *A Branch of the Blue Nile* (1986); *Macbeth* was made a part of the Mumbai underworld in *Maqbool*; and so on. The postcolonial worldwide has had a long history of interacting with Shakespeare. First taught Shakespeare as a part of the coloniser's canon, initially having viewed/read Shakespeare in English or in translation, postcolonial writers have moved on to contest, oppose, subvert and thus appropriate Shakespeare's work in terms of their own lives and histories. While engaging with Shakespeare's plays, these authors, scriptwriters and filmmakers work subaltern and postcolonial concerns into the body of Shakespeare's work and in the process also struggle against the supremacy accorded to Shakespeare by the canon as well as cultural practice. The responses to Shakespeare's canonical status are varied: Fischlin and Fortier put it neatly, speaking of not only postcolonial but all Shakespearean adaptation, "some seek to supplant or overthrow; others borrow from Shakespeare's status to give resonance to their own efforts" (6). The plots, the language and the familiarity that Shakespeare enjoys, especially in the erstwhile colonies, make him a resource that cannot be overlooked.

Queer reworkings of Shakespeare have appeared mostly on stage rather than in print or film, though there are exceptions such as Derek Jarman's 1979 film *The Tempest* and Philip Osment's *This Island's Mine* (1987) which have both tackled gay, lesbian and queer pride and related issues. But queer reworkings of Shakespeare's work are now being historicised, with early stage productions such as the 1899 production which cast Sarah Bernhardt as Hamlet and the 1900 filming of a scene from the same, receiving attention as early moments in the history of modern gender-bending Shakespeare. An all-male production of *As You Like It* was performed in 1967, another in 1991; *The Winter's Tale* was played in 2005 by an all-male cast; all-female casts have also been seen in recent years: in just one year, 2013, there were productions of *Henry V*, *The Taming of the Shrew*, *Hamlet*, *Titus Andronicus* and *Julius Caesar*. The new Globe has often presented Shakespearean productions featuring all-male and all-female casts, making it possible to examine the nuances of cross-dressing and gendered sexuality while playing with assumptions regarding the Renaissance theatrical norm of an all-male cast. There are also more comic short interludes such as the "Sassy Gay Friend" series of shorts: each of which averts a Shakespearean tragedy by bringing a gay friend to rescue the tragic heroines at the crucial point in the play! Queer readings of the plays have also been seen as ways of adapting and appropriating the plays from the normative heterosexual world to one which is more inclusive and open.

****

Shakespearean adaptations continue to proliferate, as this chapter has demonstrated. They adapt not just entire plays but sections thereof, characters from the plays, themes and significant moments. They work at endorsing, contesting, subverting, challenging and destabilising Shakespeare's pre-eminent position in the canon of English literature. However, adapters have not just stopped at the plays: Shakespeare, the playwright, the man from Stratford, the cultural icon, the

British star (or the Klingon one!), has come in for his share of the makeover process too. From biographies (*Will in the World*, 2004) and films (think *Shakespeare in Love*, 1998) to fictionalised narratives of real and imagined incidents in his life, Shakespeare has an amazing and never-ending afterlife.

Works Cited

Brooke, Michael. *The BBC Television Shakespeare* (1978–85). *BFI Screenonline*. n.p. n.d. Web. 16 June 2014.

Brown, Rebecca. "Stage History." *Antony and Cleopatra. Royal Shakespeare Company*. n.d. Web. 13 June 2014.

Classical Comics. "Education." *Classical Comics Ltd*. 2013. Web. 14 June 2014. <http://www.classicalcomics.com/education.html>.

Fischlin, Daniel and Mark Fortier. *Adaptations of Shakespeare: A Critical Anthology of Plays from the Seventeenth Century to the Present*. London: Routledge, 2000. Print.

Hutcheon, Linda. *A Theory of Adaptation*. New York: Routledge, 2006. Print.

Lamb, Charles and Mary. "Preface." *Tales from Shakespeare*. 1807. *Project Gutenberg*. 1996. Web. 13 June 2014.

Maguire, Laurie. "Shakespeare Published." *Shakespeare: An Oxford Guide*. Ed. Stanley Wells and Lena Cowen Orlin. Oxford: Oxford UP, 2003. 582--93. Print.

"Plays and Poems: Help." *Internet Shakespeare Editions*. University of Victoria. n.d. Web. 14 June 2014. <http://internetshakespeare.uvic.ca/Foyer/Texts/help/>.

Trivedi, Poonam and Bartholomeusz, Dennis, ed. *India's Shakespeare: Translation, Interpretation, and Performance*. New Delhi: Longman/Pearson, 2005. Print.

Notes

1. For video and performance archives of Shakespeare across the globe, see <http://globalshakespeares.mit.edu/#>
2. For a discussion of Shakespeare in India, see Poonam Trivedi's *India's Shakespeare*.
3. Earlier editors were men of letters such as Alexander Pope (1725) and Samuel Johnson (1765) but from the 1860s editing Shakespeare became an academic endeavour, with the publication of the Cambridge Shakespeare in 1863–66.
4. This discussion of Shakespeare editions draws its substance in large part from the Maguire essay.
5. You can see this iconic moment at <https://www.youtube.com/watch?v=jz9MfjuBB70>
6. See <http://www.imdb.com/name/nm0000636/> for an exhaustive (and exhaustingly long) list of Shakespeare adaptations, those already in circulation and those that are upcoming.
7. Watch it here: <http://www.youtube.com/watch?v=-pOjKdy7cgs>
8. See an image here <http://sevencircumstances.com/2014/04/23/remembering-the-bard-450-years-on/#jp-carousel-4065>
9. See here <http://io9.com/all-of-shakespeares-plays-converted-to-3-panel-webcom-1559458973>
10. See more details and also experience an interactive motion comic at <http://www.classicalcomics.com/education.html>
11. See <http://www.killshakespeare.com/>
12. See images from the Manga *Macbeth* at <http://www.selfmadehero.com/title.php?isbn=9780955285660&edition_id=107>

Eight

Shakespeare and Criticism

The criticism of Shakespeare over the last four hundred plus years can hardly be contained in a book, let alone a short chapter: therefore, what this chapter aims at is a chronological overview of the criticism of Shakespeare's works. It will examine, in particular, the main trends in the last hundred and fifty years of Shakespeare criticism, when criticism became the work of professionals and academics, situated in universities and institutions of higher learning. Thus we will do a brief survey of pre-1900 criticism, then move on to the major schools of criticism and their modes of analyses of Shakespeare's plays.

First, we shall study the main domains in which Shakespeare criticism has evolved over the years: from textual studies and editions, to performance studies and adaptations to criticism of the plays as print texts, wherein, in the main, they are treated as any other "literary" text.

The shifting fortunes of various plays in critical practice is also an indication of the ways in which people from different eras respond differently to Shakespeare's plays, seeing virtue where earlier none was apparent. I shall return to this theme later in the chapter.

Shakespeare Studies: Variants and Modes

Most Shakespearean criticism takes the form of essays and monographs on the works of William Shakespeare read as *literary texts*. However, Shakespeare criticism is not only critical readings of his plays and poetry. To gain an understanding of the various ways in which Shakespeare criticism is practised, one only needs to look at the Shakespeare chapter in any year's edition of *YWES* (*Year's Work in English Studies*). They begin with a discussion of editions of Shakespeare's work that have appeared in the previous year: editions of individual plays as well as collected works, noting the ways in which they improve upon earlier editions, take different decisions regarding the variants possible and determine particular readings by choosing certain phrases and words. In addition, they also consider textual studies of the plays and poems, either essays or full-length books which carefully delineate textual variations or try to demonstrate, based upon in-text references and other evidence, that a particular edition of a play could be considered as predating other editions. The discussion could also involve comparative analyses of manuscripts.

While we might find some of this work wearying and repetitive, it is necessary to understand the need for these editions. When we read a Shakespeare play published by Oxford University Press or the Norton Shakespeare, when teachers recommend buying the Arden edition or the Signet edition of a particular play, we are endorsing what we can think of as editorial criticism of one variety or another. The decisions taken by the editors and their choices, in terms of which variant of a phrase, a speech or a speaker is used, as well as the "Editor's Introduction" to the play and the choice of additional materials which are printed along with the text of the play, all go to make up a certain version of the play itself. The choice of the Norton Shakespeare editors to use the 1986 Oxford Edition of the works when preparing their own student-friendly edition of 1997 was an editorial decision, but while we enjoy reading the Norton Shakespeare, we do not think about the many transformations that have been worked through the centuries by successive editors to bring us this mammoth work. *Textual studies* focusing on specifics of Shakespeare's texts are again seen as boring by most students but such studies help us to understand the ideological views or the material realities which make certain choices necessary. Textual studies also help us to see where certain lines in Shakespeare might be derived from; and journals devoted to textual and philological studies such as *Notes and Queries* continue to showcase the efforts of textual scholars who find that particular lines have their antecedents in earlier works that Shakespeare must have known. Thus editorial and textual studies continue to be one of the noteworthy areas in Shakespeare Studies today.

If the text is one significant area of study, another is performance. *Performance studies* of Shakespeare's work includes a wide variety of approaches. There are essays and books which deal with how directors and producers have presented Shakespeare in the theatre, there are accounts of actors and actresses who talk about playing certain parts in a Shakespeare play and there are studies of the staging of a play across time and space, or the incisive analysis of one actor's work in various Shakespeare plays. While one might wonder what one can learn from reading these accounts, they provide a window onto a crucial aspect of Shakespeare's work, and one which the literature student often forgets: that these were primarily *plays*, meant for performance on the *stage,* as *spectacles*. By reading about certain productions, by reading essays that discuss the ways in which characters, speeches and movements provide signals and directions within a Shakespeare play, for the other actors, it is possible to gain a fresh new understanding of the play itself. Likewise, interviews with actors who speak about the process of acting in a Shakespearean play, and their experiences in doing so, can enrich our understanding of both the play and the character within it.

Other variants of performance studies include a focus on film and television adaptations of Shakespeare. The ways in which the medium changes Shakespeare's work, the usc of different styles in filming, the shift from Shakespeare's words to a more modern vocabulary and linguistic style, the locating of the plays in spaces and times that are radically different from Shakespeare's plays' worlds: all these and more are studied in performance studies and studies of Shakespeare on screen, and could also be classified as "adaptation studies".

Literary criticism is, by far, the largest category of criticism for Shakespeare's work. Again there are a multitude of approaches, a multiplicity of foci. Whether in terms of chronology or in terms of schools of criticism, it is a near impossible task to provide a complete overview of all the criticism that has been produced over the centuries on Shakespeare.

Early Criticism

Early criticism of Shakespeare's work dates back to soon after his entry into the theatre: Robert Greene's attack on his work (he famously, or notoriously, described Shakespeare as an "upstart crow" in a tract published around 1592), which was however without directly naming him. The next significant critic was Francis Meres who was adulatory in his praise in 1598: "As Epius Stolo said that the Muses would speake with Plautus tongue if they would speak Latin: so I say that the Muses would speak with Shakespeares fine filed phrase if they would speak English." Shakespeare's colleague and friend, Ben Jonson, renowned playwright and poet, is also remembered today for his views on Shakespeare, both those affixed to the First Folio and those published later in 1630, in *Timber, or Discoveries:*

> I REMEMBER the players have often mentioned it as an honor to Shakespeare, that in his writing, whatsoever he penned, he never blotted out a line. My answer hath been, "Would he had

> blotted a thousand," . . . He was, indeed, honest, and of an open and free nature; had an excellent fancy, brave notions, and gentle expressions, wherein he flowed with that facility that sometime it was necessary he should be stopped.

In the seventeenth century both John Milton and John Dryden wrote on Shakespeare, seeing in him a large-hearted genius who instinctively understood all humanity, even as they criticised his work for violating the classical rules of drama and for lacking a formal decorum. That trend, of recognising the universal elements while criticising the formal properties in Shakespeare's plays, continued through the Neoclassical age, with its emphases on the Classical model of drama. Eventually, the fascination with the Classical model faded but the perspective which showed Shakespeare's universal element continued till the late twentieth century. Seventeenth-century voices such as that of Thomas Rhymer and Samuel Pepys objected to specific plays in the Shakespeare canon: the former to *Othello*, the latter to *A Midsummer Night's Dream*. Rhymer's scathing criticism of *Othello* is still cited today, as a starting point for criticism on *Othello*:

> The moral, sure, of this Fable is very instructive. First, This may be a caution to all Maidens of Quality, how, without their Parents consent, they run away with Blackamoors. Secondly, This may be a warning to all good Wives that they may look well to their Linnen. Thirdly, This may be a lesson to Husbands, that before their Jealousie be Tragical, the proofs may be Mathematical. . . . But the tragical part is, plainly none other, than a Bloody Farce, without salt or savour.

This particular quotation is also instructive in that it helps us to see the prejudices of the critic as well in his criticism of the play: a viewpoint which we need to keep in mind as we read any criticism. All criticism is the product of its times, just as much as is all creative writing.

The eighteenth century began with a new mode of criticism: the publishing of a new edition of Shakespeare's work, by Nicholas Rowe: *The Works of Mr. William Shakespear; Revis'd and Corrected,* 6 vol. (1709; 9 vol., including poems, 1714), based largely upon the First Folio. Several features of this new edition were notable: he restored passages from earlier editions of *Hamlet*, *Romeo and Juliet*, *King Lear*, etc.; modernised spelling and punctuation; set out a list of characters at the beginning of each play; tried to divide the plays by act and scene systematically; provided a location for the scenes and, interestingly, wrote a Shakespeare biography, full of fascinating and unverified "facts". Thus Rowe put into circulation the story that Shakespeare left Stratford because he was guilty of poaching deer and hence got into trouble; that Shakespeare was the first to see merit in Jonson's early work and recommend it to the playing company; and so on.[1] While the anecdotal (and apocryphal) Shakespearean biography is now largely discredited, the Rowe edition is significant for the other features mentioned above: comparison with other early editions, the systematic division into act and scene, all set a precedent for later editors to follow, though the paucity of material in those early years meant that there were not many options for the editors to work with. Other significant landmarks in the eighteenth century include Alexander Pope's and Samuel Johnson's editions of Shakespeare's works, in 1725 and 1765 respectively.

In addition, the century saw the publication of much critical material on the plays as well as several adaptations, which were also critical rewritings of Shakespeare's work. The plays themselves continued to be examined in terms of the unities, their universal truths and their edifying nature, while being criticised for their wordplay and for the ambiguity which characterised them. Samuel Johnson was particularly harsh in his stigmatising of Shakespeare's penchant for quibbles, puns and such other jest, also castigating him for his low, common and often gross sense of humour, which dwelt upon matters that were not edifying and uplifting. Some of this criticism was often self-contradictory as when he praises Shakespeare's dialogue for its "ease and simplicity" while damning his style for being "ungrammatical, perplexed and obscure". Further, many of these faults were explained (away) by claiming that Shakespeare was addressing himself to the common audience and as such had no option but to gratify their low tastes.

Early critics of Shakespeare also launched a trend that continues to this day: they analysed individual characters from the plays, a particular favourite being Hamlet. Among the earliest full length studies on a specific character was Maurice Morgann's *An Essay on the Dramatic Character of Sir John Falstaff* (1777). The early 1800s saw William Hazlitt's *Characters of Shakespeare's Plays* (1817) but also the first sustained examination of the heroines of Shakespeare's plays: *Shakespeare's Heroines*, originally known as *Characteristics of Women, Moral, Poetical and Historical* (1832), by Anna Jameson. These character studies are important because they explore the characters of the plays as if they are real people, investing them with psychological depth and analysing their motivations and their inner lives. But often these character-based studies created the character anew, overlooking textual elements that were not conducive to the author's perception of the character in question. Thus Falstaff in Morgann's estimate is a kindly, large-hearted wit, not a coward or a liar. Thus he says that he does not "clearly discern that Sir *John Falstaff* deserves to bear the character so generally given him of an absolute Coward", while it seems to him that "the leading quality in *Falstaff*'s character, and that from which all the rest take their colour, is a high degree of wit and humour, accompanied with great natural vigour and alacrity of mind." He also offers proofs "that *Courage* is a part of *Falstaff*'s *Character*, that it belonged to his constitution, and was manifest in the conduct and practice of his whole life." These proofs are drawn in large part from the comments of Falstaff's fellow conspirers and in foregrounding them as the proof of the former's courage. Morgan ignores the evidence within the play which posits Falstaff as an "absolute" and "constitutional coward".

The attention paid in Victorian times to Shakespearean women characters is a feature that casts a long shadow in Shakespeare Studies. Authors such as Anna Jameson (mentioned above), Mary Cowden Clarke and Helena Faucit foreshadow the many feminist critics of the twentieth century who examined the gender politics of the plays, analysing the roles played by women, the stereotypes associated with them, the patriarchally-ordained nature of their relationships, etc. Books such as *Shakespeare and the Nature of Women* (1975), *Still Harping on Daughters: Women and Drama in the Age of Shakespeare* (1983), *The Woman's Part: Feminist Criticism of Shakespeare* (1984), *Fashioning Femininity and English Renaissance Drama* (1991) and *A Feminist Companion to Shakespeare* (2001) are the descendants of the early work on Shakespeare's women characters by the Victorian critics mentioned above. While today, on reading their work, we might scoff at their exaltation of the Victorian notions of femininity, it is salutary to remember that they nonetheless found it meaningful to consider and study Shakespeare's women characters as women who combined "feminine"' virtues with intelligence and rationality. Even as these Victorian women critics added to the body of character criticism of Shakespearean characters, they also created a new avenue of study within Shakespearean criticism.

Significant names of the century include Charles Lamb and Thomas De Quincey ("On the Knocking at the Gate in *Macbeth*" 1823, still read in Indian universities today), alongside Samuel Taylor Coleridge and Hazlitt. The Victorians are less well-known as Shakespearean critics but authors such as John Ruskin wrote at length about Shakespeare's work, giving us ways of approaching the plays which are still relevant today. His dictum that Shakespeare had no heroes, only heroines, is something that is still used as a debate initiator today. One indication of the esteem in which Shakespeare was held by this time is the fact that Thomas Carlyle included Shakespeare in his book *On Heroes, Hero-worship and the Heroic in History* (1841) as one of the heroic figures produced by England. Shakespeare as the English poet par excellence stems from this period when his works also become part of the civilisational mission of England, taught in schools and colleges as part of the best that England could export. Towards the end of the century a more scholarly approach was evident as in Edward Dowden's *Shakespeare: A Critical Study of His Mind and Art* (1875). Dowden was one of the earliest academics to engage in sustained scholarship and writing on literature. By the end of the Victorian era, in 1904, there appeared A. C. Bradley's *Shakespearean Tragedy*, and Shakespearean criticism was set on its route to the modern. Though Bradley's psychological focus on the principal characters of Shakespeare's tragedies is what he is primarily remembered for now, he remains pre-eminent in Shakespeare criticism even today, excerpts from *Shakespearean Tragedy* being required reading in most university-level Shakespeare courses. Thus the nineteenth century gave Shakespearean criticism at least two of its many trajectories: Shakespeare as national cultural icon and the intensive study of Shakespeare's women characters.

Twentieth Century and After

The early decades of the twentieth century saw two eminent literary figures presenting their views on *Hamlet*: James Joyce and T. S. Eliot. While Eliot's work, on not just *Hamlet* but much else of Shakespeare, has survived, all we know of Joyce's is that he delivered a series of twelve lectures on *Hamlet* from November 1912 to February 1913, in Trieste, Italy, the first of which was greeted with "warm and prolonged applause" as a "learned and graceful talk". Initially there were to be just ten lectures but the warm reception accorded to them caused them to be extended to twelve sessions. The lectures are said to have provided Joyce with the opportunity to think through Shakespeare and particularly the way in which *Hamlet* could be incorporated into his *Ulysses.*[2] Eliot, writing a decade later, produced his critique of Hamlet, the play *and* the character, in "Hamlet and His Problems"(1922), which declared Shakespeare's most popular and revered play a failure, while lauding *Coriolanus* and *Antony and Cleopatra* as Shakespeare's "most assured artistic success". This reversal of fortune for the most acclaimed of Shakespeare's plays is particularly noteworthy as the twentieth century saw a sudden revival in the fortunes of what was earlier thought of as Shakespeare's most troubling play: *King Lear*. Yet another acclaimed name who wrote upon Shakespeare's plays and changed the way criticism was conducted was Sigmund Freud. His remarks on the Macbeths, in *Some Character-types Met with in Psycho-analytical Work* (1916),[3] takes further the character criticism of earlier times but adds to it psychological depth and intensity, laying the ground for the psychoanalytic school of literary theory/studies in the second half of the century.

The beginning of the twentieth century also saw a new development in Shakespeare criticism: historical criticism (not to be confused with the New Historicist school of criticism) which laid an emphasis on studying Shakespeare's work as a product of his times. As more and more knowledge was coming to the fore regarding the Early Modern, as documents were retrieved and Elizabethan and Jacobean England studied in greater detail, critics such as Elmer Edgar Stoll and Alfred Harbage (to name just two) studied Shakespeare's plays in the context of their historical environment. Most of the earlier historical criticism had examined the conventions of playing companies, censorship, theatres and audiences, and analysed the plays within these contexts. The new mode of critical enquiry, thus, contextualised the plays, seeing them as fitting into, and reflecting, the modes of culture, knowledge and thought that were prevalent in Shakespeare's time. The effects of this new mode of criticism are still apparent today as contextualised study is seen as integral to an understanding of Shakespeare: why else would you need a book on backgrounds and contexts to the study of Shakespeare? (The school of New Historicists in the latter decades of the twentieth century would reconfigure the use of contexts and backgrounds adding nuances and a greater depth to the understanding of how texts and contexts spoke to each other, often undermining the strict definition of a text and so on. I shall come to this school in the section on materialist criticism.)

The 1930s and 40s were especially significant for literary study as they saw the rise of the New Critics, who inaugurated a critical style that continues to be valid and relevant even today. The *Encyclopædia Britannica*'s "Guide to Shakespeare" assesses the role and contribution of the New Critics and their work in Shakespeare Studies thus:

> At its most extreme, it urged the ignoring of historical background in favour of an intense and personal engagement with Shakespeare's language: tone, speaker, image patterns, and verbal repetitions and rhythms. Studies of imagery, rhetorical patterns, wordplay, and still more gave support to the movement. At the commencement of the 21st century, close reading remained an acceptable approach to the Shakespearean text.

Among the best-known Shakespearean New Critics were L. C. Knights and G. Wilson Knight: their work remains a valuable resource today and the title of Wilson Knight's book *The Wheel of Fire: Interpretations of Shakespearian Tragedy* (1949, reissued 2001) and that of L. C. Knights's essay, "How Many Children had Lady Macbeth" (1933), are still known to Indian students of Shakespeare. Other significant New Critics include M. M. Mahood who wrote *Shakespeare's Wordplay* (1957) and Caroline Spurgeon. The latter's *Shakespeare's Imagery and What*

It Tells Us (1935) itemises the prominent images in the major plays and goes on to show how these clusters of images can be read together to gain a better understanding of the play in question. F. R. Leavis was not strictly a Shakespearean but wrote "Diabolic Intellect, or the Noble Hero" in *The Common Pursuit* (1958), which neatly took apart Bradley's reading of *Othello* as the comparatively blameless victim of Iago's evil machinations. Several of the schools of contemporary literary theory continue to use the New Critics' mode of reading a text closely, analysing the properties of a Shakespearean play rather than the intentions and glories of the author who created it. While the decontextualising that the formalists among the New Critics advocated is not an acceptable practice in most forms of theoretical and critical understanding today, the focus on the text and the (formalist) emphasis on "what a text does, and how it does it" was the most valuable contribution of the New Critics. The approach continues to contribute to the generation of meanings in any and all Shakespearean plays.

While the New Critics held sway over most of the mid-twentieth century, the last quarter of the century saw a dramatic increase in approaches to the study of Shakespeare. Feminist, materialist, structuralist and poststructuralist, postmodern, deconstructionist, postcolonial, queer and ecocritical readings among others are the new modes of reading Shakespeare. These function in composite fashion as well so there are books such as Ania Loomba's *Gender, Race, Renaissance Drama* (1989); Kim Hall's *Things of Darkness: Economies of Race and Gender in Early Modern England* (1996), etc., which examine the intersections of race and gender in plays such as *Othello*, demonstrating as Thomas Rhymer did (in the quotation given above) the connections between the sexual, racial and gender themes. The feminist critics themselves have examined gender concerns through various prisms: the materialist, the deconstructive, and so on.

Gender and Sexuality

Feminist critics such as Karen Newman, Penny Gay, Jean Howard and others have examined various facets of Shakespeare's plays, as they relate to notions of gender and gendered modes of behaviour. These studies analyse the roles of, and expectations from, daughters and wives in Early Modern culture, the codes that would ideally govern their behaviour and situate these in the context of Shakespeare's plays, discussing how these are not just reflected but also challenged, contested, endorsed or subverted. Characters such as Gertrude in *Hamlet* and Lady Macbeth in *Macbeth* were useful "vehicles", so to speak, for examining the popular perceptions regarding wives: not just in the Early Modern but in much of the criticism of the plays through the centuries. Gertrude, earlier typified as deceitful wife and lustful widow, and Lady Macbeth, an exemplar of the wife who was responsible for her husband's evil machinations, were demonstrated to have more than just these stereotypical negative traits. Close reading of the plays in conjunction with an analysis of Early Modern norms regarding women's sexuality and the worries of their men about their sexuality, helped to demonstrate that the problem with Gertrude may not have been her raging sexuality but the efforts of her first husband and her son to control her sexuality. The women of the comedies, young, articulate and intelligent, find love and enter into marriage at the end of the comedies, demonstrating the anxiety of the patriarchal world to contain women within the institution of marriage, in effect subduing them and reducing them to mere adjuncts to their menfolk. Anxieties regarding daughters are successfully resolved in the comedies, where control of the young daughter is passed from father to husband fairly seamlessly. But the same relationship is rendered fraught and heart-rending when women try to take control of their own lives, as in *Othello*, *King Lear* and *Hamlet*, in each of which the daughters' choices are shown as faulty, leading to tragic consequences for all concerned. This endorsement of patriarchy is, however, itself shown to be flawed if the plays are read in a nuanced manner, wherein the fathers' heavy-handed controlling of their daughters is highlighted alongside their complete ignorance of their daughters' real selves and desires. Thus Brabantio, Desdemona's father, and King Lear are both shown to be unaware of what their daughters are like, as they see them in fixed ways that contribute to their own images of themselves rather than as individuals possessing independent personalities.

Critics working on gender have focused on other aspects as well: the role of friendships among women, as well as the relationships that men share within the plays with one another. Gender studies and studies of masculinity by critics such as Coppelia Kahn and Robin Wells have examined the ways in which masculinity is configured in Shakespeare's plays. It has been noted that patriarchy empowers only a certain class and age group among men: that all men do not necessarily benefit from the patriarchal structures that society perpetuates and that it actively renders some men victims. Orlando as a younger son in *As You Like It*, is an example, as is his old servant, Adam (a role said to have been played by Shakespeare himself), both of whom are routinely neglected and eventually forced to flee, due to Oliver's mistreatment of them, to safeguard their lives. Masculinity and its pressures has also come in for a fair deal of attention from practitioners of gender studies who see the tragedies *Hamlet* and *Macbeth* as partly due to the concept of normative masculinity that society constructs and endorses. Thus while Macbeth repeatedly affirms that he does all that can be expected of a man, Hamlet sees himself as conforming more to the roles of *women* who speak and express grief rather than perform the actions that masculinity demands of them, in his case vengeance upon his uncle. Most of the great tragic heroes reveal a degree of uncertainty regarding their achieving of their normative gender roles and that hesitance is seen as contributing to their tragic ends. The ambivalence of an Antony who allows his Cleopatra to wear his sword and himself dresses in her "tires and mantles" (II.v.22) demonstrates the masculine-feminine divide and its bridging that is seen as problematic, both within the world of the play and in subsequent critical attitudes to Antony's character attributes.

The theatrical practice of young boys playing the roles of women in Shakespeare's time, and the subsequent/consequent destabilising of gender roles, has also been critically analysed in considerable detail in late-twentieth-century criticism. While this practice was criticised as early as the 1583 by Philip Stubbes in his *Anatomy of Abuses,* critics such as Peter Stallybrass, Marjorie Garber, Lisa Jardine and Phyllis Rackin have focused on various aspects connected with cross-dressing. The thematic possibilities that were opened up due to young boys playing the roles of women is one aspect that received attention, but theorists also pointed to the fears that cross-dressing engendered regarding unstable gender identities, same-sex love and desire and the fear of effeminacy. These concerns were discussed particularly with regard to the plays in which Shakespeare included young heroines who then dressed up as boys and interacted with or wooed their romantic interests, in plays such as *The Merchant of Venice*, *As You Like It* and *Twelfth Night* which added additional layers of complexity to the portrayal of gender roles. This is best illustrated in *As You Like It*: a boy playing the role of Rosalind dressed up as a girl, then dresses as a man (as Celia and Rosalind flee to the Forest of Arden) and once they meet Orlando he further pretends to be Orlando's love Rosalind! The destabilising of fixed gender roles and identities that plays such as this performed has attracted considerable critical attention and further helped in understanding the politics of gender both within the play as well as in Shakespeare's England.

Practitioners of queer/LGBT studies, such as Madhavi Menon, Bruce Smith and Theodora Jankowski, have found Renaissance drama and Shakespeare's plays a rich resource. While it can be disputed whether any of Shakespeare's plays explicitly portray homosexual or lesbian relationships, queer studies has examined the homoerotic overtones to plays such as *The Two Gentlemen of Verona* and *Coriolanus*. The privileging of the male friendship between Valentine and Proteus in *The Two Gentlemen of Verona,* over the love shared by Valentine and Silvia, repudiated by Valentine on his discovery of Proteus' attempt to rape Silvia but immediately reinstated on his apology and further endorsed by Valentine's desire that Proteus should have his desire and marry Silvia, has been read homoerotically but also in terms of Early Modern contexts that advantaged male friendships and relationships above romantic involvements with women. Even a text such as *Coriolanus*, built upon the notion of Roman masculinity, shows Aufidius using metaphors and concepts that are commonly associated with love and marriage, as he greets Coriolanus in the Volscian camp:

> Let me twine
> Mine arms about that body, where against
> My grainèd ash an hundred times hath broke,
> And scarre'd the moon with splinters. Here I clip
> The anvil of my sword, and do contest
> As hotly and as nobly with thy love
> As ever in ambitious strength I did
> Contend against thy valour. Know thou first,
> I loved the maid I married; never man
> Sighed truer breath. But that I see thee here,
> Thou noble thing, more dances my rapt heart
> Than when I first my wedded mistress saw
> Bestride my threshold. (*Coriolanus* IV.v.105–17)

Similarly, the attraction felt by Olivia for Viola-as-Cesario in *Twelfth Night* and the final scene of the play wherein Duke

Orsino embraces Viola, still dressed as Cesario, along with countless other examples from the Shakespeare canon, have provoked queer readings which are carefully explicated and evidenced with textual analysis.

Materialist Criticism

If gender and sexuality has been one dominant axis along which Shakespeare's work has been analysed, another major axis is that of materialist criticism which usually includes the Marxist models of criticism but also the New Historicist and Cultural Materialist schools. Today, Marxist criticism has proliferated in various directions but a central tenet that still holds good for all the variants is that all art and literature is part of, and inseparable from, the societies that produce them and the conflicts and struggles of the times. While Karl Marx himself had some pronouncements on Shakespeare's work, early Marxist critics included Robert Weimann writing in German, Victor Kiernan and A. A. Smirnov, writing in Russian. Initial Marxist explorations of Shakespeare's plays analysed the role of the common people in Shakespeare's plays, demonstrated the ideological biases which were evidenced in the play, the strict class stratification and the consequent advantages enjoyed by the aristocracy and the royalty. Plays such as *Coriolanus* and *King Lear* can be read in this fashion where the opposition of the classes is clearly to be seen, but the comedies also came in for such criticism as it was noted that even when Rosalind and Celia relocated to the Forest of Arden and the pastoral life, they lived in a class-bound society wherein they encountered shepherds such as Corin and Silvius. In addition to the class inequalities that are rife in Shakespeare's many worlds, the Marxists have also seen in his personal life evidence of the struggles in the Elizabethan age as the society moved from a feudal society to a more capitalistic one. His move to the status of a gentleman is read in the context of an Elizabethan world wherein upward mobility was facilitated by the new conditions of the commercial theatre which made rewards for personal excellence possible. Early Marxist critics of Shakespeare also set up an opposition between the humanist criticism of his plays and their own, focusing on countering other, earlier critics and writers who saw Shakespeare's plays as an expression of the transcendent human spirit, ignoring the very real material conditions which often served to smother that human spirit.

Marxism has continued to be relevant to Shakespearean studies through the last century and continues to be so today as well. Terry Eagleton's sustained work on Shakespeare, Jan Kott's work on the contemporary relevance of Shakespeare, Bakhtinian theories of the carnival as demonstrated by Michael Bristol, the understanding of the popular voice in Annabel Patterson's work and Gabriel Egan's student-friendly work on Marx and Shakespeare, all demonstrate the continuing relevance of Marxist literary theories to Shakespeare studies. Marxism and feminism come together in the work of Dympna Callaghan, Jean Howard and others who locate gender and feminist issues in material practices which are then analysed together to demonstrate that gender issues are also class-based issues and that to speak about women in any text is necessarily also to locate them in their social class.

While traditional Marxist criticism remains a useful way to read Shakespeare's plays, it was added to and further developed by the Cultural Materialists and the New Historicists of the 1980s and after. The New Historicists include one of the most influential of Shakespeare critics today, Stephen Greenblatt, but also others such as Louis Montrose and Catherine Gallagher, who turned their attention to Renaissance drama, in particular the work of Shakespeare. New Historicism is again a school of criticism which brings together various elements. They work by situating history within texts and texts within history: the convenient formulation being Montrose's "The

Historicity of Texts and the Textuality of History" (23). Thus the New Historicists actively engage in examining literary texts for the ways in which they contribute to producing history as well. They also read literary texts alongside texts from other domains of knowledge, produced in roughly the same period: thus *Macbeth* might be read alongside James I's *Dæmonologie* of 1597; *The Tempest* alongside narratives of exploration from the late Elizabethan–early Jacobean times; and *Hamlet* analysed on the basis of the Ghost and its relationship to purgatory. By reading "literary" texts in these contexts, the New Historicists sought to demonstrate that similar discourses and ideologies were in circulation at a given time. They also analysed how power circulates, is contested by individuals who subvert the structures of power, and try to undermine them but are eventually contained within them, even as that containment makes the structures themselves stronger.

The New Historicists, primarily American, had their counterparts across the Atlantic (specifically Britain) in the Cultural Materialists who also practised a Marxist inflected model of critical enquiry. The two schools were similar in many ways, especially in reading the connections between literature and politics and historicising them both. While the New Historicists showed subversion being contained, the Cultural Materialists showed how texts actively played out dissidence. This interest in resistance was also powered by an interest in engaging with the complexities of dissident voices from the margins; so Cultural Materialism participates in dialogues with gender, sexuality, queer and class-based theoretical schools. In addition, Cultural Materialists, such as Alan Sinfield, Graham Holderness and Jonathan Dollimore focused their gaze on their own present locations, in time and space, giving a certain contemporary edge to their work, because of its situatedness in the present. Jonathan Gil Harris, writing about the Cultural Materialists, situates them as examining Shakespeare-as-institution but also studying his plays as "sites of ideological struggle over interpretation" (481). Thus even while they read the Shakespearean text in conversation with other texts from the same period, they also locate it in the present-day context and show how it continues to be a tool, to be used to control but also to express dissent.

Postcolonial Approaches

Postcolonial criticism, begun after the decolonisation of large areas of Asia, Africa, the Caribbean, etc., works at furthering the process of liberation via freeing the colonised from the cultural colonisation that accompanied their political oppression. Analysing the role that Shakespeare played in the cultural dominance of the former colonies was one of the first steps in postcolonial criticism's approach to rethinking the definitions and models handed to colonised peoples by their colonial masters. The introduction of Shakespeare in education (in the early 1800s in India, and later on in West Africa [1849 onwards], East Africa [beginning in the early 1900s] and so on) made it certain that Shakespeare's influence was strongly felt and the legacy continued, in all the previous British colonies. Ania Loomba's statement about the use of Shakespeare's plays in Indian education holds true for other colonised nations too: "As the privileged core of colonial English education, they were used to bolster ideas of English superiority over the culture and literature of the 'natives'" (212). But that Shakespearean influence, overlaid by postcolonialism, has given rise to "Postcolonial Shakespeares".[4]

So what do postcolonial critics such as Loomba, Kim Hall and others do with Shakespeare? Race and its representations are one of the central concerns of the postcolonial critic: thus they examine characters such as Aaron the Moor in *Titus Andronicus*, Othello and the Prince of Morocco in *The Merchant of Venice*, Cleopatra in *Antony and Cleopatra* and even the little

Indian boy and his mother from *A Midsummer Night's Dream*. The most basic way of doing this is to analyse the presentation of the "raced" character in terms of the stereotypes that are deployed, whether in the attitudes of other characters to her/ him or the way in which s/he is constructed/presented. Thus Othello's own character can be studied for the stereotypes it embodies regarding black men; but we can also examine the ways in which other characters speak of/to him and what that demonstrates regarding the ways in which blacks and Moors were perceived in the Venice of the text but also Early Modern England. The racism evident in Iago's and Brabantio's speeches, the animal metaphors used to speak of Othello and the accusations of witchcraft against him, all go to construct a stereotype of the black as irrational, given to superstition and bestial in nature. The combining of a postcolonial critique with New Historicist/Cultural Materialist ways of reading leads to an understanding of how Othello or Aaron are in part creations of the culture of the times, wherein the colour black is associated with evil, but also where races other than white were often conflated into one category of "otherness" which made it possible to represent them as less than human, their unfamiliar appearances and customs being ground enough to deny them a recognisable humanity.

Postcolonial critics have also found *The Tempest* a rich resource, as it offers a very clear depiction of a colonial takeover of a free space and the reducing of native peoples to colonial subjects. While *The Tempest* is the main play studied from this angle, other plays such as *Antony and Cleopatra* can also be read from this perspective: Prospero's taking over of Caliban and Ariel's island is an imaginative representation of a colonial process; but Octavius Caesar's conquest of Egypt and the consequences of that conquest are historically situated and, when adapted in Shakespeare's play, offer multiple perspectives to the reader. The historicity of Egypt and Rome remains but the Renaissance idea of imagining England as a second Rome gives a certain resonance to the activities of the Roman Octavius and the expanding Roman empire, in an English world which was sending out discoverers and embassies across the world and also looking to trade and conquest-via-trade as a very real possibility, as demonstrated by the Charter granted to The East India Company by Elizabeth I.

The postcolonial critical imperative has meant that even as the Shakespearean texts are examined for representations of race and empire, they are also used to show how the colonised attempt to talk back to the coloniser and even retaliate and fight back. *The Tempest* is again a central text for those interested in such readings: the play was earlier seen as exemplifying a benevolent patriarchy, on the part of Prospero, but the postcolonial critics exploded that myth by focusing on Caliban and Ariel and their enforced servitude. Caliban's speech regarding the use of language,

> You taught me language, and my profit on't
> Is I know how to curse. The red plague rid you
> For learning me your language! (I.ii.366–68)

is a speech that has received sustained (one could even say, excessive) attention from postcolonial readers and critics and it continues to be relevant today, as an instance of the cultural dominance of the coloniser and how that has been turned against him by the colonised.

It is not that the postcolonial critic has only examined plays within which we see two races encountering each other. Postcolonial readings of other texts have also been done and have revealed how Shakespeare can be read in terms of the postcolonial condition even when he is not addressing issues of race, colonisation, etc. *King Lear* with its emphasis on land, its ownership and distribution, has been analysed by Nicholas Visser in comparison with the issue of the appropriation of land in South Africa.[5] Some postcolonial criticism has taken the form of rewriting and adapting Shakespeare's texts, in ways that demonstrate postcolonial issues, concepts and ideas. Aimé Césaire's reworking of *The Tempest* (*Une Tempête*, 1969), Vishal Bhardwaj's film *Omkara* (2006) and Welcome Msomi's *uMabatha* (c.1972), a melding of a Zulu epic with *Macbeth*, are all variants of postcolonial criticisms. Each reworks a Shakespearean text to incorporate elements that are felt to be more relevant to the postcolonial world. In this mode of criticism *Romeo and Juliet* has arguably the largest presence as it has been consistently used to think about warring families, clans and tribes, as recently as in 2014 India, with a movie version titled *Goliyon ki Rasleela: Ram-Leela*.

Since most of Shakespeare's plays have been picked threadbare by the critics, a substantial amount of criticism by the postcolonials has taken the form of examining appropriations and productions of Shakespeare's work on stages and in films, in languages and forms that are native to the erstwhile colonies. Criticism has also focused on early productions of plays such as *Othello* and *The Tempest*, studying issues of casting and production and laying bare the racism inherent therein. The many uses to which Shakespeare has been put in the earlier colonies, whether in education or in entertainment, whether in popular forms or for the elite, remains an absorbing field of study for the postcolonial critic, even as such studies blend postcolonial criticism with adaptation studies.

Other Interpretive Approaches

If pre-1900 criticism of Shakespeare's work was largely in terms of the humanist outlook and character interpretation, the 1900s and after have seen a multitude of approaches to his work. In addition to those outlined above, there have been psychological and psychoanalytic studies, deconstructive readings, and towards the end of the twentieth century, ecocritical and posthumanist readings of his work.

Sigmund Freud's notes on various Shakespearean characters gave the initial impetus for critics such as Ernest Jones, Norman Holland and Janet Adelman to write full length studies of Shakespeare's plays, studying among other ideas, neurosis, jealousy, sexual desire, whether overt or covert, the Oedipal conflict and other such matters. While the most well-known psychoanalytic reading of all time remains Ernest Jones's on *Hamlet*, other plays have also received the attention of the psychoanalytic critics, who read issues within relationships, analysing characters and why they behave the way they do, alongside motifs and significant symbols, all of which resolve into overarching themes regarding subjectivity and the unconscious. While the tragedies have, as always, been the focus of considerable attention, comedies such as *A Midsummer Night's Dream* have also received sustained focus, especially the relationship between Titania and Oberon, their jealousy over the little Indian boy and Titania's love for the ass-headed Bottom.

Critics such as Terence Hawkes, Howard Felperin and Malcolm Evans and others have used deconstruction as a critical tool to read Shakespeare's work. Their readings have once again evidenced the longevity of the close reading of the New Critics but combined it with a rejection of coherent, self-contained interpretations that can then be used as a lens through which the text can be viewed. The deconstructionist critic focuses on the words that constitute the text even as she also pays attention to the historical contexts within which those words are, and were, situated. Thus they read the plays to show how unified meanings and interpretations of a play can be teased apart and a space created within which the play can then be reconstituted but without that reconstitution being the final word. So deconstructive critics read the plays, seeing in them the instability of language and words (given Shakespeare's love of puns and language games this has been a particularly rich resource), the self-reflexivity of Shakespeare's characters who constantly remind their viewers/readers that they are characters in a play, deception and mysteries which remain unsolved and undeciphered (why does Iago lapse into silence at the end of Othello?), fluid identities and shifting foci. Shakespeare's plays lend themselves to deconstructive readings with ease and facilitate these, unlocking "startling insights stored in the play's poetic language and theatrical techniques" (Ryan 517). Edited volumes such as *Presentist Shakespeares* continue to offer readers new interpretations based upon the fluidity and shifting nature of meaning as seen in the work of deconstructive critics working upon Shakespeare.

As the twentieth century ended new areas in Shakespeare Studies were opened up by the application of ecocritical theories to Shakespeare's texts. Critics such as Gabriel Egan, Simon Estok, Lynne Bruckner and Dan Brayton have added green overtones to the study of Shakespeare, examining his texts for ecocritical perspectives, studying ecology and environmental ethics or their lack in his works. Adaptation theorists, such as Margaret Jane Kidnie, studied Shakespeare's plays as adapted worldwide and saw that the text of a play was only a provisional text, used and altered according to the need of the user. The latest entrant into Shakespeare Studies is posthumanism: if humanist criticism was one of the major strands in Shakespearean critical enquiry, critics such as Stefan Herbrechter and Ivan Callus have extended that into the posthumanist phase, studying the idea of the human in the context of the politics and technology of the Early Modern, and speaking of the posthuman in the case of many plays, but especially *King Lear* and *Hamlet*.

It is essential to realise one key feature of Shakespeare criticism: that the fortunes of Shakespeare's plays do not remain stable through time. It has been noticed that certain plays which earlier were seen as too violent and immature (*Titus Andronicus*) or too depressing and heartbreaking (*King Lear*) are often found to be perfect in a new time. Thus the last quarter of the twentieth century has seen a flurry of criticism around *Titus Andronicus*, resulting in the production of film versions (with Anthony Hopkins, no less, as Titus) critical essays, new editions of the play and other critical apparatus. Where earlier it was regularly ignored for its spectacular violence and mutilation, its stilted language and its cannibalism, today it is studied for those very features, in essays by David Goldstein, Molly Easo Smith, etc. *King Lear*, which critics such as Samuel Johnson and Charles Lamb found so unpalatable that they could either not reread it or could not conceive of it being produced, has enjoyed a turnaround in critical opinion after the Second World War, so much so that it now rivals *Hamlet* as the most rewarding of the tragedies. The change in critical opinion is partially because of the change in the times: the violence of a *Titus Andronicus* fits right into a world which has witnessed great wars, torture of prisoners of war and random acts of cruelty gratuitously inflicted on friend or foe. *King Lear*, with its deeply despairing vision of "pelican daughters" (III.iv.72) and sons, with Gloucester's eyes being put out on stage, is suitable and indeed enlightening for a world that does not have fixed coordinates of loyalty and friendship, where justice is often subverted and cruelty rewarded. The times affect the reception of the plays as much as reading methods do.

While particular texts might resonate at particular times with critics, there are certain texts that find favour with particular schools of criticism: as mentioned earlier, *The Tempest* and *Othello* are always prime favourites with the postcolonials, *Hamlet* remains a central text for those who wish to engage in humanist or posthumanist definitions of man, and so on. But the truth remains that as new theoretical schools arrive, the test case for each one of them remains Shakespeare: Does this theory work when applied to Shakespeare's plays?

Works Cited

Encyclopædia Britannica's Guide to Shakespeare. "Understanding Shakespeare: New Criticism." David Bevington. 2014. Web. 15 June 2014. <https://www.britannica.com/shakespeare>.

Harris, Jonathan Gil. "Materialist Criticisms." *Shakespeare: An Oxford Guide.* Ed. Stanley Wells and Lena Cowen Orlin. Oxford: Oxford UP, 2003. 472–84. Print.

Johnson, Samuel. "Preface to Shakespeare." 1765. *Prefaces and Prologues.* Vol. XXXIX. The Harvard Classics. New York: P.F. Collier and Son, 1909–14; *Bartleby.com*, 2001. Web. 11 June 2014.

Jonson, Ben. "On Shakespeare." *English Essays: Sidney to Macaulay.* Vol. XXVII. The Harvard Classics. New York: P. F. Collier and Son, 1909–14; *Bartleby.com*, 2001. Web. 11 June 2014.

Loomba, Ania. "India." *The Oxford Companion to Shakespeare.* Ed. Michael Dobson and Stanley Wells. Oxford: Oxford UP, 2001. 212–13. Print.

Meres, Francis. From *Palladis Tamia.* 1598. *Elizabethan Critical Essays.* Ed. G. Gregory Smith. Oxford: Clarendon Press, 1904; *Bartleby.com*, 2012. Web. 11 June 2014.

Montrose, Louis. "Professing the Renaissance: The Poetics and Politics of Culture." *The New Historicism.* Ed. H Aram Veeser. New York: Taylor and Francis, 1989. 15–36. Print.

Morgann, Maurice. *An Essay on the Dramatic Character of Sir John Falstaff.* 1777. *Eighteenth Century Essays on Shakespeare.* Ed. D. Nichol Smith. Glasgow: James MacLehose and Sons. 1903. *Project Gutenberg*, 2009. Web. 11 June 2014.

Rhymer, Thomas. "Short View of Tragedy." *Critical Works of Thomas Rymer.* Ed. Curt A. Zimansky. New Haven, London, 1956: 132, 164; web.uvic.ca 2006. Web. 11 June 2014.

Ruskin, John. "Lilies: Of Queens' Gardens." 1865. *Essays: English and American.* Vol. XXVIII. The Harvard Classics. New York: P. F. Collier and Son, 1909–14; *Bartleby.com*, 2001. Web. 11 June 2014.

Ryan, Kiernan. "Deconstruction." *Shakespeare: An Oxford Guide*. Ed. Stanley Wells and Lena Cowen Orlin. Oxford: Oxford UP, 2003. 508–17. Print.

Notes

1. The whole of Rowe's life and critical introduction to the edition may be read here: <http://www.gutenberg.org/files/16275/16275-h/16275-h.htm>
2. Read more about these lectures at <http://jamesjoyce.ie/day-10-february/i>
3. Can be read here <http://web.singnet.com.sg/~yisheng/notes/shakespeare/mbeth_f.htm>
4. With apologies to Ania Loomba and Martin Orkin whose 1998 book has the same title
5. See Nicholas Visser. "Shakespeare and Hanekom, *King Lear* and Land: A South African Perspective". In Loomba and Orkin. 205–17.

Recommended Reading

Apart from the last three sections, the reading list is sectioned according to the chapters of the book.

Kingship and Authority

Guy, John. *Tudor England*. Oxford: Oxford UP, 1988. Print.

Kinney, Arthur F. *Elizabethan and Jacobean England: Sources and Documents of the English Renaissance*. Malden, MA: Wiley-Blackwell, 2011. Print.

Montrose, Louis. *The Subject of Elizabeth: Authority, Gender, and Representation*. Chicago: U of Chicago P, 2006. Print.

Palliser, D. M. *The Age of Elizabeth: England Under the Later Tudors, 1547–1603*. New York: Longman, 1992. Print.

Somerville, J. P. *Politics and Ideology in England, 1603–1640*. London: Longman, 1986. Print.

Family and Gender

Amussen, Susan Dwyer. *An Ordered Society: Gender and Class in Early Modern England*. New York: Columbia UP, 1993. Print.

Berry, Helen, and Elizabeth Foyster, ed. *The Family in Early Modern England*. Cambridge: Cambridge UP, 2007. Print.

Breitenberg, Mark. *Anxious Masculinity in Early Modern England*. Cambridge: Cambridge UP, 1996. Print.

Jardine, Lisa. *Still Harping on Daughters: Women and Drama in the Age of Shakespeare*. Sussex: Harvester Press, 1983. Print.

Mendelson, Sara, and Patricia Crawford. *Women in Early Modern England*. Oxford: Clarendon, 1998. Print.

Expanding Worlds and New Peoples

Alexander, Catherine M. S., and Stanley Wells, ed. *Shakespeare and Race*. Cambridge: Cambridge UP, 2000. Print.

Brotton, Jerry. *Trading Territories: Mapping the Early Modern World*. London: Reaktion Books, 1997. Print.

Gillies, John. *Shakespeare and the Geography of Difference*. Cambridge: Cambridge UP, 1994. Print.

Greenblatt, Stephen. *Marvelous Possessions: The Wonder of the New World*. Chicago: U of Chicago P, 1991. Print.

Hulme, Peter. *Colonial Encounters: Europe and the Native Caribbean, 1492–1797*. London: Methuen, 1986. Print.

Yungblut, Laura Hunt. *Strangers Settled Here Amongst Us: Policies, Perceptions and the Presence of the Alien in Elizabethan England*. London: Routledge, 1996. Print.

Theatre and Stagecraft

Chambers, E. K. *The Elizabethan Stage*. 4 vols. Oxford: Oxford UP, 1923. Print.

Cox, John D., and David Scott Kastan, ed. *A New History of Early English Drama*. New York: Columbia UP, 1997. Print.

Dillon, Janette. *The Cambridge Introduction to Early English Theatre*. Cambridge: Cambridge UP, 2006. Print.

Gurr, Andrew. *Playgoing in Shakespeare's London*. Cambridge: Cambridge UP, 1987. Print.

——. *The Shakespearean Stage*. 3rd Ed. Cambridge: Cambridge UP, 1992. Print.

SHAKESPEARE AND HIS CONTEMPORARIES

Bate, Jonathan. *Soul of the Age: The Life, Mind and World of William Shakespeare*. London: Viking-Penguin, 2008. Print.

Braunmuller, A. R., and M. Hattaway, ed. *The Cambridge Companion to English Renaissance Drama*. Cambridge: Cambridge UP, 2002. Print.

Engle, Lars, and Eric Rasmussen. *Studying Shakespeare's Contemporaries*. Oxford and Malden, MA: Wiley-Blackwell, 2014. Print.

Greenblatt, Stephen. *Will in the World*. New York: W. W. Norton, 2004. Print.

McLuskie, Kathleen. *Renaissance Dramatists*. New York: Harvester Wheatsheaf, 1989. Print.

Schoenbaum, Samuel. *Shakespeare: His Life, His Language, His Theatre*. New York: Signet, 1990. Print.

SHAKESPEARE'S DRAMATIC FORMS AND MODES

Barber, C. L. *Shakespeare's Festive Comedy*. Princeton: Princeton UP, 1959. Print.

Belsey, Catherine. *The Subject of Tragedy: Identity and Difference in Renaissance Drama*. New York: Methuen, 1985. Print.

Bradley, A. C. *Shakespearean Tragedy*. New York: St. Martin's, 1967. Print.

Danson, Lawrence. *Shakespeare's Dramatic Genres*. Oxford: Oxford UP, 2000. Print.

Felperin, Howard. *Shakespearean Romance*. Princeton: Princeton UP, 1972. Print.

Leggatt, Alexander. *Shakespeare's Political Drama: The History Plays and the Roman Plays*. London and New York: Routledge, 1988. Print.

Shakespeare Adaptations

Burnett, Mark Thornton. *Shakespeare and World Cinema*. Cambridge: Cambridge UP, 2013. Print.

Cohn, Ruby. *Modern Shakespeare Offshoots*. Princeton: Princeton UP, 1976. Print.

Fischlin, Daniel, and Mark Fortier, ed. *Adaptations of Shakespeare: A Critical Anthology of plays from the Seventeenth Century to the Present*. London: Routledge, 2000. Print.

Gross, John, ed. *After Shakespeare: Writing Inspired by the World's Greatest Author*. Oxford: Oxford UP, 2002. Print.

Kidnie, Margaret Jane. *Shakespeare and the Problem of Adaptation*. London and New York: Routledge, 2008. Print.

Shakespeare and Criticism

Adelman, Janet. *Suffocating Mothers: Fantasies of Maternal Origins in Shakespeare's Plays,* Hamlet *to* The Tempest. New York and London: Routledge, 1992. Print.

Bray, Alan. "Homosexuality and the Signs of Male Friendship." *Queering the Renaissance*. Ed. Jonathan Goldberg. Durham: Durham UP, 1993. 40–61. Print.

——. *Homosexuality in Renaissance England*. 2nd edn. New York: Columbia UP, 1995. Print.

Bristol, Michael. *Carnival and Theatre: Plebeian Culture and the Structure of Authority in Renaissance Britain*. New York and London: Methuen, 1985. Print.

Bruckner, Lynne, and Dan Brayton, ed. *Ecocritical Shakespeare*. Farnham: Ashgate, 2011. Print.

Callaghan, Dympna. "Looking Well to Linens: Women and Cultural Production in *Othello* and Shakespeare's England." *Marxist Shakespeares*. Ed. Jean Howard and Scott Cutler Shershow. London: Routledge, 2001. Print.

Carlin, Murray. *Not Now, Sweet Desdemona: A Duologue for Black and White Within the Realm of Shakespeare's* Othello. 1969. Oxford: Oxford UP, 1969. Print.

Cesaire, Aime. *A Tempest.* 1985. Trans. Richard Miller. *First-Year Foundations.* New York: Barnard College. Web. 15 June 2014.

Clarke, Mary Cowden. *The Girlhood of Shakespeare's Heroines.* London: Bickers and Son, 1880. *Archive.org.* Web. 20 June 2014.

Dollimore, Jonathan. *Radical Tragedy: Religion Ideology and Power in the Drama of Shakespeare and His Contemporaries.* 1984. New York: Palgrave Macmillan, 2010. Print.

Eagleton, Terry. *William Shakespeare.* Oxford: Basil Blackwell, 1986. Print.

Egan, Gabriel. *Green Shakespeare: From Ecopolitics to Ecocriticism.* London and New York: Routledge, 2006. Print.

Egan, Gabriel. *Shakespeare and Marx.* Oxford: Oxford UP, 2004. Print.

Eliot, T. S. "Hamlet and His Problems." *The Sacred Wood.* New York: Alfred A. Knopf, 1921. *Bartleby.com*, 1996. Web. 20 June 2014.

Estok, Simon. *Ecocriticism and Shakespeare: Reading Ecophobia.* New York: Palgrave Macmillan, 2011. Print.

Evans, Malcolm. "Deconstructing Shakespeare's Comedies." *Alternative Shakespeares.* Vol. 1. Ed. John Drakakis. London and New York: Routledge (1985), 2002. 69–96. Print.

Felperin, Howard. "'Tongue-tied Our Queen?': The Deconstruction of Presence in *The Winter's Tale.*" *Shakespeare and the Question of Theory.* Ed. Geoffrey H. Hartman and Patricia Parker. New York: Routledge, 1985. Print.

Freud, Sigmund. [Shakespeare: Macbeth] *Some Character-types Met with in Psycho-analytical Work* (1916). <http://web.singnet.com.sg/~yisheng/notes/shakespeare/mbeth_f.htm. Web. 20 June 2014>.

Gallagher, Catherine, and Stephen Greenblatt, ed. *Practicing New Historicism.* Chicago: U of Chicago P, 2000. Print.

Garber, Marjorie. *Vested Interests: Cross-dressing and Cultural Anxiety.* New York: Routledge, 1992. Print.

Gay, Penny. *As She Likes It: Shakespeare's Unruly Women*. London and New York: Routledge, 2002. Print.

Goldberg, Jonathan. *Sodometries: Renaissance Texts, Modern Sexualities.* New York: Fordham UP, 2010. Print.

Goldstein, David B. "The Cook and the Cannibal: *Titus Andronicus* and the New World." *Shakespeare Studies* 37, 2009. 99–134. Print.

Greenblatt, Stephen. "Remember Me." *Hamlet in Purgatory*. Princeton: Princeton UP, 2001. 205–57. Print.

——. "The Mousetrap." *Shakespeare Studies* 35 (1997): 1–32. Print.

Hall, Kim. "Othello and the Problem of Race." *Blackwell Companions to Shakespeare: The Tragedies*. Ed. R. Dutton and J. Howard. London: Blackwell, 2003. Print.

Harbage, Alfred. *Shakespeare and the Rival Traditions.* New York: Macmillan, 1952. Print.

Hawkes, Terence, and Hugh Grady, ed. *Presentist Shakespeares.* London and New York: Routledge, 2006. Print.

Herbrechter, Stefan, and Ivan Callus, ed. *Posthumanist Shakespeares.* New York: Palgrave Macmillan, 2012. Print.

Holderness, Graham, ed. *The Shakespeare Myth.* Manchester: Manchester UP, 1988. Print.

Holland, Norman. *Psychoanalysis and Shakespeare*. New York: McGraw-Hill, 1966. Print.

Howard, Jean E., and Phyllis Rackin. *Engendering a Nation: A Feminist Account of Shakespeare's English Histories*. London and New York: Routledge, 1997. Print.

Howard, Jean E., and Scott Cutler Shershow, ed. *Marxist Shakespeares.* London: Routledge, 2001. Print. Accents on Shakespeare.

Jankowski, Theodora. *Pure Resistance: Queer Virginity in Early Modern English Drama*. U of Pennsylvania P, 2000. Print.

Jardine, Lisa. "Twins and Travesties: Gender, Dependency and Availability in *Twelfth Night*." *Erotic Politics: The Dynamics of Desire in the Renaissance Theatre*. Ed. Susan Zimmerman. London: Routledge, 1992. Print.

Jones, Ernest. *Hamlet and Oedipus*. 1949. New York: W. W. Norton, 1976. Print.

Kahn, Coppelia. *Man's Estate: Masculine Identity in Shakespeare*. Berkeley-London: U of California P, 1981. Print.

Kidnie, Margaret Jane. *Shakespeare and the Problem of Adaptation*. London and New York: Routledge, 2008. Print.

Kiernan, Victor G. *Eight Tragedies of Shakespeare: A Marxist Study*. London and New York: Verso, 1996. Print.

Kott, Jan. *Shakespeare Our Contemporary*. 1964 (originally published in Polish). New York: W. W. Norton, 1974. Print.

Levine, Laura. *Men in Women's Clothing: Anti-theatricality and Effeminization, 1579–1642*. Cambridge: Cambridge UP, 1994. Print.

Loomba, Ania, and Martin Orkin, ed. *Post-colonial Shakespeares*. London: Routledge, 1998. Print.

Lovejoy, Arthur O. *The Great Chain of Being: A Study of the History of an Idea*. Cambridge, MA: Harvard UP, 1936. Print.

Mahood, M.M. *Shakespeare's Wordplay*. 1957. London: Routledge, 2001. Print.

Marx, Karl, and Frederick Engels. *Marx and Engels On Literature and Art*. Progress Publishers. 1976. *Marxists Internet Archive*. <http://www.marxists.org/archive/marx/works/subject/art/. Web. 20 June 2014>.

Menon, Madhavi. *Shakesqueer: A Queer Companion to the Complete Works of Shakespeare*. Durham and London: Duke UP, 2011. Print.

Montrose, Louis. "The Politics and Poetics of Culture." *The New Historicism*. Ed. Aram H. Veeser. London and New York: Routledge, 1989. Print.

Msomi, Welcome. *uMabatha*. 1969–72. *Adaptations of Shakespeare: A Critical Anthology of Plays from the Seventeenth Century to the Present*. Ed. Daniel Fischlin and Mark Fortier. London: Routledge, 2000. 164–87. Print.

Newman, Karen. *Fashioning Femininity and English Renaissance Drama*. Chicago: U of Chicago P, 1991. Print.

Patterson, Annabel. *Shakespeare and the Popular Voice*. Cambridge, MA: Basil Blackwell, 1989. Print.

Rackin, Phyllis. "Shakespeare's Crossdressing Comedies." *A Companion to Shakespeare's Works, Volume III: The Comedies*. Ed Richard Dutton and Jean E. Howard. Blackwell online: 2005. Web. 24 June 2014.

Sinfield, Alan. *Shakespeare, Authority, Sexuality: Unfinished Business in Cultural Materialism*. London: Routledge, 2006. Print. Accents on Shakespeare.

Smirnov, A. A. *Shakespeare: A Marxist Interpretation*. Translated from the Russian. New York: Critics Group, 1937. Print.

Smith, Bruce R. *Homosexual Desire in Shakespeare's England: A Cultural Poetics*. Chicago: U of Chicago P, 1991. Print.

Smith, Molly Easo. "Spectacles of Torment in *Titus Andronicus*." *Studies in English Literature* 36 (1996): 315–31. *Ebsco*. Web. 12 June 2014.

Spurgeon, Caroline. *Shakespeare's Imagery and What It Tells Us*. 1935. Cambridge: Cambridge UP, 2005. Print.

Stallybrass, Peter. "Transvestism and the 'Body Beneath': Speculating on the Boy Actor." *Erotic Politics: The Dynamics of Desire in the Renaissance Theatre*. Ed. Susan Zimmerman. London: Routledge, 1992. Print.

Stoll, Elmer Edgar. *Art and Artifice in Shakespeare*. New York: Macmillan, 1933. Print.

Tillyard, E. M. W. *The Elizabethan World Picture: A Study of the Idea of Order in the Age of Shakespeare, Donne and Milton*. New York: Vintage Books, 1959. Print.

Vickers, Brian. "The Emergence of Character Criticism, 1774–1800." *Shakespeare Survey* 34 (1981): Characterization in Shakespeare. Print.

Weimann, Robert. *Shakespeare and the Popular Tradition in the Theater: Studies in the Social Dimension of Dramatic Form and Function*. Baltimore and London: The Johns Hopkins UP, 1978. Print.

Wells, Robin. *Shakespeare on Masculinity.* Cambridge: Cambridge UP, 2000. Print.

Zimmerman, Susan, ed. *Erotic Politics: The Dynamics of Desire in the Renaissance Theatre*. London: Routledge, 1992. Print.

Companions and Guides

Dobson, Michael, and Stanley Wells, ed. *The Oxford Companion to Shakespeare*. Oxford: Oxford UP, 2001. Print.

McDonald, Russ. *The Bedford Companion to Shakespeare: An Introduction with Documents*. Boston: Bedford/St. Martin's, 2001. Print.

Smith, Emma. *The Cambridge Introduction to Shakespeare*. Cambridge: Cambridge UP, 2007. Print.

Wells, Stanley, and Lena Cowen Orlin, ed. *Shakespeare: An Oxford Guide*. Oxford: Oxford UP, 2003. Print.

Wells, Stanley. *The Cambridge Companion to Shakespeare Studies*. Rev. ed. Cambridge: Cambridge UP, 1986. Print.

Miscellaneous

Bloom, Harold. *Shakespeare and the Invention of the Human*. New York: Riverhead Books, 1998. Print

Evans, G. Blakemore, ed. *The Riverside Shakespeare*. Boston: Houghton, 1974. Print.

Garber, Marjorie. *Shakespeare After All*. New York: Anchor Books, 2004. Print.

Greenblatt, Stephen, et al., ed. *The Norton Shakespeare*. 1997. New York: W. W. Norton, 2008. Print.

Web Resources

Encyclopædia Britannica's Guide to Shakespeare: <https://www.britannica.com/shakespeare>

Folger Shakespeare Library: <http://www.folger.edu/index.cfm>

Internet Shakespeare Editions: <http://internetshakespeare.uvic.ca/>

MIT Global Shakespeares: <http://globalshakespeares.mit.edu/#>

Open Source Shakespeare: An Experiment in Literary Technology: <www.opensourceshakespeare.org>

The Complete Works of William Shakespeare: <http://shakespeare.mit.edu/>

Index

adaptation studies, 178, 179–81, 228
adaptations, 177–203
Aristotle, 47–48
authority of the father, 51–52

BBC TV Shakespeare, 188, 194–95
Bible, The, and gender, 49–50, 69
Blackfriars, 104–05
Bowdler, Thomas, 182
boy players, 111–12
Bradley, A. C., 212

chronicle play, 130–31, 140, 159
class-based adaptations, 198–99
clowns, 148
comedy, 141, 142–50
comic relief, 156–57
companionate marriage, 60–61
crossdressing, 148–49
Cultural Materialists, 220, 221, 222–23

de Witt, Johannes, 101, 103
deconstructive criticism, 227–28
Divine Right of Kings, 24–25, 26–28, 164
Doctor Faustus, 7, 82–83, 113, 130,132
Drake, Francis, 22, 71, 73
Dryden, John, 181, 208

East India Charter, 75–76, 78, 225
ecocriticism, 228
editions, 184–85, 205
Edward II, 132, 133, 159
Edward VI, 20–21
Eliot, T. S., 213
Elizabeth I, 17, 22–24, 124
English history, 141, 158, 188
exploration and discovery, 22, 64–51

First Folio, 11, 126, 141, 167, 184, 209
Freud, Sigmund, 213, 227

gender-based adaptations, 199
gender criticism, 210–11, 216–20, 221
Globe, The, 101, 102, 125
Greek and Latin drama, 100
Greene, Robert, 116, 119–20, 128, 131, 167, 207

Henry VIII, 17–20
historical criticism, 213–14
histories, 141, 158–66
homilies, 37, 45, 50, 59
honour and gender, 52–53
humanism, 4–8, 13

iambic pentameter, 14
insiders/outsiders, 84–92
interludes, 100, 159

James VI and I, 17, 24–25, 51, 78, 124, 125
Jew of Malta, The, 88, 90–91, 132–33
Jews, 78–79, 84, 87–89
Johnson, Samuel, 209
Jones, Inigo, 25, 65, 134
Jonson, Ben, 65, 76, 126–27, 133–34, 207–08

king's bloodlines and genealogy, 30–32, 164
king's two bodies, 29

kingship and spectacle, 38–41
Kyd, Thomas, 127–28

Lamb, Charles and Mary, 182, 189
Lord Admiral's Men, 102, 106, 121, 131
Lord Chamberlain's Men, 102, 106–08, 121, 124, 133

male primogeniture, 20, 56, 62, 164
Marlowe, Christopher, 116, 127, 131–33
marriage, 56–61
Marxist criticism, 220–21
Mary I, 21–22
Materialist Criticism, 220–23
Moors, 89–91
mystery, miracle and morality plays, 97–99

New Critics, 214–15
New Historicists, 213–14, 221–22

order in Elizabethan England, 35–38

palimpsests, 179, 180
performance studies, 206–207
playhouses and theatres, 101–05
playing companies, 97, 100, 102, 105, 106–08
playscripts, 108, 114, 136
Pope, Alexander, 209
postcolonial adaptations, 200
postcolonial criticism, 223–26
posthumanist criticism, 228
print adaptations, 189–92
printing press, 6–7, 9, 72
problem plays, 141, 167, 171
psychoanalytic criticism, 227

queer adaptations, 200–01
queer criticism, 214–15

Raleigh, Walter, 22, 23, 70, 73
Reformation, 9, 18–21, 37, 44, 72
Renaissance, 5–6, 8, 83, 122
revenge tragedy, 127, 140
Roman history, 141, 160, 188
romances, 141, 166–71

Shakespeare's canon, 10–11
Shakespeare's language, 8–10
Shakespeare's sonnets, 10–11
social mobility, 64, 66, 73–74, 221
soliloquy, 155
Spanish Armada, 22, 23, 74
stage props, 109–11
stereotypes about women, 66–67

Tamburlaine, 131–32
Tate, Nahum, 181, 185, 190
textual studies, 206
tragedy, 141, 150–58
tragicomedies, 142, 167–68, 171

University Wits, 120, 127, 128–31

Virginia Charter, 76, 78

Shakespeare Plays

All's Well That Ends Well, 100, 171
Antony and Cleopatra, 2, 49, 103, 110,111–12, 124, 151–60 passim, 223, 224–25, 181, 182–83, 200, 213, 218
As You Like It, 61–66 passim, 108, 112, 117, 118, 123, 124, 181,143–48 passim, 201, 217, 218
Cardenio, 125
Comedy of Errors, The, 118, 120, 145, 149, 177
Coriolanus, 124, 151, 156–58 passim, 160, 181, 213, 219, 220

Cymbeline, 59, 125, 141, 166, 169, 170, 171
Hamlet, 28–34 passim, 39, 43, 47, 57–67 passim, 98, 103, 110, 111, 113, 114, 123–28 passim, 133, 140, 151–57 passim, 177, 180, 183–84, 189, 190, 199, 200, 209, 213, 216, 217, 222, 227–29 passim
Henry V, 52, 53, 56, 87, 110, 123, 159, 161, 165, 187, 201
Henry VIII, 125, 135, 159
I Henry IV, 52, 99, 100, 123, 159, 160–65 passim
II Henry IV, 52, 99, 100, 123, 159, 160–65 passim
I Henry VI, 159
II Henry VI, 159
III Henry VI, 119, 120, 159
Julius Caesar, 123, 151, 153, 160, 201
King John, 159
King Lear, 30, 38, 54–62 passim, 67, 81, 108, 109, 110, 124, 141, 148, 151–57 passim, 177, 181, 197, 199, 200, 201, 209, 213, 216, 220, 225, 228, 229
Love's Labour's Lost, 143
Macbeth, 24, 33, 36, 41, 46, 81, 110, 124, 135, 150–58 passim, 183, 188, 191, 197,200,216, 217, 222, 226
Measure for Measure, 124, 135, 171, 182, 186
Merchant of Venice, The, 58, 78, 82, 88–89, 123, 133, 144, 146, 148, 171, 172, 182, 218, 223
Merry Wives of Windsor, 143
Midsummer Night's Dream, A, 23–24, 51–52, 57, 71, 107, 110, 113, 123, 136,144, 148–50 passim, 182, 187, 196, 208, 223–24, 227
Much Ado about Nothing, 108, 123, 144–48 passim, 188
Othello, 53, 63, 66, 69, 70, 89–90, 110,111, 124, 151–56 passim, 182, 183, 187, 196, 199, 208, 215, 216, 223–24, 226, 229
Pericles, 125,166, 169–71 passim
Richard II, 26–28 passim, 31, 33, 42, 63, 65, 81, 123, 159, 162–65 passim, 181
Richard III, 120, 141, 159, 164, 187
Romeo and Juliet, 52, 54, 57, 60, 80–81, 151, 179, 182, 187, 188, 196, 209, 226
Taming of the Shrew, The, 52, 58–59, 120, 135, 147, 179, 181, 186, 187, 196, 201
Tempest, The, 34, 57, 63, 65, 67, 79, 82, 100, 103, 125, 141, 167–71 passim, 180, 188, 200, 201, 222–26 passim, 229
Timon of Athens, 151
Titus Andronicus, 59, 89–91, 104, 110,118, 127–28, 130, 133, 151, 156, 157, 160, 201, 223, 229
Troilus and Cressida, 36, 141, 171, 172, 181
Twelfth Night, 58, 61, 108, 112, 123, 134, 143, 146–50 passim, 187, 218, 219–20
Two Gentlemen of Verona, The, 130, 143, 148, 219
Two Noble Kinsmen, The, 125, 135, 141
Winter's Tale, The, 53, 60, 67, 83, 100, 125, 130, 131, 166–71 passim, 182, 201